THE ULTIMATE QUESTION

A revelation

By a Servant of the King

Dedication

In grateful appreciation, this account is dedicated to those who take the time, make the effort, risk rejection and make other sacrifices to tell others about the grace of God in Jesus Christ.

 Published in the United Stated by The House of Yefeth, LLC.

Library of Congress Control Number: 2016904790
Date: 2013.03.21

ISBN-10: 0-9972939-0-X

ISBN-13: 978-0-9972939-0-6

Manufactured in the United States of America

Acknowledgement: To friends and family who encouraged and corrected me through the writing and editing of this book. For the guidance of God who patiently waited for me to set this account in writing and kept me from many unprofitable tangents while preparing this manuscript.

Table of Contents:

Introduction

When I was a new convert to Christianity, I was invited to dedicate my life to serving God's purposes. This seemed the right thing to do and God responded by giving a prophetic word telling me to "Go tell others what I have done in your heart." That was in 1979.

In the intervening thirty-four years, our Heavenly Father did many things in my heart. Now it appears to be the time to compile those things into a sensible narrative that puts things in proper order and context.

I have woven two stories into one. The first is about a near death experience I had in 1995 that in a matter of minutes thoroughly reshaped my understanding of spiritual matters. The other story is about the highlights of my pilgrimage through life and the lessons I learned. Together they show the way I found to a right relationship with God through the confusing maze of the world and its chaotic view on the meaning of life.

I can only guess what God's purposes are in having me tell this story. The writing of it helped me sort out the details of my belief system and drew me closer to Him. For each reader it will be different; some will also be drawn closer to God and others will be challenged to examine and revise their own beliefs and relationship with God and conduct with others. I expect some will reject part or all of what I write. Very likely most will be indifferent.

My hope is that anyone who reads this will seriously ask themselves what is the answer to the ultimate question. That is what really matters.

God's servant, East Texas, 2013

"And as it is reserved to men once to die, and after this, Judgment; so Christ having been once offered 'to bear the sins of many,' Christ shall appear a second time without sin to those expecting Him for salvation. (Isa. 53:12)" Hebrews 9:27-28 LITV

Chapter 1 – The Night I Died

It was midnight on a cold winter night in 1995. Three days earlier I had been in a gas explosion caused by a faulty heater. Pain and exhaustion had consumed me. My charred right hand throbbed; my throat was seared and my eyes burned and oozed pus. I could not eat, drink or see very well, and was desperate for sleep. The small couch I was trying to relax on was far from comfortable so I decided to lay out the couch cushions on the floor so I could at least lie horizontally. *Perhaps then*, I reasoned, *I could at least rest*. What I didn't realize was that being propped up on the couch had been keeping me alive! For the seared tissues in my lungs had been leaking fluid and it was filling the lower lobes of my lungs. As I lay the cushions together on the floor, my thoughts were only on how good it would feel to lie down and get some rest.

A moment later I stretched out on my back and enjoyed the small but significant pleasure of being able to lie full-length without my legs being bent uncomfortably or the couch armrest digging into my back. I lay there relaxing. When my hand started throbbing again, I realized I had forgotten the bowl of ice water I was soaking it in and would have to get up to retrieve it.

Only I discovered I couldn't rise.

Suddenly my body had become weak and unresponsive and I felt as if I was being smothered. Although I didn't know then that the fluid had spilled up into the upper portions of my lungs, I did know I couldn't breathe. I realized the danger I was in. It was late at night, almost exactly midnight, everyone was asleep, and no one would check on me until morning! I tried to cry out, but had no voice. I was trapped, suffocating in my own living room. I realized my only help now would have to come from God, so I began to pray silently in my mind.

Now I do know how to pray, and in those desperate moments as my life ebbed away I composed some of the most eloquent and well-considered prayers I have ever prayed. But nothing happened. I felt my mind continue to shut down as my brain absorbed the diminishing oxygen from my blood. I continued to pray, a few paragraphs, then a paragraph, then a few sentences, then a sentence at a time. No response.

My ears began ringing and my heart rate increased. I knew from swimming underwater that these were signs of severe oxygen deprivation. I became desperate and fearful, knowing death was imminent. A peaceful resignation began to come over me, but I determined to fight it. I realized it was almost over and I had only enough consciousness remaining to pray one last word. It had to be chosen carefully, it was my last chance, and it must count. I put behind it the clear intention that I sought any help God would give me on any terms He would offer and I put forth my plea… "Help!"

Suddenly the pain was gone as were the sensations of exhaustion, thirst and hunger. My mind was clear, and I felt vital and alive again. *My prayer is answered!* I thought. I was elated and immediately stood up. It was the middle of the night and there were no lights on anywhere in the house. Yet the room appeared brightly lit, with no shadows and there was no source of the illumination. All my senses seemed remarkably enhanced; I no longer needed my glasses to see, I could hear the slightest far-off noises, and everything smelled sharp and distinct. Even the chronic lower back pain I had endured for many years had seemingly dissolved. I was delighted, assuming I had been miraculously healed. Then I looked down to where I had been lying on the floor.

There, on the couch cushions, my body lay, still and silent. I had died.

How did this happen? It helps to take a few steps back in time from that moment and put the pieces of the story together.

I had recently been laid off from a contract engineering position with a local manufacturer. It was 1995, the local economy wasn't exactly booming and I was unemployed. Consequently I had little money and no insurance. A couple of years before, in better times, we had bought a little run-down single family ranch house in a working class neighborhood. My wife and I poured everything we had into making it a cozy little home for our growing family. Now, even the modest mortgage and carefully watched utilities rapidly drained away the small income I managed to earn at odd jobs here and there and we had no savings to speak of.

So, when the old, decrepit gas furnace began failing, I had to try to repairing it because we couldn't afford to replace the corroded pilot light and the rusted burners it so badly needed. Normally, I would have called the repairman but since it was winter and we had no money, I fiddled with it the best I could.

It was an older model so it didn't have a safety valve to stop the flow of gas when the pilot light went out. This meant it would continue to send fuel to the burners. Naturally, as the house became colder, the furnace would cycle more frequently and even more gas would be pumped into the air. It was a dangerous situation.

After several weeks of this, I had developed a routine. When I smelled gas or the temperature dropped that meant the pilot light had gone out. I would go to the furnace, shut off the gas and turn on the exhaust until no more gas could be smelled. Then I would relight the pilot light and watch it until it was burning steadily. Only after that did I turn on the gas to the burners and restart the furnace. As a final precaution I would stand and watch the furnace for a while to be sure it was operating correctly.

On that fateful night, I had lost count of how many times the furnace had gone out. I was groggy from lack of sleep and the gas fumes didn't help. It was about 3 a.m. when once again I felt the bite of the cold and smelled gas. Weary and frustrated, I stumbled out of bed and shuffled down the hallway to the furnace closet. I thought how simple it would be just to toss a match into the furnace and ignite the burners without the tedious safety rituals I normally did. Some other part of my mind was alarmed and warned me of how dangerous and foolish this idea was. I dismissed it as unreasonable and over cautious and was sure if I stood back far enough any burst of flame would be inconsequential. Since childhood I had tinkered with fire in various forms and always escaped serious harm, and besides, how much gas could there really be?

I gripped the large box of wooden, strike-anywhere matches in my left-hand; with one smooth motion, I struck a single match and sent the flaming splinter of wood straight into the burner section of the furnace.

I didn't even see it land.

A bright flash filled my entire vision and I felt as if a large, hot and heavy mattress had suddenly walloped me from the front. The trajectory of my body was linear and very short before my back impacted the opposite wall of the hallway and I slumped to the floor. I don't recall any sound from the explosion, perhaps a soft "whoosh!" My ears were not ringing after the explosion and nothing was in flames afterwards; everything returned to normal as if I had imagined it, not even the stubborn old furnace burners had ignited. No one else in the house awoke and I sat in the dark hallway for a moment collecting my thoughts.

I was still alive and intact, and didn't feel any pain. I sighed, realizing I had been foolish, but thankful I had escaped serious injury.

The hall light wasn't on. I didn't need it since I knew my way from the bedroom to the furnace so well and I hated the bright light after waking from sleep. So I had to feel my way to the bathroom where I turned on the light. I wanted to see what sort of damage had been done, expecting singed eyebrows and crinkled hair, as had been the case a few times before with flammable experiments gone awry. It took a moment for my eyes to adjust to the light before I could see clearly what I had done to myself.

The frightening sight and the searing pain hit me simultaneously. Both were shocking. My eyebrows were completely burned off and my face was framed by badly singed hair. My exposed right arm and my face were bright red. I looked down at my hands and the right one was red and the skin was charred about the thumb and forefinger. Instinctively I thrust my burned hand under a gush of cold water from the sink faucet. But that did little to relieve the intense, throbbing pain from the burn. I groaned, realizing what I could expect to endure for some time to come.

The next few days were dominated by two things: pain and humiliation. There was no respite day or night from the searing pain in my hand; nor was there relief from the shame of knowing that I had made an avoidable mistake. I had no money to spare for a doctor's visit, no insurance due to the cold heartedness of my ex-employer and no government assistance due to my youth and recent employment status. When even prayer brought no relief, I resorted to doctoring myself.

The injuries I sustained that weren't obvious were the worst. Rust had been blown into my eyes and flames had seared my throat and nasal passages. Infection quickly set in and soon my eyes filled with pus and my throat became so raw I could not swallow my own saliva without agony. With no medical training or access to supplies, my regime of treatment was quite primitive. I soaked my burned hand in ice water, took some antihistamines, read the Bible and prayed for relief. Reading was difficult since I had to rinse my eyes frequently, but I was desperately searching for some passage on healing that I might have overlooked. I read Ole Hallesby's book "Prayer"[i] seeking guidance too, but though I learned some valuable lessons, I did not find what I sought.

When I tried to lie down in bed to go to sleep all I could do was thrash about so I moved to the couch in the living room to keep from disturbing my wife. I knew sleep would allow my body to start healing but I was in so much discomfort I would lay there, propped up on one armrest, reading with a book in my left hand and letting my right hand rest in a bowl of ice water on the floor. My hand was like a yo-yo, going down to seek the relief of the cool water and then retreating when chilblains set in.

"But if any of you lacks wisdom, let him ask from God, who gives to all freely and with no reproach, and it will be given to him." James 1:5 LITV

Chapter 2 – The List and the Key

My rather inadequate preparation for the afterlife was an interesting and eclectic journey that brought me into contact with a variety of people and institutions. It was like searching for a needle in a haystack; a great deal of it was not very helpful or useful, but there was an overall purpose to the journey. Two events that were crucially important were developing my list of questions on spiritual subjects, and obtaining a key piece of information that meant the difference between salvation and damnation.

Years before, in 1979, I arrived at the train station in Huntingdon, Pennsylvania to begin my first year of undergraduate studies at Juniata College. I was 17 years old and this would be my first extended period away from the security, order, and comforts of home. I had no friends or family in Huntingdon and was entirely dependent on myself and strangers for everything. Therefore, I was both apprehensive and excited. My first impression of the town and college was a good one. Another student's family offered to transport me and my belongings from the train station to campus. I have long remembered this kindness with gratitude.

Juniata College was founded as a land grant college in 1876 by the Church of the Brethren as the Brethren Normal College. (A "Normal College" is focused on preparing its graduates specifically for teaching vocations.) Over the years it developed a broader scope and when I attended, Juniata had become a liberal arts and sciences college with a broad spectrum of students from a variety of religious, ethnic, and national backgrounds. Although mandatory chapel attendance had been dropped some years before, the Christian traditions were still relatively healthy and vibrant. Thus I soon became active in two Christian student organizations: the Intervarsity Christian Fellowship or IVCF for short, and the Deputation Club.

Through my fellowship with other students in these organizations, I was introduced to quite a variety of Christian authors and musicians. (My dorm mates also exposed me to a lot of other things too, for which I had no liking or interest.) Between reading the Bible and the writings of C. S. Lewis[ii], I came to read the book "Caught Up Into Paradise,[iii]" by D.O. Richard Eby. In that book, Eby told of his own near death experience and how he'd seen heaven and returned to life after his body was resuscitated. Although I found the book very encouraging and enlightening, I had been disappointed that the author had asked very few profound questions of God when the opportunity came. I had my own idea of what questions were important that the author left unanswered. So, after reading the book I composed what I thought was a good list of the questions I would ask God, if I ever had the chance.

One of my first questions arose back in 1978, soon after my conversion from being agnostic to becoming a Christian. I had been taught the gospel and the reality of heaven and hell. Even as a 17-year-old it seemed logical to me that there must be more to life than simply escaping hell and getting to heaven. Perhaps there was a hierarchy in heaven with a progression of levels? Surely a person's love of Christ and desire to serve would only increase when one arrived in heaven. I asked my pastor, the Rev Charles B. Gross, if there were more levels of advancement in heaven after a person got there. His honest answer was that he didn't know. So, my first question on my list was:

1. What is heaven like and do we continue to progress to higher orders of being, after we get there?

In the early eighties when I started college, the issue of abortion was fresh in the news and there was considerable debate among Christians on whether the life of an individual began at conception or birth and what the fate was of the souls of aborted babies. So, my next BIG question was:

2. What is the fate of the souls of people who die before they are born? Before they reach the age of accountability or who never develop sufficient mental faculties to know right from wrong?

The other questions developed as I experienced more of life and they ran something like this:

3. What is the fate of people who live and die without ever hearing the gospel? Of people who only hear a corrupted version of it?

4. Why do good people appear to suffer for no apparent reason, and why do evil people appear to escape the logical or natural consequences of their sins?

5. Why is the Biblical account of creation so vastly different from the scientific explanation for how the universe and life began, especially in terms of evolution and the time spans involved?

6. What is the nature of the soul—does it have structure and functions like the body? Do animals have souls like people do? Can a soul be destroyed?

7. How did Jesus transmute water into wine and multiply the loaves and fishes?

8. Who or what is the Holy Spirit?

9. What are demons and where do they come from?

10. Why do we pray?

11. Where is hell? What are the criteria for being sent there?

12. Is there a true church?

13. Why don't modern Christians demonstrate the same miraculous powers that are recorded of the prophets, seers and apostles in the scriptures?

14. Is there such a thing as reincarnation?

Etc.

Over the years I revised and added to my list as my understanding and knowledge grew through study and prayer. Some questions I answered to my own satisfaction and subsequently dropped from the list. However, others still nagged me. From these, many doubts arose and challenged my faith. I felt I could not fully rest or feel secure in my faith until they had been answered. On occasions when I had the privilege to meet great teachers and preachers in the faith I would pose one or more of my favorite questions to see how they would answer. Gathering answers from such leaders would surely give me the advantage of varied views. More often than not, their answers did not satisfy me. It finally occurred to me that I would have to answer them myself.

I seriously studied to understand and apply the faith as well as I could. First, I read through the Bible, savoring the clear, precise language of the New American Standard translation that spoke to me and resonated. Later I discovered Dr. Jay P. Green's "Literal Translation of the Holy Bible" which brought me to even deeper insights. From C.S. Lewis's writings, I diversified to a whole host of other Christian authors: Dr. John G. Lake[iv], Smith Wigglesworth[v], Ivan Panin[vi], Rev. E. W. Bullinger D.D.[vii] & etc. Often I spent my time reading these to the detriment of my technical studies. While at Juniata College, I used the opportunity to spend time in the library of the Stone Church of the Brethren on campus, browsing, borrowing, and studying. Later I transferred to the Georgia Institute of Technology as part of a dual degree program. There I joined the Baptist Student Union (BSU).

The BSU at Georgia Tech had an excellent facility with a small but well stocked library. I quickly appreciated this unforeseen benefit and made myself a regular visitor. During my three years of undergraduate studies there I spent the large fraction of my time studying in that cozy room surrounded by spiritual subjects. When the tedium of calculus, thermodynamics, fluid mechanics or the like became too great, I would pluck a book from the shelves there and refresh my spirit. At the BSU, I met Christians who had been raised by Christian parents and attended church all their lives. As a recent convert, the depth and breadth of their knowledge and faith humbled and challenged me but it also motivated me to be the best Christian I could. Occasionally informal contests of Bible knowledge were held and I was matched against some sharp contenders. This was good practice for me. As I studied and exercised my knowledge, my list grew and developed too. The list wasn't always on my mind, but from time to time I would update it as new ideas came to me.

After graduation, I joined the workforce as a process engineer. Work and social life kept me quite busy and my spiritual life devolved into weekly church services and daily prayer and Bible studies. I tried attending some local fellowships and Bible studies to further my Christian education, but they were chiefly for new believers and working class Christians. These were too basic to advance what I had already learned so far. Consequently, I missed the stimulating academic life, being surrounded by other analytical and spiritual people in such a nurturing environment. The vibrant ferment of academia gradually settled into a routine around work, home and church where there was only incremental progress. I needed more, I needed to be stimulated to think and test my theories. Little change occurred in my list until later in my married life.

The one VERY important exception to this was a small house church near my hometown of Princeton, New Jersey called the Plainsboro Gospel Fellowship (PGF). It met in the home of Stanton and Margaret Clark in Plainsboro, New Jersey. It was recommended to me by someone I met at the coffee house that was held at that time in the basement of the Nassau Christian Center in Princeton, New Jersey. I was looking for a New Testament style church that I felt would suit me. At first I liked PGF with its charismatic, informal, family style atmosphere and the deeply spiritual, loving, caring attitude of the congregants. But as the church grew in numbers the leadership began planning on building a regular church building. Their emphasis changed from building believers to building the infrastructure of the church. From that point it seemed to me that the fresh spirit seemed to decline. In the interim I met many real "Jesus People" whom I really liked and admired. One of these would give me the key I needed to escape the very real bonds of hell and death.

"For we know that if our earthly house of this tabernacle is taken down, we have a building from God, a house not made with hands, eternal in Heaven. For also in this we groan, greatly desiring to be clothed with our dwelling place out of Heaven, if indeed in being clothed, we shall not be found naked. For indeed, being in the tabernacle, we groan, having been weighted down, inasmuch as we do not wish to be unclothed, but to be clothed, so that the mortal may be swallowed up by the life. And the One having worked in us for this same thing is God, who also is giving us the earnest of the Spirit. Then always being fully assured, and knowing that being at home in the body we are away from home from the Lord (for we walk by faith, not by sight), even we are fully assured, and think it good rather to go away from home out of the body, and to come home to the Lord. Because of this, we also are striving to be pleasing to Him, whether being at home, or being away from home." 2 Corinthians 5:1-9 LITV

Chapter 3 – My Spiritual Body

For a moment the sight of my prone body laid out on the living room floor left me sad and fearful, wondering what the full implication was of being in the afterlife. What happened next? I was alone with my body but that was all that seemed to have changed. Then I took stock of the situation. It wasn't as bad as might have been expected. My personality was still intact and had survived the death of my body. I was still me, self-aware and a quick check confirmed I still retained all the memories of my life experiences. In fact, though ordinarily my memory is slow and fallible, my memory in that state was remarkably complete, perfectly organized and accurate, with total recall of every detail and very rapid processing and analytical capabilities. I felt alive and healthier than I had ever felt before. All pain and discomfort was gone, not just from my injuries, but also chronic back pain from scoliosis and those minor aches and pains we learn to live with.

Although I could remember easily and clearly every detail of my earthly life, I had no memory of any previous existence in that state. However, it seemed totally normal and natural to me to exist as just a spirit. I had a vague sense that I had been in this state before and my reactions to it felt as if they were habitual and well developed. I had never felt more like myself and the familiarity was invigorating. There was no period of adjustment such as an infant goes through when it matures from a helpless state at birth through childhood. The only other bodily sensations I missed were hunger, thirst and the need to breathe. At first I thought it odd not doing something automatic like breathing but since I didn't have a physical body that relied on oxygen

I felt no need to inhale and there was no desire to eat or drink. Nor did I feel any movement of air against me whether I stood still or moved. The physical human senses we accept as given were replaced with different and far more sensitive senses. Regrettably, I did not think to check to see if I was clothed or not.

I tested out my new senses, trying vision first. I found I had the ability to focus on objects near and far instantaneously with total clarity, even to the blades of grass in my neighbor's lawn across the street or microscopic particles of dust on the wires of the window screen before me. I became completely aware of what felt like everything. I could not see through solid objects like walls or trees but my field of vision appeared to be wider than when in the physical body, though it had a definite area of focus surrounded by a less defined periphery. I could not see behind myself. I also felt an awareness of things around me that wasn't sight, but more akin to RADAR or SONAR that allowed me to "feel" the proximity of the floors, celling, walls and furniture that were about me on all sides. I regret not looking in the mirror, but in the drama of the moment that did not occur to me. My sense of sight did not depend on natural or artificial illumination, but everything was clearly visible without shades or shadows. Though the colors and hues were somewhat different (colors as I saw them in the spirit were generally lighter in shade and more intense than I the material) from what I regarded as normal, everything was recognizable.

My hearing became extremely sensitive as well; I could hear small animals and insects moving about inside and outside the house. I could distinctly hear traffic on the main road over five blocks away. Normally this would have required sophisticated listening devices to detect. This sense of hearing was very directional and I could pinpoint the locations of the sound sources with accuracy and precision.

My sense of smell was also quite keen. Years earlier, I had lost most of my natural sense of smell from a severe case of influenza in 1980. Yet in my spiritual state everything around me had a distinct and pleasant odor that I could easily identify. Even ordinary, inert things like paper, fabric and wood were easily recognizable. Living things like plants, people and pets had an especially nice fragrance.

I could feel that I had two arms and two legs and used them normally as I had in those of my physical body. When I held my hand in my field of vision, I did not clearly see a hand as I did the physical objects around me. It was more like a faint wisp of steam that maintained its shape. I don't clearly recall any distinct sense of touch. This is natural, since I could not significantly interact with material objects. As I passed through doors I felt a mild sensation like I was pushing through a curtain of falling dust. I have a vague recollection that I felt a very light pressure against the soles my feet as the touched the floor, it was on the order of a few ounces, rather than the hundreds of pounds I normally felt in my physical body. I didn't look to see what my face looked like or if I have the normal anatomy for an adult male for it didn't occur to me to check. I feel that was a grave oversight. Had I thought of it, I also would have looked in a mirror and experimented with trying to forcefully impact liquids such as water or light objects such as feathers or dust. But unfortunately my thoughts were far from running a battery of tests and experiments, I was dead after all.

Next, I began to go about the house, testing my ability at locomotion. It was not exactly walking. Rather I willed myself to move in a direction with a certain velocity and that's what happened. It seemed perfectly natural and effortless as if I had always done this at some previous time. I suppose I could have floated up and flown, or dived beneath the floor as easily as I moved in the horizontal plane. However, my mind was still conditioned to moving in one plane and it didn't even occur to me to try either of those stunts.

Once I had my bearings I decided to check on my children.

"And you, child, will be called Prophet of the Most High, for you will go before the face of the Lord to prepare His ways, (Mal. 3:1) to give a knowledge of salvation to His people by remission of their sins, through the tender heart of mercy of our God, in which the Dayspring from on high will visit us, to appear to those sitting in darkness and in shadow of death, to direct our feet into the way of peace. (Isaiah. 9:2)" Luke 01:76 LITV

Chapter 4 – Early Encounters With Death

That fateful night in 1995 when I actually died was not my first close encounter with death. In fact, my life seemed to be shadowed by death, regularly punctuated with near misses.

My mother told me the story of the first such event occurred when I was a mere two months old. In late 1961 we were living in an apartment in Cambridge, Massachusetts where my parents were finishing their graduate studies. Although I appeared otherwise healthy and was growing normally, I started vomiting up my food at every feeding. Concerned, my mother contacted our pediatrician, the renowned Dr. Barry Brazelton. Vomiting in infants is not uncommon, so Dr. Brazelton advised waiting to see how things developed.

By that weekend the vomiting, grew worse. In fact, it became more and more frequent, and violent. Now very concerned, my mother telephoned the on-call doctor at Boston Children's Hospital. From my mother's explanation the on-call doctor realized that the vomiting was what is known as "projectile vomiting." She came to our apartment and confirmed this and diagnosed pylorus stenosis, a failure of the sphincter muscles in the duodenum of the stomach to develop normally. This prevented food from passing from the stomach to the upper intestine. So, although I was being fed regularly, I could not retain my food and digest it and was slowly dehydrating and starving.

In earlier years there was no treatment, and children with this condition usually lived or died based on whether or not their bodies could correct the condition before succumbing to starvation. It is an inherited trait, striking alternate generations, and my paternal grandmother had barely survived it. Coincidentally a pioneering surgery to correct this had been developed right in Cambridge, Massachusetts where we lived. The surgery was performed at the Children's Hospital and I recovered. However, it left a great scar on my tiny belly that migrated over the years to my right side.

When I was about three years of age our family moved from New England to New Jersey. My father had earned his PhD from the Massachusetts Institute of Technology in optical physics and landed a research position with Bell Laboratories in Murray Hill. Like most New Jersey residents, in the summer, we would escape the heat by going to the shore. On one such outing when I was about four years of age, I was allowed to wander the beach by myself to pick up shells and play in the surf. While beachcombing, I saw how the other children enjoyed swimming in the surf and decided to try it too. I wandered into the deeper water, enjoying the movement of the sea and the cool firmness of the sand between my toes.

Suddenly a wave knocked me over and pressed me flat against the sand under the water. A strong undertow then pulled me away from the shore. I was too weak to rise up in the light green waters and had not yet learned how to swim well. Instinctively, I began crawling upwards along the sandy bottom as the dense brine rushed past me. I could see the sunlight shining through the water ahead of me and knew there would be shallower water where I might be able to rise and breathe again.

I held my breath and kept crawling for what seemed like forever. Soon my lungs were burning for air and I was feeling weaker. When it seemed I could not hold out any longer, the level of water suddenly dropped around me as a wave receded. With the pressure dissipating, I was able to rise up on my knees and get my head above water. It felt wonderful to breathe again, but soon the water began to rise around me as another wave rolled in. Fearful of being trapped underwater again, I forced my tired and weary limbs to scramble towards the shore to safety.

I lay in the shallow surf for quite a while recovering my strength. As I lay there I looked around at the adults and children playing nearby in the sand and water. No one seemed to notice me lying there and none showed any concern for me. I felt that was terribly wrong. I had nearly died a frightful death from drowning and it seemed no one noticed or cared. When my strength returned, I got up and walked back to the spot where my family had laid out their beach blankets. The summer sun felt warm on my cold body and I lay down on a blanket to sleep. It felt really good to be alive! When I told them what had happened, only my mother really believed me and she seemed more cross than concerned. It was my first encounter with disbelief but far from the last.

The next encounter with death was even more harrowing.

My father's advances in his career allowed us to relocate from our apartment in Plainfield, New Jersey to nearby Mountainside where we moved into our first real house. There I had my own bedroom and a yard to play in. It was a beautiful house and I especially liked the double French doors that opened outward onto the back yard and gave a view of the hillside garden. This was a time of major changes. For soon after our move to the house on Deer Path, I started public school for the first time and was also introduced to organized religion through the local Presbyterian Church, as well as the brotherhood of mischief all boys my age shared.

My parents had left the Christian Science Church after my paternal grandfather, also a member of that cult, had died of untreated diabetes. Some adherents of Christian Science, like my grandfather, refuse to acknowledge the reality of illness and avoid necessary treatment for it. The death of my grandfather, combined with other issues, turned my parents, and especially my father, away from religion in general. However, my parents did briefly try the Community Presbyterian Church down the street. Though their attendance wasn't regular, we did become good friends with the pastor, Rev. Elmer Talcott, and his family. I also liked to play with their children and was friends with their sons Malcolm and Scott. They lived two houses up the street, next to the church. Between our house and the Talcott home lived the O'Konski family. My mother became friends with the Irene O'Konski, and it was she who saved my life this time. Across the street from us lived another family with children my age, the Shields.

It happened one summer day in 1968 when I was in the first grade; we came home to a locked house and my mother couldn't find her house key. She left me and my siblings in the back yard while she went to get the spare key she left with Irene. Being good friends and having no apparent reason to hurry, they chatted amicably on her front porch.

Meanwhile, my friends Chris Shields, David O'Konski, and some others, gathered in our back yard and we began talking. Teasing me was one of their favorite past-times and they were quick to make fun of our predicament. My mother seemed to be taking a long time retrieving the house key and the boys took full advantage of the absence of adult supervision to tease me mercilessly. Then I remembered how the French doors didn't latch well, and even when locked, could be pushed open from inside with a firm shove. So, I thought I would do my mother a kindness and show my tormentors that I was smarter than them and could solve the problem myself.

Leading the group of boys onto the back porch I confidently announced that I would open the doors with a mighty rush against them. Then, with my audience watching, I ran with outstretched arms full force at the doors. However, the doors only opened outwards and no force I could exert would cause them to open inwards. When my hand hit the glass pane of one of the many windows, it shattered and my arm went through the jagged opening. In panic I hastily pulled my arm out again. In two swift motions my right arm was thoroughly shredded. The skin had been flayed off of my upper arm and I could see cream-colored bones and purple muscles laid bare in the sunlight. Arterial blood gushed out in spurts from there and a long gash in my wrist, quickly turned the whole arm bright red.

I immediately went into shock, I felt little pain, but terror gripped me from what I saw and the surprise of the sudden injury paralyzed the other boys into inaction. My first thought was to run to the Talcott home for help. The pastor's wife, Brucie Talcott, was nearly always home and welcomed us children whenever we visited. So, I ran straight towards their house, intending to cross, as I normally did, through the O'Konski family's back yard and head for the Talcott's back door. However, as I passed through the gate between our yards, a strong impulse hit me to run to my right, around the front of the O'Konski house, a way I seldom went. (David O'Konski later told me he felt an angelic presence at that moment.) This made no sense at the time, since it was a longer way to go and I nearly always cut through the O'Konski's back yard to reach the Talcott's back door rather than the front. To go to the Talcott's front yard required a relatively longer detour around the fences and hedges in the respective front yards. But I followed that impulse and as I came around the front of the O'Konski house, I saw my mother and Irene standing on the front porch.

Seeing her child running, screaming and covered in fresh blood must have alarmed my mother. But she kept her presence of mind and stopped me to keep me from running further. Mrs. O'Konski dashed inside and grabbed a handful of clean diapers. She used these as a compress to stop the bleeding. Then, while my mother held the diapers on my injured arm, Irene called for police and an ambulance. A police officer soon arrived and administered more conventional first aid. After the ambulance arrived, I was whisked away to the hospital, lights blazing and sirens screaming; my wounds were closed and I was able to recover. I recall the Emergency Medical technician in the ambulance trying to calm and distract me by explaining the use of the siren and lights.

In an odd twist of fate, I was placed in a ward with two brothers who had given each other the very same injuries as I had that same day. I wondered at the coincidence and suspected a connection. It is certain that detour around the front of the O'Konski house saved my life. For the Talcott family had left on vacation earlier and no one was at home. Had I gone there, it is likely I would have quickly bled to death waiting vainly for them to answer the back door because no one would have known where I'd run off to.

At that point in my life I already believed in God and felt I had a purpose for being alive. However, my concept of spiritual matters was quite limited. In a frightening experience one morning before the accident with the door, I had actually seen a demon while preparing for school. It said nothing when I tried to speak to it. The demon only glared at me menacingly before disappearing. It was a hideously ugly dwarf-like creature with mottled skin and malformed facial features. Sensations I recall from when I saw this demon and before I charged the door suggest to me that something demonic had urged me on to foolish behavior and something angelic had guided me around the O'Konski's house to safety. However, these concepts were very vague in my mind at the time, so I didn't ponder them very deeply.

There were many more situations where my life could have easily been taken as I grew older: falls, fires, explosions, electrocutions, poisoning, exposure to radiation, automobile, motorcycle and bicycle accidents, attacks by gangs and animals, abductions, armed robbery, and the like. Along the way I accumulated a variety of scars, fractured bones and emotional trauma because of all this. By the time I was nine I was sure I would not live to be eleven! By my twenties such events seemed so commonplace that they became almost routine. "Oh no! Not again!" was my typical reaction.

I was the victim of an attempted armed robbery in 1984 and it is one of the more interesting stories.

It was the early part of the year and I had returned to my undergraduate studies at Georgia Tech for the winter quarter, but classes had not started yet. Heavy snow had fallen the night before. That morning I bought my textbooks and groceries for the term and had most of the afternoon free. Having grown up in the north, I was used to snowy conditions and was well prepared with jumper cables, anti-freeze and snow tires. However, many of the locals were not so well prepared. So I decided to be a good neighbor and drove around the area helping to jump-start stalled cars and free other motorists from the snow.

On my afternoon of Good Samaritan acts I stopped at a gas station near campus to refuel when a young black man in a fatigue jacket came up to me and asked if I had cables and could jump-start his car. I had been doing that for much of the day and thought nothing of the request. I asked him to wait while I paid the attendant for the gasoline. The young man told me his car was in a nearby low-income housing development, Techwood Homes. So I took him as a passenger and we drove across the overpass to Techwood. He seemed uneasy and his directions and description of his car were vague. I began to wonder what his motives really were. My concerns were realized when he directed me behind an apartment building and then pulled out a small nickel-plated revolver.

“Now don’t get nervous man,” he said, “this is a stickup.”

At first I was shocked, then afraid, then angry all in a matter of seconds. I had only been trying to help the man, and he used the occasion to try to rob me at gunpoint. This was beyond simple opportunism.

“I just want your car,” he explained.

Just my only means of transportation, I thought, *along with my groceries for the month, my textbooks and all my tools in the trunk of the car.* I had just spent most of my savings and realized I could not get through the quarter if he took off with all these things. I also remembered that I was a Christian and not afraid of death and that stealing was a sin.

So armed only with these basic truths I replied, “Mister, I’m a Christian and I’m not afraid to die. And stealing is a sin. I can’t let you do that.”

He was clearly surprised at this unexpected response. While he hesitated, I began to back the car towards the street where there were many people and potential witnesses that could discourage him.

Then he reached over and turned off the ignition, but left the keys there.

My anger mounted, and I restarted the car, astonished and thankful that he had not taken the keys and that the finicky starter motor actually worked on the first try. “Don’t touch my keys!” I retorted sharply as I resumed course to the street.

This obviously wasn’t going like the robber had expected and he froze for a moment to rethink his plan while I backed out of the parking lot into the driveway.

Then he tried to step on the brake pedal, but I kicked away his leg and shouted, “Keep your foot away from my brake pedal!”

I was now so angry I didn’t even think about the gun at my side.

I floored the accelerator and tried to speed backwards down the driveway. However, I cut the corner too tight and smashed into the apartment building, crumpling the rear fender of the car.

Immediately after impact the robber opened the passenger side door and fled. The last I saw of him he was running away into the apartment complex.

When I reported the crime to the campus police, the desk sergeant at Georgia Tech shook his head slowly and told me I was lucky to be alive. As I pondered these words, fear finally set in and I began trembling at the thought of what I had just been through. Perhaps the robber lacked the nerve to shoot, the gun might not have been loaded or it even could have been a fake. I didn’t know. Still, again, I was grateful to God to be alive and also thankful to still have a car and all that went with it. I suppose that if the robber wanted my car, he was planning something more involved. I hope that never materialized.

1I visited my daughter and tried to wake her.

"See My hands and My feet, that I am He? Feel Me and see, because a spirit does not have flesh and bones, as you see Me having." Luke 24:39 LITV

Chapter 5 – Visiting My Children

Just standing in my living room looking at my dead body didn't hold my attention very long. After a moment to think, the first priority that came to mind was to check on my family. They had no idea what had happened to me.

First I went to my daughter's bedroom to check on her. The door was closed and I found my hand could not grip the doorknob but passed through it. So I stepped through the door and stood by her bed. I noticed that my vision was temporarily obscured, but not completely occluded as I moved through the door. My intention was to wake her and tell her what had happened. I felt it important to assure her I was OK and was going to watch over her. However, I could not make any sound or touch her in a way that would wake her. So I just looked at the sleeping child and felt sorrow that I would not be able to comfort her or hold her again. Alexandra was only three at that time. Her little face looked angelic and peaceful in sleep, framed by her long golden locks. At that moment I realized my children would be without a father to raise them and I became concerned and agitated.

I returned to the hallway and turned into my son's bedroom and watched him sleep. I couldn't wake him either; so I just stood there and wondered what his fate would be when I was gone. This made me sad as I looked at his peaceful face half buried in the pillow, blond hair tousled in sleep. I had been so busy with my career and fixing up our recently purchased home that I had neglected many opportunities to spend time with Christopher. I thought with mixed joy and sadness about the times we had enjoyed together and the realization that there would be no more of them.

I could have just walked in a straight line through the walls from room to room, but force of habit made me go back into the hallway again. From there I decided to return to the living room. I thought that maybe if I examined my body more closely I would be able to see if there might be a way to reenter and reanimate it. As an engineer by profession, I regarded all problems as something to be resolved. Being dead was certainly a problem, but there was no point in giving up immediately. My plan was to examine the situation, see what resources I had to work with and go from there. With my mind newly freed of corporal encumbrances and working at a level far above the norm I felt it was worth a try. I reasoned that there might be some capabilities in the spirit that I had yet to discover, and fixing the problem became my highest priority.

Back in the living room I stood pondering at the feet of my body for a short while. Suddenly I began to sense the presence of something evil. It was like the malevolent presence that had troubled me since early childhood. It was akin to that moment of suspense created in a horror movie when nothing is overtly seen, but there's an atmosphere of expectancy that something really frightening is about to happen. If I had been in my body, the hair on the back of my neck would have been rising up to full attention. Emanations of passionate hatred were unmistakable. Uncertain what was going on I stepped back from the body. My new heightened senses seemed to know more than I did.

"There is a way that seems right to a man, but the end of it is the ways of death." Proverbs 14:12, 16:25 LITV

Chapter 6 – My First Experiences With Religion

The Community Presbyterian Church in Mountainside, New Jersey was my first encounter with organized religion. My best friend at the time was Scott Talcott, the son of the church's minister. We were neighbors of about the same age and I regarded him as my closest friend and sought to play with him whenever I could. However, he often disappeared for much of the day, especially on the Lord's Day.

When I asked him about this, Scott explained that he had to go to church related functions rather than play. Eager to be with my friend, I proposed that I would go with him and so it was arranged. At that age I really didn't understand what it was all about and found the structured lessons and rites very tedious. It was not nearly as fun as playing out in the woods or on the church playground. I was also disappointed that I could not spend time with Scott, since we were all made to sit quietly at desks or on benches while adults talked to us. Scott and the others seemed to understand what was going on, but it was all over my head. My one positive memory of those Bible classes was that they gave us grape juice to drink and crackers to eat. I thought these were tasty, but the significance escaped me at that time.

My interest in church peaked but was abruptly cut off when I followed Scott's example and joined the children's choir. It was rather fun at the beginning. We gathered in a large room at the church and some kind ladies taught us how to sing. I had listened to music before, but had never formally tried to make it myself until then. So naturally I was not very good at singing but enjoyed the expression and the way it made me feel. The best moment came when we had our picture taken as a choir and it was published in the local paper. Then the bad news came.

The children's choir was ready to perform, and we were all going to wear choir robes. The robes for the children's choir were short, white, puffy dresses with large red ribbons about the neck. My first impression of them was how girly these anachronisms looked and my opinion rapidly declined from there. My parents, especially my mother, tried to comfort and reassure me that this was just fine. She emphasized that all the other children would be wearing the same outfit. I didn't feel any better but reluctantly I went along until the day of our debut came.

We gathered in the practice room to don our robes and make final adjustments. Then we were marched single-file to the sanctuary. I was near the rear. As we emerged into the sanctuary I looked from side to side at all the staid, well dressed adults seated in the pews awaiting our performance. I was unsure of my ability to sing, and terrified that all these neighbors and social elites would see me dressed like a giant piece of beribboned popcorn. I tried to keep the rush of panic at bay but I only made it a short distance into the sanctuary before shame and humiliation overcame me. I turned and fled crying back to the narthex. After that experience, I flatly refused to go to any more church functions with Scott and it seemed they were relieved to be done with this stubborn, awkward child too. I felt humiliated and so out of place. That was my last choir performance for over forty years and the end of my interest in organized religion for nearly a decade.

My parents also lost interest in the church at the same time as their relationship deteriorated. In 1969 they divorced and my mother moved with my siblings and me to Trenton, New Jersey. There she married an English professor, Dr. Jonathan Thomas, and we moved into his home on Carlton Avenue. "Jack," as he asked to be called, became my stepfather and something of a mentor. Unlike my father who was preoccupied with his research, Jack took an active role in parenting. Dr. Thomas had already raised a son and daughter from a previous marriage and therefore had some experience in parenting. As a college level English professor he was also well educated in the Bible, but chiefly as literature. He did not regard the Christian faith with any serious or practical interest, and therefore did not apply it to parenting. The concept of religious ideals in the daily life was put on hold. He did give me many scholarly lectures on morality and proper, just behavior, but seldom if ever invoked spiritual values. There were several copies of the Bible in his personal library, and I began reading it there for the first time along with many other excellent books.

My mother and Jack did sporadically attend the Unitarian Churches in Ewing and later Princeton, New Jersey for a while. The services did little for me though, being on par with book reviews and mild-tempered social commentary. It was far from what I needed as a spiritual home and it lacked the regularity and stability of friendships with fellow church-going children. However, this church did have what were termed "extended family weekends" periodically where a number of families would spend the weekend staying overnight in the sprawling facilities. These were quite fun for us children who happily played in and around the church buildings. A charismatic boy named Rick Smith dominated the social scene for the children though. He and I had some sharp differences, so eventually I kept apart from them and enjoyed my own company. This furthered my isolation and kept me from reaping the fruits of a full spiritual life.

Since my time at that church didn't cultivate any significant friendships I did what any rejected kid does and retreated to the library. The church library was extensive and housed many kinds of books It was the first time I had seen so many books on religion. Bibles were relatively scarce there, but there were many commentaries and topical books. An adolescent at the time, I read the ones about sex education first. After exhausting this topic, I began reading other titles too. Though most of them were far beyond my ability to properly comprehend at the time, it did create awareness in me that there was a whole body of literature on spiritual subjects. I was becoming cognizant that there was more to believing in God than simply acknowledging that He existed and that life had purpose, meaning and goals. For the first time it occurred to me that God had expectations of people.

The adults also enjoyed the extended family meetings, perhaps too well, for they saw the demise of my mother's second marriage. Jack became interested in another woman and eventually married her. This naturally caused some strains in the respective marriages not to mention between the families. My mother and Jack did try a variety of things to address the issues troubling their marriage. On one weekend our family and the Smiths went to a gestalt therapy session in Mays Landing, New Jersey. Gestalt therapy is a humanistic approach to satisfying immediate perceived needs without addressing the root causes of personal issues. The shortcomings of this feel-good approach should be obvious as well as detrimental to young minds that don't fully understand romantic relationships.

The counselors there attempted to heal marital problems by encouraging intimacy through therapy that included people baring both their heart and bodies during the sessions. Children included. Being very modest, and not understanding how my nakedness would help my family, I declined to disrobe as others in the group did. But the sights and sounds from that weekend still deeply disturbed me regardless. From that point on a new element of sexual lust was added to the evil thoughts that troubled me. If I had not been demonized up to that point, it is sure I was after that!

Since it ignores sin, even the radical, experimental gestalt therapy offered no real cure. Rather it ameliorates the symptoms and only makes the patient feel better while in fact they are still getting worse. Therefore, in the course of things, Jack and my mother divorced, as did the Smiths. Jack eventually married a woman who was a regular at the "Extended Family Weekends." My mother also remarried yet again. All this was quite distressing and embarrassing to me. I resolved that when I married, I would do all I could to avoid divorce. Thankfully we left the Unitarian Church and the gestalt therapists behind when we moved from Trenton to the vicinity of Washington's Crossing Park, on the New Jersey side, to be in a better public school system.

Our new home in Titusville overlooked the Delaware River and occupied a pleasant and attractive lot with large trees and grassy lawns. At the time, the Belvidere-Delaware Railroad operated along the Delaware-Raritan Canal between our property and the river. In between the canal and the river was a narrow strip of forest that became one of my favorite places to wander and explore. It was nearly a paradise for a boy my age. It would have been an ideal place to live except for two things: the local gang of boys and a spirit that haunted our house, particularly the attic. Moreover, without a regular father figure in my life, my interests tended to drift leaving me open to outside influences.

The gang of boys was led by two brothers, Steve and Bobby Service. They had long picked on another boy, Jon Tyson, before my arrival. Since I was a new kid, both of us were outsiders to the local social order. Thus it was natural that Jon and I soon became friends since the Service brothers made sure to keep us on the receiving end of their bullying. So, I tended to keep to my own yard or the forest once that kind of treatment commenced.

We moved there in 1974. Around 1977 weird things began to happen. Across the street from our house was a large apartment building with a bar called the Tally Ho on the first floor. Drunks would often exit the bar with loud shouting and profane comments late at night. The noise of cars starting and squealing tires as well the regular loud sounds that accompany drunkenness would keep me away nightly. By comparison, the passing freight trains across River Road were inconsequential. But what disturbed me most was that sometimes I could hear their thoughts in my mind, as I lay awake in bed late at night. The confused, unrestrained mind of a drunk was shocking to a teen raised in a peaceful home where drunkenness and profanity were otherwise unknown…

Another strange thing began to happen at night. I would hear footsteps clearly ascending and descending the attic stairs. This went on night after night. Frightened but curious, I would turn on the lights and investigate. I never saw anyone in the hall, on the stairs or in the attic but I knew what I heard and it was very distinctive. When I checked on my siblings and my mother, all were fast asleep. None of them claimed to hear the footsteps when I asked them about this. Shortly before we moved from there in 1979 the footsteps stopped.

Occasionally I would also have very vivid, detailed dreams of mundane events. Within a day or so of having the dream, the events portrayed would actually happen. One of the most vivid and disturbing dreams/visions ended in a scene where I was looking down into some dead, brown leaves while drops of blood fell from the right side of my vision and spattered onto the leaves. Although I knew I had dreamed more, I could only recall the last part. It seemed like a warning, but without more clues it was hard to know what I should be looking out for.

Later that day I was walking in the woods above our neighborhood. It was a part I had never been in before. Following a narrow deer trail, I came to a very tall Japanese Larch. High up near the top I spied a branch that would make an ideal quarterstaff. (I wanted one because my friend Jon and I were interested in things medieval and we planned to learn how to spar like the knights of old.) However, the lower limbs of the tree were all dead. I knew from years of tree climbing that a climber should never trust their weight on a dead tree limb. But I wanted that particular branch very badly.

After some thought I decided that if I stayed close to the trunk of the tree and kept a firm grip on a branch at all times, I would be OK. Even to me this was obviously a bad idea. Yet though my conscience sounded an alarm, I climbed up about twenty to twenty-five feet to where I was nearly in reach of the branch I wanted. (Later I would learn where these bad ideas really originated.) As I took hold of the next branch, it snapped off easily in my right hand. Unconcerned, I dropped it and reached for another. Then the branch in my left hand broke off. Only mildly concerned, I reached with both hands for other branches. Then the branches under my feet suddenly snapped! I became *very* concerned!

It seemed that I hung in the air for a brief instant—long enough to realize my predicament and to compose a short prayer.

"God, if You get me out of this alive," I promised, "I won't do this again!"

I must have hit my head on something as I plummeted earthward, for I do not recall any more of the descent. I awoke from unconsciousness face down in the leaf meal at the base of the tree. As I pushed myself up I could see the very same pattern of leaves before me that I dreamed about earlier. Immediately blood began dripping from my lacerated right ear and spattering on the leaves. It was eerie to see in my waking state what I had dreamed that very morning. This was not the first time it happened, nor would it be the last. Yet the extreme clarity of the dream and the exact match of the view down to the veins in the leaves made it unusually memorable and precluded mere déjà vu. Later I realized the significance of this experience—our lives are very carefully scripted by God, down to minute details. And He sends us warnings! I just needed to learn how to read those warnings and react accordingly.

I was otherwise unhurt and stood up to assess the damage. Looking upwards, I saw that my falling body had broken off all the branches on one side of the tree, leaving jagged, knife-like protrusions sticking out from the trunk. The broken branches formed a large pile leaning up against the trunk. Their splintered ends pointed skyward like spears. I had landed just to the side of the pile and had missed being impaled by inches. The thought made me shudder. Once more, I was very grateful to be alive.

That happened on a weekend and my mother worked at that time as an English teacher. So when I arrived home, I found my mother in her usual occupation of grading the papers of the students she taught. She turned to look at me when I announced I had something that needed her attention. My dear mother expressed initial shock at seeing me standing there, clothes torn and dirty, broadly grinning, with blood caked all over the right side of my head and neck. Then her composure returned and she requested an explanation. I told her the story as we drove to the doctor's office. She was not impressed with my daring adventure but she was becoming more and more accustomed to my injuries. The doctor put a few stitches in my ear and sent me home with some good advice about staying out of trees with dead branches. I mostly heeded him and kept my promise to God.

The most profound experiences for me while we lived there were the out of body experiences I began to have. My interest in spiritual matters had been piqued by some of the more unusual books in the library of the Unitarian church. I was also looking for explanations for the paranormal experiences I was having. Without the guidance of my parents or a stable church environment, it fell solely on my shoulders to try to make sense of my experiences. So, I ordered more books from ads I found in the back sections of some magazines we had. These were not about Christianity, but about ESP, mind reading, and astral projection—occult themes.

Using techniques learned from a source on mind control I ordered, I learned to detach my spirit from my body. Mostly it was just for a few seconds before some disturbance broke my concentration and I was sucked back into the body. However, sometimes I could float up and out and hover about my bedroom. In this state I first realized that there was another dimension to reality. For in the spirit I could see that my bedroom was noticeably different in the spiritual realm than in physical reality. The differences puzzled me until I realized that not only was I leaving my body, but also entering a parallel world to the physical one I had previously known. Without my physical body the way I reacted and interacted with my surroundings also changed. There were subtle differences between them regarding the physical laws such as the propagation of light, spatial relationships and the flow of time, but my visits were too brief and infrequent to examine these phenomena closely. In that state I also felt an evil presence there that frightened me. There was a sense of danger that had been following me throughout my life and I wasn't any nearer to finding out what it was or why it was.

The experiences were not only disturbing, but also difficult to achieve. So, fearful of hidden dangers, troubled by the amplified feelings of evil and discouraged by the arduous effort involved, I eventually abandoned experimenting with these things. My limited dabbling in the occult frightened and disgusted me. However I still desired to learn more about spiritual things, but I realized I was looking for something pure, clean and safe. I also yearned for a father.

That primed me for what I found during Christmas break in 1978. I was watching television and idly changing channels looking for some interesting programming. After much flipping back and forth between channels I came across a program called "Show My People." It was broadcast from Bob Jones University (BJU) in South Carolina. There was a speaker, Dr. Bob Jones III, who was telling the television audience about Jesus Christ. I had never seen anyone on television before talk plainly about Christianity and decided to watch for a while. Eventually Dr. Jones said something that I could relate to.

"Do you feel an emptiness in your heart?" he said with a quaint southern drawl.

That grabbed my attention, for it was true.

"That's because you need Jesus Christ in your heart," he explained.

There was a clear connect in my thinking. This one statement made more sense to me than all the books I had read, songs I had heard, and sermons I had listened to up to that date. I wanted to know more. So I grabbed a pencil and paper and wrote down the telephone number Dr. Jones invited us to call. After the program I called the number and was given an address to write to for more information.

Writing that first letter began the journey that lead me to the very gates of heaven and hell!

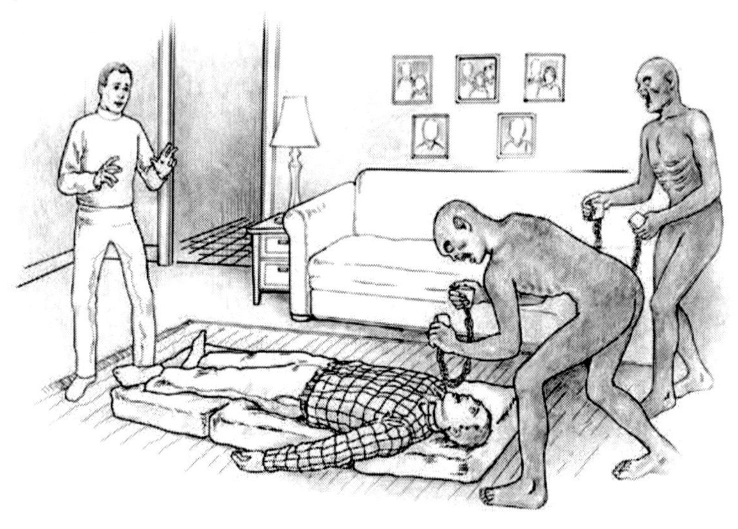

Two demons came to bind me with chains and drag me into hell!

"Behold, they are all My souls. As the soul of the father, also the soul of the son, they are Mine. The soul that sins, it shall die." Ezekiel 18:04 LITV

Chapter 7 – At the Gates of Hell

My body was still lying on the floor of our living room when I returned. I stood near the feet and was wondering if there was a way to revive it when I felt a new sensation. It was akin to the feeling when fear builds up because some unknown danger is approaching in the darkness. It was that kind of fear that makes the hair on the back of one's neck rise up. A palpable feeling of evil began to permeate the room and I felt distinct emanations of intense hatred.

Suddenly, through the southwest corner of the living room came two dark, man-sized figures. They looked like tall, gaunt, muscular men, covered entirely in short, coarse, black hair. They had gleaming yellow slits for eyes and curving black claws on all ten digits. Each of them carried a set of manacles and they were laughing. As they laughed I could see into their open, red mouths which displayed short, white fangs. As they approached, the creatures began to communicate with me.

They didn't speak to me in the conventional sense, but projected their thoughts directly into my mind. It was a raucous burst of thoughts, emotions and images. They had very wild, chaotic minds. Thoughts of hunger dominated their thinking. And that hunger was directed towards me! It was clear to me that they didn't regard me as a person, a human being with personality, awareness, emotions, feelings and purpose, but merely as food and fuel. They intended to capture me and take me back with them to hell for consumption and endless, brutal torture to satisfy their perverse, sadistic pleasures and feed their condemned spirits.

The whole exchange lasted less than the blink of an eye, but the amount of information exchanged was staggering. I had a glimpse of hell, which showed me clearly that it is a mind-blowing, horrific place of suffering, chaos, insanity and abuse that is beyond the pale, constrained efforts of human language to describe. Excruciating pain, hunger, exhaustion, sickness, extreme thirst, trauma, and torment dominated the images they shared. It was horror beyond human comprehension, without relief, without hope, without respite. I received a vision of senseless, lawless, chaotic, disjointed, purposeless existence at the mercy of implacable, fiercely hostile powers. I was horrified and desperate. Yet to them it was home, and they seemed perfectly adapted to such a perverse environment. These were truly awful creatures, monsters and they wanted to use me and take me with them.

I protested that this was not right. I was a believing, practicing Christian. Church leaders and teachers of eternal salvation had assured me that I would be admitted to heaven when I died. I had publicly professed Christ as savior, been baptized, studied the scriptures, prayed and attended church regularly, donated money and time. I had even been a Sunday school teacher, a church trustee and gone on short-term mission trips. I was considered a model Christian by some and had done all that the church had taught me, well beyond most of my peers. I seemed to be among the last Christians who could be criticized for not being a good Christian.

The creatures laughed at this. My pain and my confusion as well as my panic were a welcome joke to them.

They flooded my mind with a remarkably complete and well-organized list of all the sins I had not properly confessed and repented of during my life. From late childhood through to the present they recalled everything from a filched paperclip to an unpaid bill. They knew of every instance of an unkind word, rude behavior, indifference to others, cheating on exams, absolutely every lie, each selfish act, etc. Thankfully they did not appear to have known my personal thoughts, but that was little consolation. For I could feel they were extremely powerful and my own strength was inadequate to resist or argue. In a moment I would be dragged away helplessly to eternal damnation.

As they approached, the creatures went on to gloat that they had been with me all of my life and they had been constantly working towards this moment. They had been trying to tempt and kill me so they could compromise my relationship with God and harvest my soul. They were singular in purpose and knew more about my life than I thought possible. Images came to mind of the many times I had narrowly escaped death and I realized they had been behind every one of those situations. Because of God's protections, they couldn't kill me outright, but they could manipulate mine and other's feelings and perceptions to cause us to make bad decisions that lead to tragedy. The incident with the furnace was only the latest in years of devising ways to trick me and lure me to death. Now they were ravenously hungry and impatient to have the fruit of their labors.

I felt this wasn't right, and I searched my mind desperately for some way to escape this fate. The must be some principle or precept I had missed. The creatures (I suppose they were demons, but they did not name themselves) were closing in on me and I knew there was only one last opportunity to escape them and it had to be good. Then I remembered what a man had told me once at the house church meeting in Plainsboro. He was an unusual fellow and often talked about miracles, demons and spiritual things outside of the normal, officially discussed church subjects. He was charismatic in his beliefs and had given me books on the gifts of the Holy Spirit, exorcism and such that I had dutifully read and shelved after making little tangible, practical progress on the subjects. However, one thing he had said to me came back from memory.

"If you ever meet a demon," he said, "rebuke it in the name of Jesus Christ."

I don't even recall his name now, but he literally saved my life, my eternal life. Looking back I wish I had told more people what he told me. This might have helped them too.

Immediately I sent the thought to them, "I rebuke you in the name of Jesus Christ."

Instantly they were gone, as if a wrecking ball had hit them dead on and sent them back where they had come from.

Once again I stood in my living room alone, with my body lying on the floor. I looked around and wondered what my fate would be now. Was I rejected from both heaven and hell? Would I wander disembodied until Judgment Day perhaps or for eternity? Would those beings come back for me? I didn't like that thought and was just imagining that there might be other dangers and perils out there for a disembodied spirit when the third remarkable thing happened.

"Therefore, I said to you that you will die in your sins. For if you do not believe that I AM, you will die in your sins." John 08:24 LITV

Chapter 8 – I Realized My Need for God

After contacting him through the television program, Dr. Jones and I corresponded for several months and he went into more detail about who Jesus is and what our relationship with God requires. As a teenager, I was profoundly impressed that a university president would show an interest in me as an individual and take the time to write letters to me. The knowledge he shared with me was incredible and I learned a lot. After he was satisfied that I understood the basics of the gospel, Dr. Jones recommended that I meet in person with a local pastor who could respond more directly to my questions and teach me in greater detail. This seemed like a good idea, so I asked for his recommendation. Dr. Jones referred me to a graduate of BJU, the Rev. Charles B. Gross. I was sent confidently on my way to continue developing my spiritual life so I contacted the pastor; he arranged to meet me at our home with my mother's permission.

Rev. Gross came to our house that spring and in his humble, quiet way explained the difference between righteousness and sin, the relationship between God and mankind, and my need for salvation from death and damnation. His patient explanation included a warning that rejecting God's plan meant dying and going to hell for eternity. God had promised to admit those who accepted His plan into heaven where they would have eternal life. I believed what he said, it made sense and I could see how this fit what I had observed in my short life to that date. I also knew I didn't want to go to hell. Going to heaven was appealing, but he was rather vague on what heaven was like and what made it desirable. I had to know more, and I wanted to experience it.

"What do people in heaven do?" I wondered. Eternal life naturally seemed much better than death. But I did wonder why both believers and unbelievers still had to suffer physical death. Pastor Gross explained that everyone has to die, and God separates out the saved and damned on Judgment Day. This was not very satisfactory to me, and many things seemed to go against my understanding of what God wanted for us. I reasoned that if Christ already died for us, why should we still have to die if our sins were forgiven? I had a problem with this point, but could get no better answer. So I set the question aside to investigate the subject more thoroughly later. Dying in any sense bothered me greatly.

The main point I grasped was that there was a distinction in behavior between righteousness and sin. Righteousness is doing God's will and sin is opposing God's will. God will reward obedience with eternal life in heaven with certain rewards and punish sin with death and torment in hell. What was not clear was the basis on which good and bad were defined. Surely God would be clear as to what the criteria were for something so critical. It seemed to me everyone had different, arbitrary opinions and there were obvious difficulties in consulting God directly. I hoped Pastor Gross would clarify this, but he just referred me to the Bible and I was left with no more insight than I could glean myself. It was not discussed then, but I would have to wait until someone else explained the role of the Holy Spirit.

At that stage in my education, this merely complicated the matter since the scriptures were way beyond my modest adolescent ability to comprehend such things. Late in the winter of '78-79 he gave me a good start by suggesting reading Psalm 119. As a high school graduation present he also gave me a Scofield Reference Bible. That helped; for it inspired me with a respect for God's laws and lead me to study them in depth.

The third and most interesting point that I realized for the first time was that there could be personal interaction between God and me. A relationship. This was profound. I could have my questions answered finally. I had believed in God as long as I could remember, but now I understood for the first time that I could have interaction with Him. What was missing from the conversation was an explanation of the principles on which this whole system operated. That would come years later when I learned about more complex subjects like respect for God, faith, and selfless love.

What primed me for this moment?

I have observed similar conversations where the gospel was clearly presented and the listener flatly rejected it, or indefinitely put off making a decision. This is difficult for me to understand because the general subject seemed crystal clear to me as Pastor Gross explained it. Even at 16 years of age I could look about me and see that I am an amazingly complex and wonderfully designed being living in a world of constant miracles and wonders. It is true that it seems warped and twisted by evil because of the wickedness of some people and the chaos and disorder that colors our environment. But for me it was like being a savage standing among the ruins of a great civilization and observing the magnificent works of my predecessors. I was ignorant of what had gone before my time. Yet there was no doubt that things had been very different before, better, perhaps even wonderful, and something had gone very wrong and changed things. The theories of a causeless, purposeless universe I had been taught in public school seemed like gibberish to me.

My memories go back to an age somewhere between two and three when my family lived in Pineview Apartments in Plainfield, New Jersey. Some of those earliest memories include an awareness of a spiritual presence about me. Sometimes it was good and assumed to be God, but more often it was evil. I couldn't understand what invoked this evil presence. I disliked the evil presence and longed for the good. I also felt a sense of destiny and purpose. It is difficult to say where that comes from. Neither my parents nor my teachers ever tried to instill such thoughts in me. Yet, the idea that life didn't matter and we couldn't change anything, so we were victims at the mercy of fate was not my understanding. I knew my life existed because it has a purpose. This might be compared to my sister's habitual neatness and passion for organization—something I lack. Asked where it comes from, she will answer, "It is just something I was given." So, it seems the same with me. My spiritual awareness is just something God put in me from the start. Though I suspect part of it was in answer to my maternal grandmother's prayers. Mildred Green was a devout woman and prayed for her family regularly. After she died in 1987, the only other person I knew who prayed for me regularly was a young woman I discipled while in my undergraduate studies at Georgia Tech, Rosemary Good. Mildred and my mother were the only members of my immediate family who encouraged me in the Christian faith.

In short, it just seemed natural to me that God exists and I could relate to Him person to person. It is such a fundamental part of my personality that it greatly astonishes me when other people think differently. I am so grateful for that gift. Although it makes me different from most people, and puts me in conflict with some, I gladly accept the difficulties it brings when I see the effects on the lives of those who lack it. The gift gives me a passion to search for truth and meaning in life, to seek out God and learn about spiritual things. It makes me sensitive to spiritual forces about me and warns me when danger or diversion is near.

The sense is far from reliable or accurate and I still grope about blindly in many regards, but it is so much better than having no spiritual sense at all. For I see those who lack this sense single-mindedly pursuing transitory things which ultimately have no real value: sensual pleasure, popularity, temporal power, material wealth, control and influence over people, and such things. They miss both the call to seek greater riches and the warnings that they are putting their very souls in peril. I can also see patterns in the world around me that are like the signature of a master artist at work. These are subtle, but deliberately left for those who seek them. These experiences make me yearn for greater levels of this gift and wish that more people shared it with me.

For then they could embark on the same amazing journey that took me into the eternal family of the believers, into the very embrace of God, into His church! And Oh my! God has a most interesting family!

"And everyone living and believing into Me shall not die to the age, never! Do you believe this?" John 11:26 LITV

Chapter 9 – Face to Face with Christ

I began to feel another emotion, like the hatred I had felt earlier, but this time it was a profound sensation of love. It was even more wonderful than the hatred had been awful. A moment after I felt it, Jesus entered the living room from the southeast corner and stood facing me. There was no mistaking in whose presence I stood. He looked just as I might have imagined Him, a Caucasian with shoulder length brown hair, a short, full beard, hazel eyes and a white robe that hung to his sandaled feet. He had a light blue cape slung over one shoulder as it often is portrayed in the popular paintings I had seen in many churches. He did not speak to me, but as the demons had, shared His thoughts with me telepathically.

First and foremost, Jesus let me know that while He was perfectly aware of my sins and flaws, He accepted me just as I was and loved me deeply and unconditionally. My relief was tremendous because I was expecting a severe rebuke given the list of sins I had just been accused of by the demons. He also let me know that He was appearing to me as I expected Him to look so that I would be comfortable with our meeting and He could appear any way to anyone as needed.

Words fail to describe what it was like to be in the presence of Christ. My eyes beheld a man of average height and build dressed in simple first century garb. As the scripture says,

"For He comes up before Him as a tender plant, and as a root out of dry ground. He has no form nor magnificence that we should see Him; nor form that we should desire Him." Isaiah 53:02 LITV

"For think this within you, which mind was also in Christ Jesus, who subsisting in the form of God, thought it not robbery to be equal with God, but emptied Himself, taking the form of a slave, having become in the likeness of men and being found in fashion as a man, He humbled Himself, having become obedient until death, even the death of a cross." Philippians 2:5-8 LITV

What I *felt* was entirely different. Instantly, I knew I was in the presence of God, which in this case was the person of the Son, Jesus Christ, one of the three persons in the Trinity. For in that spiritual state communication is far, far above what it is in the body. It is not linear and confined to a narrow bandwidth of sound like speech. It is instantaneous, complete and covers a broad spectrum of mediums that include sight, sound, feeling, thought, emotions and entirely new and wonderful modes that have no earthly equivalent. This wasn't just some exalted being or a great spiritual force. Jesus *is* His credentials. I knew it was *Him*. I knew who *He* was, and it was equally clear who *I* was and the vast, vast difference between us.

I pity the backslidden Christian, the false Christian, the agnostic, the atheist, the pagan and especially the Satanist on Judgment Day! The warnings were clear. There will be no arguing with God and He will accept no excuses, I knew this. The unbelievers and everyone else will know exactly where they stand and the terrible, terrible, terrible, terrible, terrible, terrible, terrible (there aren't enough "terribles" in all the dictionaries in the world to express what I mean) mistake of denying Him. On Judgment Day I expect the communication will be essentially entirely one way, from God to man. For there is no possibility of anyone arguing with God in His presence. He is awesome and limitless in His perfection, His holiness, His inerrancy, His fullness, His knowledge of us, and in every other attribute. The most amazing defense a person or any gathering of people could devise has absolutely no chance of enduring the scrutiny of God! He is a loving God to be sure, even merciful, but He is also mortally terrifying in His greatness, completeness and perfection!

Oddly, the experience wasn't overwhelming. Jesus didn't shine with brilliant light and He wasn't surrounded by a host of mighty angels. There was a permeating sense of calm and quiet joy. There was no crown or scepter to mark His status and Jesus didn't need a herald to introduce Him. He didn't require any trappings of deity to communicate His status. His presence was enough to establish who He was, in my mind. There was no mistaking it, I may have never seen Jesus before but I truly felt Him and that's how I knew it was Him. The only analogy I can make is that it was something like being in the presence of true royalty. Jesus' composure, the way He stood, the way his eyes regarded me, the perfectly timed and controlled gestures He made all marked Him as THE AUTHORITY. His person inspires unmitigated awe. He radiated absolute assurance. His very thoughts to me were so utterly perfect in every way that they seemed inevitable. In comparison my own efforts to present myself and compose my thoughts seemed hopelessly awkward and incoherent. Yet I didn't detect the slightest element of rejection, revulsion or a condescending attitude in His demeanor towards me.

His total awareness of me also made me feel, in a sense, naked, even worse, utterly transparent. Nothing was hidden from Him. With less effort than a thought He made it clear to me that He was aware of everything about me. In one way it made me feel terribly vulnerable but in another way it was reassuring. For it was equally clear that Jesus was there for my benefit, not to condemn or harm me. He cared deeply for me. He is a true shepherd and knows his flock more intimately than any man ever knew his wife or children. Jesus knew me far better than I knew myself. I had read this in the scriptures but encountering it first-hand was still a revelation. If it impressed me that a university president could show a direct and personal interest in me, I was amazed that God valued me so highly that He gave me such in-depth, detailed attention!

If I felt fear and disgust when the demons revealed their knowledge of my sins, it was shame and despair I felt when I understood how thoroughly all my failures were known to God. In the absence of the standards of His holiness, against which to measure myself, I had come to think of myself as a pretty fine person. This did not endure being face to face with the All mighty. In the presence of Jesus, that illusion was blown away like smoke in a strong wind. Things I regarded as triumphs were revealed as feeble, failed attempts. I was eternally humbled and forever thankful that I was allowed an audience. Qualities I regarded as noble were exposed as exorable weaknesses. Towering deeds that led me to believe I was pleasing to God looked like slapstick, comical errors. Yet all this wasn't like a scolding or a harsh criticism. It was simply the truth, quietly, plainly and lovingly revealed. Jesus wasn't trying to beat me down, but show me the way up. He wasn't telling me I wasn't good enough he was showing me that I could be better.

The first important point I had missed was that even the good things I had done were done with the wrong motives! I had done things of real benefit for others and made genuine sacrifices of my effort, time and resources. However, all my motives were self-serving: to earn a place in heaven, to achieve some status, to deserve a reward, to please others, etc. What I had missed was that I should have done them because I loved God, to please Him, to bring glory to Him. This wasn't to stroke God's ego—it has nothing to do with that. I wasn't a ploy to gain brownie points for my own benefit. It had to be totally for God. Giving glory to God is a high privilege that exalts the one giving it. Its purpose is to draw others to Him and to build relationships with God. There are generally only three activities of eternal value:

1. What we do to improve ourselves spiritually (i.e. in character after Christ's likeness)
2. What we do for others (esp. what others can't, not won't, but can't do for themselves)
3. What we do to please God (i.e. show our love for Him)

Little else really matters!

Another key point that came out of all of this was that I had tried to live on my own terms, in my own strength, depending on my own intelligence, using only my own resources. God never intended anyone to live solely that way. I, like many others, had believed a crafty lie of the devil. That is the lie that we can do anything apart from God. This pernicious lie is a set up. The devil cannot fight God directly nor can he fight us directly when we are one with God. In truth, Satan is already defeated. The only way he can defeat us is by getting us to separate ourselves from God and expose ourselves. To reject God and faith so we are vulnerable to be enticed by their poisonous lies. If we believe the lie that we can live and act independently from God, it makes us easy prey for the enemy. This is the fundamental error of pride—believing we know better, can do better and are anything or have anything apart from God. We are made in His image, we have no other purpose than to serve Him and exalt Him. If we do declare independence from God, by default we become the devil's property!

"I am able to do nothing from Myself; just as I hear, I judge; and My judgment is just, for I do not seek My will, but the will of the One sending Me, the Father." John 05:30 LITV

"The one who is not with Me is against Me, and the one who does not gather with Me scatters." Matthew 12:30 LITV

That is not to say we shouldn't use the abilities and skills we do have. However, these are just starting points. When we do use them, these must be used for God in service to others. This attitude makes us partners in God's work. God then becomes involved in our work and empowers our deeds with a vast array of subtle but very efficacious powers and purposes that greatly augment the effect we have. He works with us as a partner. In this way our words and deeds take on a life of their own and a process is initiated that continues to create results long after we have ceased to be actively engaged. That is why so much more can be achieved when we do things with the right motives. For what we do only in our own strength and for our own purposes begins and ends with just those actions with which we are directly engaged. When obeying God is the goal, we are truly selfless and genuine servants of God. The difference is as great as night and day!

Besides knowing I was in the presence of God, I also knew I was in the presence of a master teacher. It reminded me of my days of undergraduate studies when I was struggling to understand physics. I would wrestle fruitlessly with a problem or concept for hours. When I finally admitted to myself that I could not make further progress, I would go to my professor's office, Dr. Ray Pfrogner. I would explain the problem and he'd have me put it up on the chalkboard (that was before the day of white boards and digital touch screens) and set up the problem. Dr. Pfrogner had a special way of talking his students through a problem that didn't directly reveal the answer, but opened the student's eyes to see it. He let me set up the problem and work through it as far as I could go. Then Dr. Pfrogner would say a few words and the intractable became obvious. More than once I had just laid out the problem on the board for him when it was suddenly clear to me how to solve it. The ease with which he made it clear was embarrassing to me. For I also saw at once how simple the problem really was and how I should have been able to solve it myself.

It was the same only more so in the presence of Christ. For He showed me that through obedience to God, anything is possible, within God's will. One point I will always remember with surprise and shame was that the church could have won the entire world for Christ in any generation from the time of the apostles to our present age. Only laziness, selfishness, timidity and unbelief (and mainly the latter) have held back the church. In my own case, I thought I had struggled mightily to achieve the modest progress I had made as a Christian. Yet in a moment it was clear that I had not really been struggling to achieve God's will at all, but to resist it! Worse, to try to impose my will on God's purposes!

We are made to obey God and it is really the most natural thing for us! Yet I was afraid to yield because I would have to give up sins and worthless habits that I enjoyed more than fellowship with God. It was really awful to see these things clearly. I had been afraid that God would ask me to do something I didn't want to do, couldn't do or would involve incurring embarrassment or the rejection of others. In retrospect I saw how foolish those thoughts were. True there were obstacles, but for every obstacle, God provides a remedy. It was excruciatingly mortifying for me to see how simple the truth was and how convoluted and complicated I made my life to avoid admitting what I really knew all along. The pain and shame I felt didn't come from Jesus, but from within me. I realized that I had not found the answers because I really didn't want to find them.

By that time I had been a Christian for about 16 years. I had read the Bible through several times in several different translations. I had also listened to innumerable sermons and read the equivalent of a small library of books by Christian authors. I knew the truth. I knew even more than that and I forgot how thinking this way left me open to the devil's work. For everything I needed to know was in the scriptures. After all, that's just what Jesus had to start with in His mortal life! If Jesus did it why couldn't I? But like the rich young man described in chapter 19 of the gospel of St. Matthew, I loved the familiar and comfortable more than God's way. I had cherry-picked my way through the Bible. I selected what I wanted to believe and discarded what I didn't like or substituted something I thought made more sense than God's word. It was easy, since those around me were doing the same thing and they appeared to be doing just fine. In fact I felt I belonged at the top of this list because I was leading the way. It was far from the truth.

Those ideas of godliness and perfection thoroughly dissipated in the presence of the true man, Jesus Christ. I knew then I wasn't doing fine. I knew my teachers, pastors and fellow Christians weren't doing fine either. There are no excuses before God. Jesus is the standard and He had proved in His own person that the impossible was possible. I could not deny it.

What I had missed, or rather rejected, is the simple truth that we must seek obedient oneness with God. Three prime clues to this are the verses:

"And the man Moses was very meek, more than any man who was on the face of the earth." Numbers 12:03 LITV

"But the meek shall inherit the earth; yea, they shall delight themselves in abundant peace." Psalm 37:11 LITV

"Seek Jehovah, all the meek of the earth who have done His justice; seek righteousness; seek meekness. It may be you shall be hidden in the day of the anger of Jehovah."
Zephaniah 2:3 LITV

Meek doesn't mean weak. It means obedient.

Christians overcome the devil by obedience to God. An obedient Christian has the full protection, power and provision of God behind them. However, the moment they depart from obedience to God, they are on their own—within certain limitations. And that's where Satan wants them.

A great difficulty is in knowing God's will for a given individual. Extrapolating from the scriptures to the details of daily life is often challenging, for we are typically subject to innumerable conflicting demands and impulses. The key here is starting in obedience and continuing progressively in it as the relationship with God grows. Obedience starts with the revelation of God's will in the Bible. The Decalogue is a good pattern to start with followed by the revelations of the prophets and the teachings of the apostles. Yet everyone has a different starting point, and throughout life there are regular challenges, exercises and tests. To keep from failing, a person must develop a close relationship with the Holy Spirit. There is no other way. It is sin: personal, inherited, and associated that interferes with that. The Holy Spirit is usually communicating to us what we need to know at any given moment, but we either don't know how to listen, or don't want to. Sin and unbelief in our lives also makes it difficult to hear Him.

This can seem like a closed loop from which escape is impossible. How does a person cleanse themselves of sin so they can receive the Holy Spirit and keep from sinning? The particulars of everyone's case are different, but the principles are universal. Read the Bible (or listen to someone else read it if illiterate). As often as a sin is identified, repent, renounce, reject, reform, forgive and then reinforce the virtue that protects against it. Most of all, forgive. Be like the great reformer Martin Luther who prepared himself for his historic life's work by confessing and repenting of everything he could think of from the greatest to even the least sin. Luther then repeated the process over and over again until it became habitual.

This example shows that we must passionately cleanse ourselves, not once, but regularly! And this involves the grace of God too. For the basis for obtaining any forgiveness from God is that:

- we believe we are sinners.
- Christ paid the penalty for that sin.
- repent of that sin.

- make restitution for that sin.
- forgive those who sin against us.
- and also forgive ourselves and our ancestors with whom the sin originated!

It seems like a monumental task, but in reality most of this could be done (aside from restitution) in less than a day for the average person if done in a focused and systematic manner.

Once sin is out, the Holy Spirit must be invited in. Then He can transform our nature so that we aren't even tempted to sin. We don't even desire it. Moreover, He gives us new desires for righteousness, holiness, perfection and best of all, a love for God. There is no room for anything or anyone other than God; everything we do must be for Him. Anything less and we become a creature of hell. Here is where deliverance ministry becomes so important. Most of our ungodly desires and tendencies are rooted in having demons in or about us that occupy the role intended for the Holy Spirit. Removing sin from our lives removes the spiritual legal basis that allows the demons to work in our lives and influence us to rebel against God. Remove their influence; invite the Holy Spirit to fill those parts of our being the demons have vacated, and the good and proper influence of God becomes natural and easy. Leave them alone to do their diabolical work and they will work tirelessly, ceaselessly and diligently to separate us from God and destroy us. Another important point is the role of praise, worship, and prayer in a Christian's life. These are our protection, our tools, and our weapons respectively. This is a vast subject, and anyone neglecting these has already surrendered to the enemy. If we don't learn to use these, the temptation is to use carnal devices which ultimately only exacerbate the problems.

Again, it takes more time to explain all this than it took me to comprehend it in the presence of Jesus. And these poor words cannot truly begin to do justice to what Jesus helped me to understand. This is the merest of outlines. Yet, it is very important to achieve this, because until we do, we cannot make real progress in life. It is helpful to know that Jesus passionately wants us to achieve this and is ready and willing to help those who sincerely desire it and diligently seek to achieve it for the right reasons. The Holy Spirit is ready and willing to help us through the details of this process. Acknowledging this before Jesus was the step that opened up my way back to life. For just as the accusations of the demons brought upon me condemnation and damnation, the judgment of Christ, with my acknowledgement of my sins and repudiation of them, brought me justification and salvation.

When I had grasped these things, Christ indicated it was time to move on.

Then Jesus told me He had something to show me.

"For Moses writes of the righteousness which is of the Law: 'The man doing these things shall live by them.' (Lev. 18:5) But the righteousness of faith says this: "Do not say in your heart, Who will go up into Heaven?" (that is, to bring down Christ); or, 'Who will go down into the abyss?" (that is, to bring Christ up from the dead.) But what does it say? 'The Word is near you, in your mouth and in your heart' (that is, the Word of faith which we proclaim) (Deuteronomy 30:12-14). Because if you confess the Lord Jesus with your mouth, and believe in your heart that God raised Him from the dead, you will be saved. For with the heart one believes unto righteousness, and with the mouth one confesses unto salvation. For the Scripture says, 'Everyone believing on Him will not be put to shame.' (Isaiah. 28:16)" Romans 10:05-11 LITV

Chapter 10 – I Repent and Pray for Salvation

Back in the spring of 1979, Pastor Gross and I sat on the couch in my living room in Titusville and he led me in the classic sinner's prayer. Together we had prayed something like:

"Heavenly Father, I confess that I am a sinner, and I ask for Your forgiveness. I believe Christ died for my sins and rose from the dead. I repent of my sins and ask You to forgive me. I invite You to come into my heart and life. I want to trust and follow You as my Lord and Savior. In Christ's name. Amen."

Pastor Gross assured me now that I was saved from hell and nothing could take away God's promise of eternal salvation. I felt relieved, but asked him if people would also forgive me too—for I understood that most of my sins were wrongs done to others, and only indirectly against God, though there were these too. He smiled and shook his head. No, that was another matter. I was on my own when it came to reconciling with people. This was a bit disappointing, but helped me to realize that I needed to be more careful about how I treated others.

For several weeks after that, Pastor. Gross came to our house and taught me from the Bible. When he felt I was sincere in the faith and ready for more, he arranged to take me to the weekly church services where I was reintroduced to Bible classes and sermons. It impressed me that the pastor of the church would make the 20-mile round trip from Trenton to Titusville before and after the service to make it possible for me to attend. It was somewhat disappointing to me that neither my mother nor any of his grown children could relieve him of that duty. I felt I was a burden on him since I didn't drive yet.

Charles B. Gross was the pastor of Brae Burn Bible Chapel, a small, non-denominational congregation in Trenton, New Jersey. I related much better to this church than the one in Mountainside. First of all, I was older and more teachable. Secondly, there the gospel was taught simply and plainly. In the small congregation I also received the direct attention and personalized instruction I needed to understand and grow in the Christian faith. I always did better in a closer environment. Larger churches seemed to lack something I needed. The services were more informal than I had observed previously and there were no medieval traditions with strange clothes and unfamiliar rites to confuse me. The people were down to earth, working class people, friendly, hospitable and caring. His son, Steve Gross, taught the Bible classes and I took them at least as seriously as I did my regular schoolwork. Soon I surpassed my peers because most of the other youth were compelled by their parents to attend and did not put as much effort into the subject. Few would have believed me if, as a recent convert to Christianity, I told them that I found Bible classes and Biblical study boring.

One thing did trouble me. From time to time I still felt an evil presence within and about me. I had expected it to be banished when my salvation became official. I was even more astonished when I still sensed it following me to church and the presence continuing even in the midst of the worship services. Here I was in church, God's house, and I was still feeling the pull of evil. How was it possible for this evil to exist in this setting? I asked Rev. Gross about this, but he had no idea what I was talking about.

This matter troubled me, and I searched through the small church library for anything I could find that would explain this. I found books on systematic theology, eschatology, commentaries, concordances and a great variety of Bible studies and inspirational stories. But I didn't find anything that explained what I was feeling. I borrowed and studied what I could but was not satisfied. Had no one experienced this before? Perhaps those that had were too ashamed or confused to say anything.

I did enjoy the spring and summer church activities. From the sunrise service celebrating the resurrection of Christ to the pancake breakfasts, it was inspirational and fun. I liked the organized activities: volley ball games for the youth, church picnics and special musical programs. These were new and interesting for me. With few exceptions, my life had until then revolved around the routine of family, neighbors and school with a short stint in the Cub Scouts and an occasional summer camp.

During this time, high school graduation came and went. Then it was time for me to leave for college. At my request, Pastor Gross arranged an introduction for me to Calvary Baptist Church in Huntingdon, Pennsylvania where I would be attending Juniata College.

However, I didn't start attending Calvary Baptist right away. The congregation had hundreds of members and occupied a large commercial-grade building off highway 26 on the north side of town. It was quite different from the small, home-like chapel I had just left and the idea of meeting a large crowd of strangers daunted me. The smaller homegrown assembly was where I excelled. I wasn't entirely decided that I was ready to return to a formal church environment like the one I had known in Mountainside. So, instead I joined a Christian student organization, the Intervarsity Christian Fellowship. Two members of the group, Nancy Hershberger and her roommate, Karen Kunkle, invited me out to a retreat the IVCF had planned that fall. I had never been on a retreat before and it sounded interesting. I continued to learn and grow as I experienced new and different ways to worship and interacted with other Christians.

We were part of a group of about a dozen students staying in a large cabin out in the Pennsylvania woods for the weekend in the autumn of 1979. There was singing, Bible study, and times of testimony. The informal, deeply personal approach really appealed to me. In between the organized activities we shared stories from our lives. Being a recent convert, I had little to contribute relative to the others, so I mostly listened to amazing stories of healings, miracles, revelation, testing, trials and triumphs. At the same time, no one made me feel small or inadequate for not being a life-long Christian. The show of support and respectful fellowship was encouraging. On the second evening, Nancy and Karen asked me if I had ever heard of the baptism of the Holy Spirit or the gifts of the Holy Spirit. At that point I had not. So they read to me from the twelfth chapter of St. Paul's first letter to the Corinthian Christians

"But concerning the spiritual matters, brothers, I do not wish you to be ignorant. You know that being led away, you nations were led to voiceless idols. Because of this I make known to you that no one speaking by the Spirit of God says, Jesus is a curse. And no one is able to say Jesus is Lord, except by the Holy Spirit. And there are

differences of gifts, but the same Spirit; and there are differences of ministries, yet the same Lord. And there are differences of workings, but the same God is working all things in and to each one is given the showing forth of the Spirit to our profit. For through the Spirit is given to one a word of wisdom, and to another a word of knowledge, according to the same Spirit; and to another, faith by the same Spirit, and to another, gifts of healing by the same Spirit, and to another, workings of powers, and to another, prophecy, and to another, discerning of spirits, and to another, kinds of languages, and to another, interpretation of languages. But the one and the same Spirit works all these things, distributing separately to each as He wills." 1 Corinthians 12:01-11 LITV

Nancy asked me if I could speak in "tongues." I told them I had studied French and German in school and even invented a language for a story I wrote. They explained, this wasn't what they meant, but that they meant a spiritual language that is not learned. It is a language of prayer given as a gift from God. That was new to me and I asked them to show this thing to me. So Nancy spoke in a language that I didn't understand and Karen interpreted it into English. The words in English sounded vaguely like scripture and were chiefly praising God or reassuring those present of His love for them.

I was impressed, so when they asked if I wanted this gift too, I said, "Yes."

The young ladies prayed for me and I felt a tingling and flowing warmth come over my body, which they said was the Holy Spirit. After several attempts, I began to speak slowly and hesitantly in a strange tongue, but I did not interpret. I had acquired a new talent and a new tool to further my journey of praise. This was quite remarkable and I was very grateful to them for teaching me about this. This was another piece of the direct communication I could have with God. Later this gift would develop into a fluent prayer language and become an essential part of my prayer life. For even when I had no idea how or what to pray, the Spirit was always ready with something to say.

That night there was a guest speaker who also spoke on the Holy Spirit and the spiritual gifts He bestows on Christians. The speaker also emphasized the importance of giving back to God, namely giving ourselves. She said that those who gave their lives to God would be guided and blessed to fulfill their purpose in life. This appealed to me since I had this sense of purpose and drive that I couldn't shake. So I was first to stand and dedicate my life to God's purposes. The speaker and the others prayed for me and then the speaker began to prophesy. I had read of this in the Bible, but never seen it before. Again I was actively adding to my spiritual life and learning the answers to the great mysteries of human existence. It seemed very important so I wrote down the words that were spoken:

"Karl, My son, you have done well to choose to walk the path I have chosen for you. Go and tell others what I have done in your heart. My blessing rests upon you."

The prophecy was merely three sentences; but they said so much! God knew me by name and considered me His son—family! I knew now there was a purpose and a plan for me! And God had chosen to bless me! Moreover, as I listened to the other prophecies given for the students with me, I saw that the miracles I read about in the Bible were real and relevant for this age too! Likewise I saw for the first time that God was directly concerned about the lives of each person and still communicated directly with them. I was ready and wanted to communicate directly too.

This was so different from the images I had of myself and God until then. I had thought of myself as an insignificant individual among billions, a product of random events with no specific purpose and an uncertain future. Moreover, with all the difficulties, disappointments and dangers I had already faced I felt cursed, not blessed. This really turned my thinking around! I also adopted the reverent but affectionate attitude towards God I saw in others. Others I had emulated previously treated God as so holy and great that He was unapproachable directly and the details of our lives were too insignificant for His attention. This had led me to believe we were helplessly caught up on the vast currents of His activities. It gave me both joy and apprehension to know that this was not true. It is one thing to think you are an insignificant spark of life in a vast creation, and entirely different to know that God is personally aware of you and holds you accountable for what you do with your life!

After the retreat, I felt more confident about my future as a believer and decided to start attending a regular church. A few weeks later I contacted James "Jim" Thorn, a student who drove the shuttle bus for Calvary Baptist Church, and asked him to take me to the services on a regular basis...

Jack S. Palmer was the pastor of Calvary Baptist Church and he was a very different kind of man from Charles B. Gross. But both were fine Christian leaders. Charles was a short and stocky man, quiet, humble, studious and a talented pianist. He was very learned in scripture, ancient Greek, and theology. They both had good Christian wives and large families. In contrast, Jack was a tall, lean outdoorsman, direct, plain spoken and practical. He played the trumpet enthusiastically, but not particularly well and his seminary education was secondary to his leadership and organizational skills.

Charles had recognized the importance of bringing me to a saving level of knowledge, understanding and faith regarding the gospel. Jack saw that I needed to make a public declaration of faith and to be baptized. The church elders questioned me regarding my beliefs and practices to determine if I was a proper candidate for baptism. After they were satisfied, it was arranged for me to be baptized the following spring along with the other new believers. I looked forward to the occasion for two reasons. First, it would be my first opportunity to publicly declare my faith, and second, I hoped that baptism would relieve me of the evil presence that continued to trouble me.

I regard March 9, 1980 as my re-birth day. The regular service was rearranged to accommodate a baptismal service for new believers at the conclusion. From the baptistery I was allowed to address the congregation to whom I declared my repentance of sins, my belief in Jesus Christ as savior and my gratitude to God for calling me to the faith early in life. Pastor Palmer baptized me by full immersion in the name of the Father, Jesus Christ, and the Holy Spirit. It was a joyful moment for me, and I welcomed the loving approval of the members of the congregation. However, the evil presence was still with me afterwards. I realized there was more yet to be done.

I had confessed Christ as my savior, been baptized in the Holy Spirit and been publicly baptized in the name of the Trinity by full immersion. At that point I had done everything I was told was necessary to become a Christian. Most of the other believers I fellowshipped with, especially the new ones, spoke of a wonderful peace and joy they experienced and I could see it evident on their faces and hear it in their voices. But it still escaped me. I still felt an evil presence about me and was tormented by a crippling lethargy, short temper and persistent temptations. I really disliked this state and wanted relief. Why was I different? No one I asked could tell me what was missing and I was ashamed to admit I was different.

After three years of studies at Juniata College I transferred on a dual degree program to the Georgia Institute of Technology. As part of the five-year plan I would repeat my sophomore year there and ultimately earn bachelor's degrees from both institutions. It was a major move from a small-town college to a big city university. It was one of the happiest times of my life but also one of the more difficult periods. The evil presence troubled me constantly, making it difficult to study, take exams, even rest. I had to focus so intensely on academics most other things were ignored. This also included my spiritual life. This persisted even when I moved to Atlanta. There I struggled terribly with constant tiredness that regularly caused me to fall asleep in class and while studying. Somehow I managed despite this difficulty that doctors couldn't diagnose or treat.

Pastor Palmer recommended that I join the Baptist Student Union (BSU) on campus and indicated they would help me find a local church. So I arranged for the BSU intern to meet me at the train station in Atlanta when I arrived with my belongings. He welcomed me to Atlanta and brought me to campus. The campus minister, Al Rahn and his secretary, Harriet Clardy, the staff and students at the BSU also welcomed me with true southern hospitality, despite being a Yankee from up north. They helped orient me to campus life and soon I was enrolled and busy with classes. A progressive dinner to the local area churches for new students helped me select a home church. I settled on North Atlanta Baptist Church largely since it was close to campus and I had no vehicle.

The BSU was an ideal place to study: spacious, well furnished, open early to late and best of all it had a well-stocked library. The small, cozy library became my favorite place to study. It was quiet but had a nice view of the central part of campus through the large windows. Although engineering was my main emphasis of study, I continued to develop my knowledge of spiritual matters. When most other students were devoted to their academic studies or social activities, I would still make time for reading quality Christian literature, As often as I could, (and more often than I should have regarding my grades) I would pluck a book off the BSU library shelf and feed my spirit for a while. It was one of these books that caught my attention and held it firmly from cover to cover.

Glenna Henderson wrote an account of her deliverance from demonization in "My Name is Legion."[viii] She was a faithful member of a Lutheran congregation and was a sincere believer, dutiful wife and loving mother. Glenna was a leader in community service and considered a role model. However, she was also tormented by ugly, violent thoughts, abnormal lusts and intense temptations. Glenna sought counsel from her pastor who eliminated other possibilities and finally concluded she was demonized.

This was a situation where a person is not demon possessed, but is still strongly influenced by demons in or about them. By examining her personal history he determined that they had first come into her through abuse Glenna had experienced in childhood. The pastor ministered deliverance to her through confession of sins, forgiveness, fasting and prayer over about two years and eventually the demons were expelled and disposed of. This gave Mrs. Henderson the relief she sought. The book chronicled the deliverance process that they developed by trial and error since the pastor had not been trained in this matter in seminary.

I asked the campus minister, Al Rahn about the book, but he didn't know how it got there. He also didn't care for the subject and removed it from the library. I had heard that the Assembly of God (AG) churches were more likely to be informed about the gifts of the Holy Spirit than the Southern Baptists at that time. So I arranged an appointment with an associate pastor of one of the larger AG churches nearby. When I told him about the book and asked about deliverance ministry, the pastor angrily denounced the book, saying it was heresy and ought to be burned! He assured me that Christians could not be demonized and told me that he doubted the author was even really Christian and questioned my status as a believer. How could this be, it made sense to me and there seemed to be plenty of evidence to support the idea. Surely a pastor and Bible scholar would see this as well. Yet he didn't. I found this meeting less than helpful and regretted the time and trouble to make the trip.

About the same time, I befriended another Tech student, Henry "Hank" Ziemer who attended North Atlanta Baptist Church with me. In the course of things I learned that Hank was also interested in deliverance ministry and was learning from and being counseled by a deliverance minister, Tom Hodgins. This was an incredible turn of events; I would have first-hand information at my disposal and an expert to ask questions of. From what Hank told me of his experiences, it sounded like the evil presence I experienced was demonization. So I arranged to meet with Mr. Hodgins. Beforehand Hank loaned me some tapes to listen to that explained the process. It was scriptural and made sense to me, so I went to meet Mr. Hodgins for counseling. He had me confess my sins and prayed for me. I felt no change, though he did insist on payment for his services. I paid him well but left disappointed. I wondered why this worked for Hank but not for me. If anything I felt cheated after not feeling any change and also having to pay him.

That was in 1983. I resigned myself to live with the situation and managed as well as I could. But the temptations, bad temper, faulty memory and other ills persisted and highly complicated my life. I continued to study the Bible and advance spiritually, but my zeal and enthusiasm were considerably dampened. I felt real progress was eluding me until I dealt with this issue.

I knew I had a serious problem and I needed answers but wasn't finding them. I was jealous of Mrs. Henderson who had a competent pastor, supportive Christian friends and understanding spouse. I felt there must be a way to resolve this, but didn't find it at that time. I believe God never leaves us without the necessary resources. However, it appears He is very subtle about how they are presented, for I had unknowingly missed an opportunity several years before.

In 1979, the summer after I became a Christian, I was interested in spending the summer break with Youth With A Mission (YWAM). But to do so required me to raise my own financial support and somehow also pay for the next year of college. My immediate family did not support this idea and insisted that I work that summer to earn money for school. This seemed fiscally responsible, so I worked to earn money for school instead. What I didn't know then was that YWAM takes their volunteers through a very thorough counseling program that is quite similar to what Pastor Robert E. Nichelson did for Glenna Henderson. I had no idea I was possibly missing my big chance for clarity and understanding, and freedom from my demons.

I wonder how things might have been different had I followed my heart and volunteered with YWAM instead. In 1984 I did volunteer with the Children's Sand and Surf Mission (CSSM) in Ship Bottom, New Jersey. With the support of my maternal grandmother I did manage to finish school and graduate the next year despite losing some summer earnings. But the CSSM program did not include any special counseling for the volunteers like YWAM did. This seems to me, God's way of showing me I could have done this earlier if I had exercised the faith to try.

Because of my unbelief, it wasn't until 16 years later that I had a breakthrough, and nearly 35 years before all the pieces came together.

Christ shows me how to use the gift of healing to restore my dead body.

"Surely He has borne our sicknesses, and He carried our pain; yet we esteemed Him plagued, smitten by God, and afflicted. But He was wounded for our transgressions; He was bruised for our iniquities; the chastisement of our peace was upon Him; and with His wounds we ourselves are healed." Isaiah 53:04 LITV

Chapter 11 – Healing My Body

Suddenly the scene shifted and I found myself in a vision standing with my Lord on the banks of a river in a subtropical, semi-desert climate. Papyrus reeds grew tall and thick along the banks of the river and swarthy, dark haired people in simple, ancient dress were fishing and washing in the river. I presumed it was the Nile in ancient Egypt, but was given no explanation. The Lord told me to build a boat from the reeds. I did as I was instructed and made a vessel out of the reeds. It was constructed like a canoe with a flat bottom and high prows such as I had seen in books on archaeology. All the tools and materials were readily at hand and it seemed to take little time or effort to build the boat. I was superhuman in the task and didn't expect anything less. It seemed very real and miraculous but not outrageous. (Normally in my dreams the images are not vivid, and the surroundings shift and change in such a manner that completing a task like this is nearly impossible—so I knew I was not in a dream state but a vision.) I understood we were to launch the boat into the river and sail downstream. Jesus stepped into the boat and I followed, using a long wooden pole to push off and guide the boat out into the current.

Jesus sat amidships while I stood in the rear of the reed boat. Soon, we began to pass a long, low island in the river. Superimposed on the island was my prone body. It appeared translucent and I could see through the skin, bone and muscles to the organs within. All the healthy organs were transparent, but those damaged in the explosion were colored. They eyeballs were sooty looking; the throat bright red and the lungs were a mottled gray-blue/green. Jesus told me that when I had been made by God, He had put the ability to heal in my spirit. Then He instructed me to stretch out my hands toward the damaged organs and they would be healed. So I did as He commanded me. As I stretched out my hands towards each organ in turn, it became clear again as I felt a current of energy flow through me to my prone body. I was partway through this process when suddenly the demons returned and disrupted the vision. I found myself back in the living room standing at the feet of my body. Jesus warned me that I had to expel the demons if I wanted to finish healing my body. So I rebuked them again and they disappeared without returning. With Jesus guiding me, I knew I was on the right path.

The vision resumed where it had left off and I touched my eyes and watched them turn transparent. The healing was complete and the vision ended. I don't know why the vision was necessary to effect the healing or what the symbols in the vision meant. There was no explanation. As soon as the vision ended, I was back in the living room, standing before Jesus.

I felt only love, acceptance and kindness from Him, but he sternly communicated to me that my sins had grieved Him and put me in a terrible, dangerous predicament. I had no idea that I was so far from salvation and that my sins were not as obvious. They needed to be dealt with, correctly and thoroughly. I expressed my sorrow and regret for them and added my deep gratitude for being rescued from damnation. Then suddenly I remembered the list of questions that I had intended to ask God if I was ever in His presence.

However, as I stood there I realized that I had just escaped from eternal damnation by the narrowest of margins and owed everything to Christ. He owed me nothing, let alone answers to questions that now seemed so lame and trivial in His awesome presence. What I failed to realize was that all my thoughts were known to God, so He knew that I was thinking about the list, even if I did not intentionally communicate anything to Him about it. Jesus indicated that He knew my thoughts, about my list of questions, and was willing to give me a response.

I was about to have one of the most incredible experiences I think anyone can relate.

"O Jehovah, return, deliver my soul; save me for Your mercy's sake." Psalm 6:4 LITV

Chapter 12 – Deliverance

After graduation from college, the next fifteen years of my spiritual life was largely on hold. I started my career, married, fathered two children and attended a variety of churches. Each church was like a grade in school and from each one I learned new things. But they were about the mechanics of being a Christian. There were few overt miracles and much repetitive sameness.

Then a crisis hit.

My career took an interesting direction and I moved the family to Europe to work in a new plant Eaton's Vehicle Switch Electronics Division was building in Gdansk, Poland. Both the move and the job were very stressful on me and my family. I was really thrilled to be in Europe and enjoyed the excellent food, rich history, refined culture, friendly people and a welcomed change in climate from hot, humid Texas. My work as the New Product Supervisor tested all my skills to the maximum and kept me working long and arduously. Yet, I enjoyed my work and was glad to advance my knowledge and skills. I also enjoyed working with the Germans and Poles there who were highly intelligent and very industrious. On weekends I regularly attended a local congregation, the Church of the Green Light. This was a Pentecostal church in Gdansk. I was also active (though less than successful) in evangelizing on my own among the Poles.

When we first arrived in Poland there was a brief respite from the evil presence that troubled me. However, in a few weeks it returned with a vengeance. (Later I learned that some demons are territorially limited, and some of those that tormented me needed to arrange for others to take over their roles regarding me in this new country. Some of these new spirits were confined just to the city of Sopot, so I noticed the interesting phenomena that they would come and go as I crossed the city limits into Gdansk!) This presence appeared to feed upon my stress at work and the difficult adjustment my family went through living in Poland. Turmoil disrupted our home until it was nearly dysfunctional. In the worst moments I discerned a sharp increase in the malevolent presence. Therefore, I concluded that I was dealing with a spiritual problem, though one that was compounded by ordinary ones. This prompted me to revisit the subject of deliverance ministry. At that date the Internet was now widely available, including in post-communist Poland. So I used this powerful tool to research the subject in a way not feasible back in 1983. The resources that I found were multitudinous and I ordered a substantial number of books. Two authors, Ed Murphy[ix] and Charles H. Kraft[x] provided me with the best material I could find at the time.

Going through their books I engaged in what may be termed, "self-deliverance." After a fitful start and some digressions, I finally found something that worked. That feeling of evil plagued me for so long I could hardly believe I may have found a solution. It was essentially the same as I had read about in "My Name Is Legion" with the additional knowledge that I could claim direct power and authority to exorcise demons on the basis of my faith in Christ alone. Although they were very helpful, a pastor and intercessors were not absolutely necessary. As I had long suspected, the evil presence that had plagued me was a demon! In fact, it was several of them I had acquired in childhood through various traumas, from the teasing and tormenting I had experienced from other children and also during the turmoil of my parents' multiple divorces. As I prayed and struggled against them I could feel them leaving my body. It was a new and wonderful sensation! After nearly twenty years I finally had the relief I had been seeking. The lethargy, lustful thoughts, extreme emotions, poor memory and a host of other things were gone or significantly reduced. I finally felt normal and realized in retrospect how ill I had really been. I was deeply grateful to God and eager to enjoy my new state.

However, my relief was short lived. I found that the demons were back within a week or two. My knowledge and experience with demonization helped to be more aware now, and I realized where they were coming from. Through my intimate relationship with my wife they were finding an entrance back into my body. This was a huge problem. My wife was only nominally Christian. Therefore she had little interest in spiritual matters. It had taken me nearly two decades to comprehend and accept what I had just learned, and that was the result of a passionate pursuit of truth. In her case I had no idea even where to start. Still, I tried to tell her about what I had discovered, read to her and the children from the books I had bought. Why she couldn't see the truth that seemed so clear to me, I couldn't understand. I also prayed and fasted. Really prayed! To no avail. She neither believed me nor cared about such things and was so estranged by that time that I had little influence with her.

I realized I needed outside help. First I canvassed the local churches but found no one knowledgeable on the subject. Then I contacted Charles Kraft's ministry. After some negotiations I arranged for two of his assistants to travel to Poland and give a workshop on deliverance ministry. I contacted several local churches to invite the pastors and members and put out flyers and ran ads in the local papers. If I expected a warm response, I was seriously disappointed. Few people came and the assistants, though sincere and caring, were not very capable. Despite my efforts and my need for them to be here to support me, they just couldn't help. They ended up closing the conference early and taking a tour of Poland instead. Before leaving for home they did minister to the family, but with little effect. I was particularly disappointed when they declared that, as policy, they did not minister deliverance to children. I was back where I had started and had expended considerable resources and goodwill getting there.

At least I knew what I was dealing with now, and had some hope of solving the problem. But that just added a tantalizing factor to my frustration.

And this is the confidence we have toward Him, that if we ask anything according to His will, He hears us. 1 John 05:14 LITV

Chapter 13 – The Choice and the Question – Part I

The Lord is the ideal gentleman and perfectly capable of anticipating and responding to the cleverest challenge any person can present Him with. In my case He dismissed my list and offered to answer His own list of questions instead. The thought stunned me. What kind of list of questions would Jesus have? He knew everything. He created everything. What kind of questions would He have a need to answer? He was the reason behind everything! It was obvious to me that whatever list Jesus might have would be far superior to what I had composed. So I accepted and was invited to share His mind because my mind was too small and inadequate to comprehend either the questions or the answers that He proposed.

The moment I agreed to it I became one with Him and shared the mind of Christ, or at least a portion of it. I was perfectly conscious of my own self. My personality with all my memories and awareness of self was intact, but I also shared Christ's mind and knew His thoughts and knowledge related to the subject. At least He shared with me that portion of His mind dedicated to mankind. I sensed there were other vast portions of His mind relating to other things, but what I was allowed to share was only that which related to human history. As vast as that was, it was only a miniscule fraction of the total that seemed boundless in the brief glimpse I had of it. His mind is very dynamic, perfectly orderly with absolute harmony and has an analytical capacity that is beyond imagination let alone description!

If I had been impressed at the capacity and speed of my mind in the spirit, I was absolutely awed by Christ's mind. It held every detail of every person that had ever lived and would ever live. This information was perfectly organized and could be retrieved, reorganized and analyzed effortlessly without delay or hindrance at the merest thought about it. His mind was faster than anything a human could comprehend and the sheer volume of information contained in it was staggering to say the least.

The Lord then took me through a unique exercise where he began by showing me the whole of human history from start to finish. It took but a moment to comprehend it in that state. Then we began to look at how a change in some event, a decision, an action, a twist of nature, or any possible variation could affect that history. We started off small, seeing how changes in personal decisions affected individual lives. Effortlessly we saw how this change spread through time and circumstances and what the effects were on the whole. Then it became increasingly more complex as more events and more individuals were involved. I was allowed to propose variations on any given scenario. When I did, the Lord would show me how that would turn out and then proposed other variations and demonstrated what a full set of variations would result in. From this vantage point it became obvious that there is a wonderful harmony with purpose and structure to human history that is not nearly so apparent from an individual perspective.

There was a particular way He visualized this that made human history more easily understandable. The course of a person's life was like a thread that wove through the continuum of space and time. It began when they were conceived in the womb and terminated when they died. There were four colors of threads, brownish, white, gold and red. Parts of an individual thread might be white or brown depending on how they had lived at that time—white for selflessly, brown for selfishly. When a life had run its course, the thread turned either red or gold. The vast majority, perhaps 98% were red. The threads twisted together to form bundles, which represented social organizations: families, schools, communities, nations, etc. Individual threads passed from bundle to bundle as relationships changed or were rearranged, often returning to mingle with bundles they had departed from earlier. Bundles of life-threads came together periodically at nodes that represented critical events such as migrations, wars, mass movements and other historical events that affected large groups of people.

Jesus explained to me that at the junctions were nodes, where the history of mankind was particularly malleable and informed, capable individuals could exert tremendous influence on the fate of mankind at those times. That was in 1995. He showed me the next critical juncture of a majority of the bundles would come in 1998, others would follow with nodes occurring at different times in different places until they came together again in the near future. I was being shown how the future would play out and how God's plan worked. Not just the faith that is worked, but the actual spiritual forces and mechanisms.

We continued the exercise until we had looked at the ramifications of every possible variation in human history. While this may seem like an impossible task from a strictly human perspective, it was effortless for

God and takes more time to tell about it than the actual exercise involved. That is how great the mind of our Lord is!

At the conclusion of the exercise I realized there had been a common factor in all of the lines of questioning we had followed. No matter how simple or complex, short or long, minor or major, they all had one ultimate point when considered as a complete sequence. There was one question, which when answered addressed what was truly relevant about all other questions. That question was, *"What does this have to do with selfless love?"* All other issues were neatly resolved or were of no consequence when a given sequence of history was fully played out from start to finish. Only that one question had ultimate eternal value.

That was a truly profound revelation for me. There was more to this experience though.

"And having called His twelve disciples, He gave them authority over unclean spirits, so as to cast out, and to heal every disease and every weakness of body...And going on, proclaim, saying, The kingdom of Heaven has drawn near. Heal sick ones, cleanse lepers, raise dead ones, cast out demons. You freely received, freely give." Mathew 10:01-08 LITV

Chapter 14 – Deliverance

Nearly ten years after our return from Poland passed before I finally found what I was looking for—deliverance again! I had largely given up on myself and stopped trying. Though I had searched and inquired, I didn't find a competent deliverance minister and my efforts at self-deliverance were fitful and never lasted more than a few weeks. Struggling in the spirit for that peace I had tasted before took too much fasting, prayer and discipline to sustain while I was responsible for a professional career and family. Trying to repair the damaged relationship with the mother of my children it was analogous to shoveling sand uphill. It was exhausting and left me little strength for the regular demands of life. Abandoning the effort was a costly mistake though. In the interim the troubles created by the demons continued to grow and ultimately my marriage, career, education and a small business I had started all failed due to the turmoil they created. It was a terrible state to be in, but one I was resigned to endure. For I didn't know what else to do.

However, in 2011 a close friend began behaving erratically and I suspected demonization. So, for her sake, I started looking into the subject again. A search online turned up Tom Hodgins again, but he was in Georgia and we were in Texas. A real help was the Spiritual Warfare Ministries Deliverance Ministry Directory. I had not seen anything like this back in 1999 and found it a godsend. There I browsed the ministries in East Texas and found several nearby. After telephoning the nearest ones and learning the details of their beliefs and practices, I settled on Little Sparrow Ministries in Lindale, Texas. It was a small ministry, operated out of the home of Judy Farris-Smith. I decided to learn more about her and the ministry, personally, before recommending them to my friend.

In person, Judy didn't strike me as a great spiritual warrior for God. She was a short, plump, garrulous, middle-aged blond with a cheerful personality. She looked as harmless as her little pet Chihuahua. This was a far cry from my expectation of someone who routinely exorcised demons. I honestly didn't know what to expect. Right away I recognized I had found someone different though. I could feel the Holy Spirit about her and in her home very distinctly like I had never encountered before. This was what it felt like to be in the presence of someone who is filled with the Holy Spirit. Judy was quick to introduce me to her husband and associates, then move on to the matter at hand. I was already well acquainted with the principles of spiritual warfare and deliverance so we wasted no time in getting down to serious work with the Holy Spirit.

Judy also introduced me to a book by Drs. Jerry and Carol Robeson, “Strongman’s His Name, What’s His Game”[xi] on which (with permission from the authors) much of her book and ministry were based. The Robesons had long been involved in deliverance ministry and had learned that demons characteristically organized themselves into hierarchies. This was an important breakthrough. For lower ranking demons were bound in a hierarchy to their lead demon termed a strongman. Therefore the whole lot could be expelled as a group. In all, she and her intercessors cast out 15 of the 16 strongmen demons listed in the Robeson’s book. This partially explained the great difficulty I had previously encountered. In comparison, Glenna Henderson had only one strongman cast out of her. Why there was so great a difference was not explained, but hugely different number of strongmen had me understanding why things had been for hard for me to master.

I suspected that the abdominal surgery I endured as an infant was a key factor though. When I was about two months old, I was operated on for pylorus stenosis. The surgery opened my body rather dramatically for an infant. This trauma and the exposure my body and spirit were subjected to greatly compromised my spirit. Surgeons, even today, take precautions against microorganisms infecting their patients, but have no thought for spiritual contagions that are just as deadly if not more so. Based on my experience, my suspicion is that opening the body for surgery can introduce demons if care is not taken to prevent this.

Two other key points in her ministry were the breaking of ungodly soul-ties and repentance for ancestral sins. Doing so closed the “doors” through which demons routinely came back in after being expelled.

This was very different from the tedious, time-consuming, demon-by-demon approach developed by Glenna Henderson and pastor, Robert “Bob” Nichelson. Judy also had a list of sixteen strongmen demons and their subordinates derived from the Robeson's book. We prayed and asked for the help of the Holy Spirit and for discernment about what my condition was. Another key point I had not found in either Kraft's or Murphy's book was the role of inherited curses and ancestral sins. These had to be dealt with in addition to personal sins. It was mentioned in another book I read, "Unbroken Curses"[xii] by Rebecca Brown M.D. and Daniel Yoder, but they did not provide a systematic, comprehensive way to deal with the subject.

As I suspected, I was heavily demonized, so with her two assistants praying, she went right to work, laid hands on me and lead me through confession of sin and prayers she had standardized in her book. After confession of my personal sins, one of the first things we did was sever soul-ties to the demons and repent of sins in ancestral lines through which they established their claims on me. For the first time since '99 I felt again the power of the Holy Spirit flow in me. From her hands it coursed through my shoulders and chest and out through my limbs, and I also felt movement internally. It was shocking but not unpleasant.

After about a quarter hour of prayer I felt the first demons leave. It is a unique sensation. The nearest analogy I can make is that it felt like having a tattered wet sheet drawn out of and off of me. I have since learned that some demons have an appearance similar to octopi or squid, with long tentacles. What I was feeling was the tentacles that had anchored them in my body and to my spirit uncoiling and releasing their grip. I could distinctly feel their main bodies leave me like a bubble bursting forth and the tentacles slithering out of me. Though the feelings were easily discernible, I did not see anything visible or hear anything going out. It felt strange but the relief that came afterwards was wonderful! Unlike Tom Hodgins, Judy didn't require payment for her services. This was a godsend, since I was unemployed and broke at the time. Not forgetting how she helped me, I later sent her a substantial gift when my situation improved.

I came back for a few more deliverance counseling sessions and continued self-deliverance outlined in her and the Robeson's books. For the demons that were expelled (or others like them) were very persistent in trying to return to me. It was a constant, sometimes losing, struggle to keep free of them, but there was real lasting progress for the first time. Once the soul-ties to the strongmen demons were severed and the head demons cast out, it was far easier to keep them out and expel them when they returned. Previously they had just slipped back in and the strength of their hold on me was a strong as ever. Now they had to fight to get back in and could be expelled with relatively little effort. I was encouraged by Judy's example to know it could be done, and was soon advancing upon her techniques in new areas. After years of spiritual stagnation I was finally moving forward again.

Unfortunately when I tried to introduce my friend to deliverance ministry, she adamantly refused even to try it. Her pastor (who later resigned his position), forcefully (and ignorantly) assured her that Christians couldn't be demonized (which is not true). On his advice, my friend cut off all communication with me and went to another church. That didn't stop me from ordering more copies of books on deliverance and resuming my studies. For once in my spiritual life I felt like I was making progress and that I was in more control and less vulnerable. I also attended conferences on the subject and exchanged material with individuals I found receptive. An important step was attending a retreat at the Lake Hamilton Bible Camp in Hot Springs, Arkansas that is devoted to deliverance ministry. There I learned more details and refined what I already knew. I was sad for my friend and her family, but glad to finally have the necessary tool-set I was looking for to move forward in my Christian life.

One of the side effects of being delivered was that for the first time in my life I could plainly hear the voice of God talking to me. It was quite different from what I had expected. Instead of being a strong, deep, commanding voice with profound sayings and high, lofty commands, the voice of God was something very different. He spoke in a quiet gentle way about ordinary things. The voice itself was not overpowering, but I could feel ultimate confidence and authority in the even, measured way He spoke. God expected to be obeyed—these were not requests but clearly in the imperative. It was definitely a masculine voice with proper, grammatical English and concise wording. Oddly, there were no explanations with the directives—just what to do, not why it was to be done. That became plain enough afterwards. God didn't tell me to go out and conquer the world or raise up a mighty ministry for Him. It was simple commands and instructions: "Karl, it is time to wake up." (I habitually like to sleep in a little bit in the mornings.) "Do not forget to put medication in the water for the turkeys." And such things like that. (I didn't know it, but one of the turkeys I was raising at the time had the scours.)

One of the most effective techniques I developed was calling down the judgment of God on demons. Many times in frustration with troublesome people I had petitioned God to judge them for their sins.

He generally ignored such requests. However, when I asked Him to judge demons that troubled me the response was immediate and powerful. I didn't learn this from any deliverance minister or conference though. From the account of the fall of Adam and Eve, I realized that God judges not only people, but any being that rebels against Him. Only people are protected by grace, not demons, therefore the unmitigated response. So whenever I felt a fresh demonic assault, I prayed, "Heavenly Father, please judge this demon as you judged the serpent of Eden." Quite routinely and swiftly the demon was gone and its attack ceased. I do not yet know exactly what happened to them, but I suspect it was quite effective. Not only have I become sensitive enough to discern different kinds of demons, but to discern individuals among the demons. To date I can say that, to the best of my knowledge, the individual demons so judged have not returned, though many of the same kind took their places.

Again, I emphasize that binding demons together under their head demon, or strongman is an essential technique. Demons are commonly organized in hierarchies, and the whole lot can be dealt with as one group. This saves tremendous effort and time in exorcising them. Praise also weakens them; so worshipping God with praise, music and dance sets up a favorable "atmosphere" for battling with them. Fasting helped too, but is at least an order of magnitude less effective than praise and worship. Confessing and forgiving ancestral sin and renouncing ungodly ancestral covenants were very effective even essential. Declaring and ordering a spiritual divorce and manumission from the devil (worship is an intimate act comparable to sexual intimacy as in marriage) also were helpful. Persistence was central to success in the endeavor, as much in resisting temptations as in contending with demons.

It was essential to purge my home of all ungodly artifacts and printed material. Pornography is about as demonic as outright idolatry. I never permitted either outright in my home, but went to the point of blotting or cutting out references to them from the books in my library or purging the same from my computers. I also sanctified my home, property and livestock through prayer. The more knowledge I gained and the more experienced I amassed the better I was equipped to find the hidden faults that would let demons back into my life, where they waited patiently for their opportunity.

Through these efforts I had tantalizing glimpses of what might be possible with a complete deliverance from demonization and full investing of the Holy Spirit: perfect memory and rock-solid sanity with constant peace and joy, physical activity without fatigue, super-human strength, telepathy and even an end to sickness, aging and death! I realized a lot more was at stake than just feeling better!

"Even youths are faint and fatigued, and young men stumbling shall stumble; but the ones waiting for Jehovah shall renew power; they shall go up with wings as the eagles; they shall run and not be weary; they shall walk and not be faint!" Isaiah 40:30-31 LITV

However, after the initial successes, I gradually lost ground to a constant day and night assault by demons seeking to reclaim their influence over me for an unexpected reason. For even when I was diligent in resisting them during my waking hours, the assault continued as I slept and they began to slip in and reestablish themselves. How could I keep up this fight when I couldn't sleep for fear of demonization? I learned that when we sleep, our spiritual defenses subside and become vulnerable.

I also discovered something profound in the words of Elihu the Buzite.

"Why do you contend against him, saying, 'He will answer none of man's words'? For God speaks in one way, and in two, though man does not perceive it. In a dream, in a vision of the night, when deep sleep falls on men, while they slumber on their beds, then he opens the ears of men and terrifies them with warnings, that he may turn man aside from his deed and conceal pride from a man; he keeps back his soul from the pit, his life from perishing by the sword." Job 33:13-18 LITV

That is, when we sleep, we become open to spiritual influences, both good and evil. I realized that we must choose who, God or the enemy, we receive such instruction from. So I prayed, "Holy Spirit, I give You and You alone sole authority to speak to me and to commune with me as I sleep."

The night time invasions stopped.
I knew now there was more to this still to be discovered. So I began anew an in depth study of the Bible to see what was missing.

"For this God is our God forever and ever; He will be our guide even unto death." Psalm 48:14 LITV

"You shall guide me by Your counsel; and afterward You will take me to glory." Psalm 73:24 LITV

Chapter 15 – The Question Part II

Once things were seen from God's perspective, the order in creation and the centrality of selfless love was perfectly clear. Whenever someone was living based on selfish principles, their life-thread was the dull brown. Whenever they lived based on the principle of selfless love, it turned white. If they lived and died outside of God's purpose, the thread turned permanently red and terminated in the much larger bundle or red life-lines that eventually ended in nothingness. Those were the ones whose lives were not given to God. They rejected God and ultimately perished. Their entire lives were meaningless. They are food and fuel for hell. When a person lived and died for God's purposes, the life-thread turned golden and became part of the bundle that continued on throughout time and into eternity. It was a much smaller bundle, but far richer than the other bundle in the quality of the lives lived. When a thread turned red or golden, it would change over its entire length once the person's life was over. This was a graphic representation of how even a person's mistakes (or successes) can be transformed to fit God's purposes (or made of no consequence) depending on whether or not they give their lives to Him.

It was clear throughout the exercise that God is always perfectly in control and no detail escapes His attention or involvement, no matter how much we know that He created everything, it never ceases to amaze. Nor could one person directly alter another's eternal destiny. They could influence them, but it was always ultimately the individual's attitude, decisions and responses that counted. Although sin certainly mattered, the key point was not so much the magnitude or frequency of their sins or even their good deeds, but whether or not they rejected God. The only way to be absolved of sin is to accept God and live for Him only. While there are many facets to the life experience, the singular purpose of it is to test and prepare a person for oneness with God. Every soul that goes to hell had at some point in their life clearly and consciously rejected God. It just astonished me that the vast majority of people do so. Many, many of the damned are very religious too, but they embraced a false image of who God is and rejected His holy, loving, righteous nature. Instead, they justified themselves by inventing a god that accommodated them.

I should interject my understanding on one particularly poignant issue that I expect some readers still want an answer on. “Why is there so much loss and suffering in the world?” If it seems wasteful and pointless, that is because for the lost it is. However, suffering for a saint is an opportunity to grow and become stronger and more mature—to advance to higher levels of being, in short, to become more Christ-like. Sin and the consequent suffering cannot happen in heaven and the sufferings of mortal life provide a unique opportunity for people to be transformed into the children of God they are intended to become. Consciously choosing a course of action that involves suffering for divine purposes not only advances a person spiritually, but also is richly rewarded in heaven. (However, self-inflicted suffering would not generally qualify for this. Nor would creating situations that caused others to suffer.)

"Sorrow is better than laughter: for by the sadness of the countenance the heart (will/consciousness) is made better.' Ecclesiastes 7:3 KJV

Naturally we should not seek to create situations where we, or others, suffer unnecessarily, but when it comes to us, it should be seen as an opportunity and embraced even more eagerly than pleasure. Suffering is used to exercise virtues such as patience, endurance, perseverance and etc. Just as sensibly, when the opportunity to escape suffering comes, let it go if it has accomplished its purpose. But a person should not use unrighteous means to avoid suffering—if they do they add to their sins and lose the opportunity to grow. In some cases, there are other ways to accomplish similar goals, but suffering is particularly effective and God may use it when we avoid the other opportunities He gives us.

That is, our progress towards oneness with God is simple and direct when we are attuned to and obedient to the Holy Spirit. God freely and gladly works in us to transform us into His image as we seek that very thing. When we pursue other purposes, God sets barriers in our way that use suffering to warn us that we are straying from the mark and turn us back towards His goals for us. He actively guides us on our path to oneness with Him. If we utterly reject Him, He ceases the transforming process and assigns roles to become the source of tests and trials for the rest. Even in one's rejection of God, He still uses them to help guide others. This is a very bad state to be in, for it sets a person up for divine justification for ultimate annihilation.

Alternatively, we can choose suffering as an intense, expedited means to achieve goals that would otherwise be involved or lengthy. It pleases God when we willingly suffer for His purposes, for then it opens new, higher opportunities for advancement in the transforming process. For example, it increases our capacity to receive more of Him in us, the ultimate form of true wealth.

A startling revelation for me was that God also suffers. He even chooses to suffer on a scale that we could not endure merely the awareness of! His passionate love for us makes God vulnerable to the consequences of our sins. If we truly understood what our sins do to Him and had the least love for God, we would immediately stop. He willingly allows us to grieve Him for higher purposes so we may learn through our mistakes how to become more like Him. If He is allowed, He will lead the way and bring us to join with Him, and be with Him. To become like Him we must also love passionately, accepting the same vulnerability that this entails, and endure the consequent suffering, including disappointment with others.

One really needless source of suffering is unrepented, inherited sin. The Bible clearly states the penalties for sin: death, banishment, illness, loss, violence, poverty, barrenness etc. God is the author of the principles that govern creations and God must enforce them for He is self-consistent. Tragically, the descendants of the sinner inherit the penalties for some sins. The descendant may have no idea what sins their ancestor(s) committed, but they are still subject to the penalties. As much as God loves those individuals, He must execute judgment impartially. Ignorance of or disbelief in the principles offers no protection from the consequences. The devil is fully aware of this system and eagerly exploits it and our ignorance of it, especially to hinder believers.

Another key point is attitude. While we have free will and free choice, our options regarding our actions are really far more limited than we would expect. For God fully anticipates our every thought and action. Accordingly He ordains events around this to achieve His purposes. All we really fully control is our attitudes – how we receive and react to things. In simple terms, a positive attitude is desirable and a negative one is not. Therefore, our focus should be on seeing the positive side of things and responding in a positive, constructive and thankful way, regardless of circumstances. For circumstances are ultimately neither good nor bad, but it is what we make of them that counts.

After the exercise was complete, I was gently separated from His mind and returned to my normal state. I felt a moment of loss as the incredible experience of oneness with God subsided. The memories of the details of individual lives were not retained because I neither had the capacity nor a reason to keep them. The incomparable experience of being part of God has endless ramifications that are beyond the scope of this writing to elaborate on. Sensing my disappointment, Jesus assured me that similar experiences are possible in heaven.

“But You are holy, being enthroned on Israel's praises.” Psalm 22:3 LITV

“I will praise the name of God with a song; I will magnify him with thanksgiving. This will please the LORD more than an ox or a bull with horns and hoofs.” Psalm 69:30 LITV

Chapter 16 - The First Key: Praise Leads to Love for God

Once I had most of the elements necessary for a full and robust relationship with God in place, things began to turn around for me in a remarkable way. Besides merely feeling better, physical changes began to take place. Though my diet and exercise routine did not change dramatically, my health improved in measurable ways. My resting heart rate and cholesterol dropped measurably in the course of a year. Even my hair, which had receded dramatically during the two years period of my divorce proceedings, began to grow back! Acquaintances who had also been through deliverance had reported even more dramatic results from partially being cured of diabetes to wholly cured of terminal cancer! One family reported major behavioral changes in their child whose emotional instability kept them out of school for over a decade. He returned to school and placed only a year below grade level! It was clear that demonization had kept me, and others, from fully living a life for God and suffering for Him only.

I could tell I wasn’t there yet myself and something was lacking. I wondered why I could feel there were still some demonic holdouts and what would dislodge them. For months I racked my brains seeking an answer. I prayed, fasted, read scripture, gave charitably, did good works etc. in the hopes that something would provide a breakthrough. These all helped in modest ways, but I needed something more effective and lasting. In response to my prayers for guidance a memory came back to me.

In 1997 I was working as a contract engineer for FMC Sofec in Houston designing an anchor pull-in system. Engineering jobs were scarce in Longview at the time, and I was very glad to even find work out of town. Just a few weeks into the assignment, influenza swept through the office and didn’t spare me. I quickly became so ill I could barely function. However, the work had to progress or they would find another contractor. My young family needed the income badly, so my options were limited. Anti-viral drugs like Tamiflu were not readily available then, and I was already in the most debilitating phase of the infection by that time anyway. I needed a miracle to be able to manage at work the next day.

So, I went to a local church that night where they had a regular prayer meeting. It was about all I could do to drive my battered pickup truck there and sit, silently suffering through the meeting until it came to the part where people could request prayer. After all, this is what a good Christian does, right? You need healing or help from God so you pray for it. I put my hope in the scripture:

"Is any among you sick? Let him call the elders of the assembly, and let them pray over him, anointing him with oil in the name of the Lord. And the prayer of faith will save those being sick, and the Lord will raise him up. And if he may have committed sin, it will be forgiven him." James 05:14, 15 LITV

The church elders could see I was very ill and were willing to anoint me with oil and pray for me. Yet though the requirements of the scripture were fulfilled, I felt no change. Disappointed and trembling with fatigue I rose to leave. Seeing this, one of the elders whose name I did not know, stopped me.

“I felt a check in the Spirit,” he said. “I sense that what you need to do is praise God.”

I looked at him in disbelief; praise was one of the last things on my mind that night. “Thanks,” I replied, “I’ll think about that.” However, I felt this was an absurd idea and had little intention of actually doing it. I let myself out of the meeting hall thinking I had wasted the trip.

The walk back to my truck was probably less than 200 yards, but it took all my strength. A cold winter rain fell on my uncovered head but I was too miserable to care. Driving home, I pondered what the man had said. There wasn’t the least bit of motivation in my whole being to praise God at that moment. I couldn’t have forced a thought of praise let along vocalized it. For I felt, somehow, God was responsible for my illness. I resented the particularly inopportune timing that interfered with a critical assignment. ‘Why should I praise Him when He is the reason I am sick,’ was my thinking. When I arrived back at my rented room I slumped onto my bed and just lay there until my strength returned sufficiently to think clearly.

“Well,” I concluded after some thought, “praising God doesn’t cost anything and I have nothing important to do with my time. I’m too miserable to sleep." It did not seem that this would cause any harm. Therefore, there was no excuse for not trying.

But I just lay there. I couldn't summon the words to praise God. My mind was deeply mired in resentment and self-pity. However, I viewed this as a problem to be solved and looked around the room to see what resources I had to work with. Then I spied my Bible. I knew that the Psalms contained words of praise, so I opened the scriptures randomly to the middle of the book of Psalms. I began reading aloud at the first psalm I came to. Between fatigue, congestion and despondency, the words were flat and mechanical. Nothing happened. I read the psalm again and still there was no change. I paused, looked at the clock and saw I had over an hour to go until my usual bedtime. I decided to continue.

I read another psalm, then another. Perhaps twenty minutes went by without a change. Finally I stopped watching the clock and continued reading aloud. Soon a feeling of lightness of spirit came over me. I paused, did a double check and confirmed what I had sensed. This encouraged me, so I resumed reading. Was I actually starting to get it? Was it really working for me? Perhaps about an hour into reading the psalms I felt the blockage in my sinuses break loose. The feeling of lightness increased and I could sense tingling start all over my body. The Holy Spirit was at work!

It was necessary to take a break and work my way through a box of tissues as the congestion began to rapidly clear. My hope and confidence rose. The praise became genuine as I continued to read. Praising God was no longer drudgery, but the words flowed freely and easily. I was passionate about praise and it became truly selfless. It was about bedtime when I finished the book of psalms and I felt the flu had been broken. I was still weak and somewhat congested, but the aches in my joints were gone and my strength and morale was restored. So I laid the Bible back on the nightstand and tucked myself into bed with a prayer of gratitude for this healing.

The next morning I awoke with no more than a little residual congestion and was able to resume work with my usual vigor. I had not recovered from the flu so rapidly before and I excitedly shared the story with my colleagues. They showed polite interest, but because of their strong technical focus, did not relate to anything spiritual. This disappointed me, but I was glad to be able to keep my job and resumed work sincerely thankful for God's mercy.

In books by John G. Lake I had learned that illness has both physical and spiritual root causes. Addressing the spiritual root cause, such as sin-induced demonization, often results in partial or complete healing. The Rev. Lake, a Pentecostal minister, strongly advocated prayer combined with fasting, praise and worship as the remedy for otherwise intractable ills. In the above example I had proved his method in my own person. Praise not only became a potent resource in my spiritual tool set, it became a necessary part of my relationship with God. For later I came to realize that God designed people for the purpose of praising Him. It is one of our essential functions. As with anything we are intended to do "for" God, it is really for our own benefit to do so. Though He passionately desires our love, God really needs nothing from us. Praise is the means by which God connects us to Him for our own sustenance just as praying to Him aligns us with His will.

My attention had been so tightly focused on my family and career, that I had devoted little time to praise and worship outside of the twenty minutes a week that was included in the church service between the announcements and the sermon. I read the scriptures daily, prayed regularly and meditated on spiritual things almost constantly. But praise wasn't habitual for me, not yet and I was wondering exactly how it could become a habit because every second I wasn't in praise left me dangling like a worm on a hook. My lack of habitual praise left a huge opening for the demonic to operate. For it was equivalent to trying to feed my body on a diet lacking in protein! I could function almost indefinitely, but gradually grew weaker spiritually as my internal resources were depleted.

Regrettably, it was years after the incident with the flu before I made praise a regular routine. After a while I discovered that just reading the psalms wasn't sufficient in many situations. I needed something better, more effective. It occurred to me that psalms were meant to be sung, but typical English translations of Hebrew poetry don't really lend themselves to singing. So I persuaded our pastor to give me a well-worn copy of the 1940 Broadman Hymnal. I liked these classic hymns and was familiar with the musical scores. The best routine that developed was to prop up the hymnal on the windowsill above the kitchen sink and sing while I cleaned up after a meal. When I had memorized them, I sang while driving. It was a routine like this that would lend itself to habitual praise and keep me on my spiritual route.

This became one of my most important resources when I was going through the divorce. This was a time of deep despondency and fierce anger. Emotion ran so rampant that I had to cut it off just to function. The only remedy was to praise God. My natural reaction was to blame others and circumstances, and to complain; but this just exacerbated the problem. Real relief came when I set aside my bitterness and praised God! All those years of struggling to become a truly righteous servant in His eyes were part of God's plan to bring this answer to my earthly tests. I now knew how to praise Him. Those were years of extreme darkness for me. But I remember those times spent in private praise and worship as oases of joy and peace that had always been in God's plan.

During the time when I set aside my cares, concerns and complaints and expressed my thankfulness, appreciation and awe for God the darkness dispersed and peace reigned. Those precious moments gave me the strength and confidence to continue again and again after repeated setbacks and failures. They gave me hope to believe I could prevail. The reassuring touch of the Spirit reminded me I was not alone and gave me faith that better times would come that were worth persevering through the present difficulties. Most importantly, they gave me the strength to resist the temptation to give in to either resignation or retribution. They motivated me to never give up and to not stop because stopping would be like rejecting God.

It was clear that this pleased God, for I often felt the Holy Spirit come down gently on me as I sang. These praise and worship sessions refreshed me, and weakened or altogether drove away the malevolent presence that regularly tried to trouble me. As an added benefit, after months of conditioning it strengthened my speaking voice and significantly improved the range of notes I could sing. Moreover, in the presence of the Holy Spirit, topics for prayer presented themselves. So, I would interject short prayers in between the hymns. As answers to those prayers came about, it became clear that this was also an effective technique for intercessory prayer.

The positive atmosphere this created was contagious too, I noticed as I spent significant amounts of time in praise and worship, an aura of positive feelings developed about me. When I was in the presence of others the attitude was contagious. They also perked up and were more responsive. Normally outspokenly negative people were more subdued and easier to deal with too. It was like I was exuding the calm and peacefulness that was inside me, like I was a beacon for God to shine into other's lives. This was a revelation to me. For normally it took a lot of thought and effort to motivate others and defend against critics. But the presence of God developed through praise and worship seemed to cut through all of that with remarkable ease. These observations restored my confidence to such a degree that I even accepted an invitation to join the church choir!

My conclusion from these things is that God intentionally designed us to praise Him. It doesn't seems right to attribute to God the kind of ego that *He needs* praise, so it seems reasonable that praise of God is something *we need* to do, for our benefit—even a necessity for countering the devil's devices. So, just as prayer is for our benefit, praising God is for our benefit too. Having been in the presence of God, I can emphatically state that He absolutely inspires praise just by His awesome presence. In contrast I have heard accounts from those who have seen hell where the devil must force his followers and captives to praise him by threats and torture, praise of God is inspired by His greatness.

Praising God is a natural response that should require no prompting or compulsion. The fact that people here on earth have the slightest negative attitude towards God implies that the devil is actively working to obstruct the praise of God—or worse, direct praise to himself. Somehow, praise must be involved in invoking the presence of God, or the presence of the devil (as when people complain about God or glorify Satan). When God's presence is enhanced by praise and worship, it facilitates His will to be done here. When you accept God and strive to be as He is and exist only for Him, then He will be with you. Explaining how the process works is difficult, but the empirical evidence is that it does.

Worship. Praise. Prayer. Thanksgiving. Essentially thoughts and words. In a world where bucks, ballots, bullets, blades and bombs seem to be the choice instruments of influence, these three things seem at first to be feeble resources indeed. Yet, it takes hundreds of millions of dollars and vast technical resources to launch and land an ICBM on a target half way around the world. Yet I saw that from my own home, with a cast-off hymnbook, I could, through prayer, affect things a world away or even next-door! This should not be surprising. For it is ultimately through words that God accomplishes His purposes. He has made sure it was written down after all.

It was wonderful to be alive and to see again!

"And the Word became flesh and tabernacled among us. And we beheld His glory, glory as of an only begotten from the Father, full of grace and of truth." John 1:14 LITV" Jesus said to her, I am the Resurrection and the Life. The one believing into Me, though he die, he shall live. And everyone living and believing into Me shall not die to the age, never! Do you believe this?" John 11:25, 26 LITV

Chapter 17 – Returning to Life

I was humbled and starkly aware of how pitiful my list now seemed. It was not lost on me how gracious God had been to answer me in the fullest, most extraordinary way. A sense of loss tinged my thoughts as I could feel the memory of the experience already fading. My much-reduced mind struggled vainly to retain the vast knowledge and analytical capacity it had shared with Christ. I took some consolation in the thought that I could at least retain the one principle I had learned, *the fundamental centrality of selfless love*.

True to my nature, I still had one last question to ask.

"What will become of my children?"

Jesus showed me that by invoking Him, even when I was dead and damned, I had fulfilled the most basic requirement for going to heaven—calling on His name for salvation. I had also demonstrated genuine repentance for my sins. I could go to heaven now, or I could return to my body and resume responsibility for my children. At that point my progress as a saint was not worth mentioning and I couldn't expect any special rewards in heaven either. He added the warning that if I returned, I would have to deal promptly and thoroughly with my sins, and be careful not to be exposed again like I had been. There was a real risk of still going to hell if I returned, as there was for all the living at any moment. Even though He knew what I was going to do, He gave me a choice and a chance to praise Him even more! Moreover, He sternly warned me that I could not expect to invoke Him again as I had just done should I find myself damned again.

The teaching "Once saved always saved" that I had encountered in some of the churches I attended is absolutely not true! This is dangerous heresy that has landed millions of sincere people in hell! A person can lose their state of salvation at any time by rejecting or denying God, though I believe this is not necessarily true if this occurs under extreme duress such as torture or threats against loved ones. The thought of going to heaven and being forever secure from hell was very attractive; but I also thought of my children. Christ showed me with abundant clarity that in my absence their situation was very perilous and that there were more children I was supposed to father and raise to fulfill my purpose in life. It was not God's plan for me to die then.

I thought of the children and the lesson of selfless love was fresh in my mind. So I decided to return to my body. I dreaded putting it on again with all of its limitations, vulnerability to suffering and physical needs. But the fact that Jesus had already arranged for it to be healed made it obvious which decision He wanted. The instant I agreed to this than I found myself back in my body.

Immediately the pain, exhaustion and weariness returned, but were nowhere near as intense as they had been. I felt my body like a heavy, thick weight around me as I rolled off the couch cushions onto my knees. Already I missed the feeling of lightness and freedom that I had experienced in the spirit. It was like getting out of the pool after swimming when your limbs feel heavier and your feet drag, but only many times greater. It was dark again in the room, but I couldn't see anyway because my eyes were bleary with pus. Shaking slightly with fatigue, I rose and stumbled down the hallway to the bathroom where I intended to rinse my eyes out.

It was just after midnight on a cold winter morning in East Texas in 1995 as I groped my way down the hallway from our living room to the hallway bathroom. Even if the lights had been on, I couldn't have seen anything through the pus. Keeping my burned right hand tucked against my chest, I felt for the bathroom door with the left and pushed my way in. I advanced cautiously until I felt the cool tiles of the sink against the front of my legs. I fumbled with the faucet until I heard water gush into the sink and then splashed the cold water into my face, rinsing my eyes and cooling the scorched skin of my face. When my eyes were clear again, I groped around until I found a towel to dry off my face. With my good left hand I felt along the bathroom wall until I found the light switch. Bright light flooded the small room and for a moment I was too dazed to see anything.

Then my vision cleared and I looked into the mirror above the sink. After a few blinks I could see again. *I could see!* That alone was wonderful. The searing pain from infection and the rust particles that had lodged in my eyes from the explosion were gone. Moreover, the pus, which had constantly blurred my vision, was gone too! It was wonderful! I looked at my face and noted that the singed hair was still there and my eyebrows were still gone, but the red, second degree burns on the skin of my face were faded and nearly gone! I grinned in delight, not minding that my hair was a mess and I looked otherwise rather pale, even for winter. Only two small patches of burned skin remained on my thumb and ring finger. I had been given this gift and I needed make sure I was worthy of it. I will probably bear these faint scars for the rest of my life as a tangible reminder of the experience.

I WAS ALIVE!

I had always been aware of how special it is to be alive. From time to time I had reflected on this incredible miracle and taken joy from many simple things like hot showers, drawing a deep breath, gazing at a sunset or idly flexing the fingers of my hands. But that morning it all had a new and more powerful meaning for me. My heart pounded in my chest and my mind reeled with excitement at what I had just experienced. “What’s next?” I wondered as cool water from my damp hair ran down the side on my face and dripped into the sink from my chin. I reflected back on what had brought me to that moment. I had been given the second chance of all second chances. What was I going to do with it?

Soon after that I found a new employer and went back to work. The Lord was quick to remind me of my perilous state due to unrepented sin and lack of restitution to those I had wronged. I had hardly received my first paycheck when an epidemic of viral meningitis swept through our area. I was among the victims. Again, I was without resources for proper medical care. After being gravely ill for several days, I recovered enough to return to work. During my recovery I searched the scriptures to learn what sins I was guilty of and repented of them. As soon as my next paycheck came I began contacting those I had wronged and arranged to make restitution. I had learned this was serious business that should not be delayed! God has no use for excuses.

"And He said to them, It is not yours to know times or seasons which the Father placed in His own authority; but you will receive power, the Holy Spirit coming upon you, and you will be witnesses of Me both in Jerusalem, and in all Judea, and Samaria, and to the end of the earth." Acts 1:7 LITV

Chapter 18 – The Final Key – Praise Leads to Love for Others

Back in 1979 the prophetic word I received told me to "…go and tell others what I have done in your heart." I took that directive seriously and, over the years, put considerable time and effort into sharing my faith with others. I went door to door, gave away Bibles and tracts, participated in short-term mission trips, testified before audiences and have had numerous one-on-one conversations as the opportunities occurred. I even published my philosophies of life in a book. However, the response was quite disappointing. Very few of the people I shared my faith with chose to become Christians, and fewer still of those kept the faith. What seemed so centrally important to me failed to interest most of those I met. How could something so beautiful, so vital and so necessary escape those who needed it most?

Even among practicing Christians, few could relate to my testimony of prophesy, miracles and revelation. This really astonished me. Oddly, the two groups I thought would be most receptive were in fact the least so. When I approached church leadership to even mildly suggest that there could be areas of ministry being overlooked let alone errors in their teachings, the reactions ranged from indifference to being expelled from the congregation by them. The other group was Christians in crisis. It was clear that something was going terribly wrong in their lives. Having been through similar circumstances and solved similar problems, the roots causes and cures for their problems were quite plain to me. Yet typically these people dogmatically insisted on continuing on as if the difficulties were a test of loyalty to God from which they could not deviate. The mere idea that there could be some error in their relationship with God offended them. This kind of thinking is most dangerous for a Christian, as I had found out. When you think you are doing everything right and you are destined for eternal salvation only to find out, when it's too late, that you didn't even get it close to right.

After decades of this pattern it was clear a different approach was called for. There was nothing in the directive from God that told me what results I should expect, but it was discouraging to have such consistently negative responses. I reasoned that even though I was doing what God wanted, perhaps the method was at fault. About that time I was laid off from work and had a long stretch of free time. So I decided to reread a select number of the books that had influenced my faith and read some others I had been meaning to study.

So I reread through a good number of the list of recommended texts in the appendix of this book. Some I had not opened in decades. It was humbling how much I had forgotten and how much I had overlooked on the first readings. The insights the Lord had developed in the interim opened these author's writings in new and refreshing ways. This helped to fill in critical gaps in my understanding of spiritual things and corrected some errors that had crept in.

I also sought out some of the more mature and insightful believers I had known to renew our acquaintance. We brought each other up to date on what the Lord had done in our lives. In some cases it was quite interesting and encouraging to see we'd been on parallel tracks. This was especially true of deliverance ministry. This confirmed to me that this is a critical time for this ministry to be brought into the mainstream church.

"Iron sharpeneth iron; so a man sharpeneth the countenance of his friend." Proverbs 27:17 KJV

I renewed my efforts to clear up past sins. I prepared a list of every one of my sins that was in the Bible and spent several days confessing, repenting, repudiating and asking God's forgiveness. Another step was to identify and break bad habits and cease activities that might bring reproach on the body of Christ. As I did this, I could feel demons of various strengths automatically leaving. So I repeated the self-deliverance exercises I had learned as well. It was humbling to discover how much of the old problem had crept quietly back in—but it was relatively easy to expel it again. I had become more efficient and effective at self-deliverance because I had become better at praise, worship and selfless love.

With each step I took towards a closer relationship with God, I felt better and stronger. However, these were incremental changes, and I felt I needed something more efficacious.

I felt a need to develop a loving relationship with God and my neighbors. So I gave charitably and performed acts of kindness for some who needed it. I spent more time encouraging and counseling others and also worked on my interpersonal skills. All these efforts saw me improving and growing closer to Christ.

However, only one thing made a fundamental difference.

It is a truism that the most important thing we possess is our time; rich or poor, great or small; all of us have only twenty-four hours to spend each day. A good portion of that is devoted to necessary things like, sleeping, eating, grooming and ordinary chores and other obligations. The discretionary time we have left over is our most valuable resource.

I decided to revisit the lesson I had learned about praise and give that time to God, as a gift. I already give time every day to reading the scriptures, prayers and devotions. These are good, but in the Spirit, I felt these were not what really pleased Him. What truly pleased God was worship.

So, I took all the free time I could spare and devoted it to worshiping God. Primarily this took the form of praise and singing. I even dusted off my old acoustic guitar and resumed teaching myself how to play so I could improve my singing and learn new scores. Immediately I felt the presence of the Holy Spirit come, sometimes intensely. I have been told by those that see in the Spirit that God caresses, embraces and even kisses us. His presence was so delightful I can believe this! It was wonderful to realize that, regardless of my actual skills and talents for worship, God is ready at any moment to receive our love.

A side effect of this was that I felt better; my health improved, my mind was clearer, my outlook more positive and temptations fewer and weaker. I also noticed that my positive mood was contagious. I would talk with people throughout my day and they seemed to "catch" my good mood. That was a nice bonus. It was as if the guardian angels, which I am told are our constant companions, drew some strength from this activity and became more active and spread the good spirit about me.

An even more profound side effect was that small problems that had long bedeviled me without resolution began to resolve themselves without any effort from me. Financial shortcomings, interpersonal conflicts, logistical and scheduling complications, household repairs; they all just seemed to take care of themselves. I even had the best garden in years with no more effort than usual!

At first these times of praise and worship were a bit awkward and scheduling them seemed to interfere with my other priorities. Yet as I saw how they improved my mental and spiritual state and had a collateral effect, I realized this had greater value and a broader effect than I had anticipated! I resolved that I would try to make this a permanent part of my daily routine and try to organize my life about it. I took a cue from the psalmist who wrote:

"Seven times a day do I praise thee because of thy righteous judgments." Psalm 119:164 LITV

That works out to about every three hours in a given 24-hour period. So I scheduled my times of praise and worship about three hours apart.

This worked so well, I decided that if I should become an employer, I would try to give my employees breaks every three hours just for this! I wish to God I could find such an employer.

This led to two things. For the first time in my Christian walk, my respect for God began to transform into genuine love. I needed God, respected Him, feared Him, and admired Him and much more. But I hadn't yet begun to love Him and didn't know how to summon up the emotion. A clue for me was in C. S. Lewis's book "The Four Loves." There he wrote that if we don't feel like loving, we should go through the motions until it becomes habitual and then natural. I regret that I had to start that low on the scale, but it worked for me.

God had rebuked, prodded, encouraged, warned and chastened me in a great variety of ways throughout my life. But I do not recall Him being ever so responsive as He was to my efforts to love Him. This feedback naturally encouraged me to love Him more. I had finally come home and conquered one of my worst sins. I could finally keep the first and foremost commandment, to love the Lord your God!

The other outcome of this was my love for others was likewise stimulated. Previously I had regarded service to others and sharing the gospel as a duty. The scriptures clearly state we should bless others in need and share the gospel. I tried to perform these duties professionally and competently. Imagine my puzzlement when previously I noticed that others so engaged were having more and better results than me who were not half as zealous, informed, prepared, strategically guided and persistent as I was. Not that those things were wrong, but although I had plenty of conviction, due to a lack of love I also lacked compassion. That was the difference.

Now I had both.

My love for God transformed my attitude and gave me compassion for others because I could see them as He does. The self-centered veil of pride was lifted and the light of heaven could finally shine through me. It brought back to mind another prophetic word that was spoken to me by prophetic minister Ed Traut during one of his meetings of his ministry, Prophetic Life, in Austin, Texas.

"The Spirit says to you, 'I will rebuild all that the devil has torn down.'"

When I realized all that was kept from me and stolen from me because no one had ever taught or preached this simple truth to me, I might have been angry. However, I took comfort in the scriptures:

"In every matter of trespass, for ox, for ass, for sheep, for clothing, for anything lost of which it is said that it is his, the case of both of them shall come to God. Whom God declares guilty, he shall repay double to his neighbor." Exodus 22:09 LITV

And

"Men do not despise a thief, if he steal to satisfy his soul when he is hungry; But if he be found, he shall restore sevenfold; he shall give all the substance of his house." Proverbs 6:30 LITV

As I enjoy the growing love of God, I also look forward to seeing how the devil will be made to repay what he stole from me and others!

"Wash yourselves, purify yourselves. Put away the evil of your doings from My sight; stop doing evil. Learn to do good, seek justice, straighten the oppressor, judge the orphan, strive for the widow. Come now and let us reason together, says Jehovah: Though your sins are as scarlet, they shall be white as snow; though they are red as the crimson, they shall be like wool. If you are willing and hear, you shall eat the good of the land." Isaiah 1:16-19 LITV

"But if any of you lacks wisdom, let him ask from God, who gives to all freely and with no reproach, and it will be given to him." James_1:5

Chapter 19 – Analysis and Conclusion

This book describes two parallel journeys and the lessons God taught me through them:

The first journey is my discovery of God and the journey to oneness with him that lead me through the following stages:

1. Awareness of God in the triune being of the Father, Son and Holy Spirit

"I and the Father are One!" John 10:30 LITV

"And when the Comforter comes, whom I will send to you from the Father, the Spirit of Truth who proceeds from the Father, that One will witness concerning Me." John 15:26 LITV

There is indeed one God, as it says in Deuteronomy 6:4. In fact, everything comes from Him, exists in Him and returns to Him. His being permeates everything. Belief in God is a natural condition of mankind and came to me as easily as learning to breathe. What He had to reveal to me and teach to me was first that He exists in three distinct persons; a Trinity, with distinct roles: the Father who is the Godhead and directs all things, the Son, Jesus Christ through whom He created everything good and redeemed all things from sin into perfection and the Holy Spirit through whom He realizes and perfects the spiritual maturity of His creation.

The necessity for God having multiple persons in one being was extremely difficult to grasp until I understood two things. The first was how my own person fit so perfectly into the person of God when He permitted me to experience oneness with Him. Sin separates us from God and from His other children so we cannot see how well this works. Yet we are made for that purpose and the triune nature of God is perfectly expressed in our own design. When we are perfected in righteousness and holiness the tendency to unite is inevitable! What was most profound to me is how harmoniously our person integrates with His so that nothing is lost in the union of our identity, and His person is perfectly expressed through us. Likewise, although God exists in three distinct persons, they are perfectly and harmoniously integrated.

The other point that I understood, which demonstrates the necessity of God having three persons, is that life itself comes from the exchange of love between persons. A god that could neither give nor receive love is a dead god. God must have existed before His creation and must have had life to impart to creation to give it life. The life force that comes from God is generated by the tremendous love that flows constantly between His three persons. Our mortal life is a temporary gift that, while augmented in small ways, is steadily consumed over time. If it is not replenished by the exchange of love, death results when life is exhausted. Eternal life is possible only when we enter a loving relationship with God and unreservedly exchange love with Him.

When the Christ emptied Himself and came to earth in mortal form, only two persons of God remained in heaven, the Father and the Holy Spirit. Love continued to be exchanged between those two; otherwise life itself would have ceased! Had God been only one or two persons, it would be impossible to have a savior, the Messiah. More than three persons in the essence of God is not necessary. Though since He created us, it's obviously not a limit either. Any or all of the Trinity may appear on earth as a theophany (essentially a projection rather than the true essence of their beings); but at least two persons of the true essence of their beings must remain in heaven for life to exist or even heaven itself. For at its simplest, heaven is the active, loving presence of God.

2. Awareness that God intends us to have a personal relationship with Him but that sin, rebellion against His will, prevents that relationship and condemns a person to damnation and destruction in hell.

"For the wages of sin is death, but the gift of God is everlasting life in Christ Jesus our Lord." Romans 06:23 LITV

From my earliest childhood I wondered why God could be so present and yet so difficult to communicate with. It seemed like He would want to communicate easily with us. I felt this was very wrong and didn't accept the standard explanation that He was impersonal and unapproachable by nature. The problem is Satan, who cannot create anything good. He depends on using us as resources to accomplish his will. He knows sin separates us from God and exposes us to his predations. Every resource the devil has must be stolen from God through His disobedient children. The devil is incapable of confronting God directly, so he must work to turn God's creation against the creator in his attempts to steal from or displace God. To accomplish that in us, the enemy tries to entice, deceive, terrorize and ultimately force us to turn on our loving Creator. But this is impossible when we have a full and robust relationship with God. For that relationship makes us like God, Who cannot be enticed, deceived, frightened or forced in any way. A person who yields to the devil has demonstrated themselves to be unlike God, and therefore incapable of ultimately achieving oneness with God. This type of behavior puts a person at odds with God, they are rejecting Him and His love. The alternative to conformity to God's character is to be like the devil who must be destroyed in hell. Those who try to play both sides automatically fall into Satan's camp. To accommodate even a single defect in character is to choose the devil's path. For he began with iniquity and the rest of the story developed from there.

3. Awareness of reconciliation to God through grace through the substitutionary sacrifice of Jesus Christ for my sin.

God, who made us and the creation we live in, foreknew us and what we would think, say, do and become. He knew the devil's devices were so pernicious and effective that none of us but the Christ Himself could overcome sin. God loves us and was not willing that any should be damned with the devil and his angels, so He prepared a means of salvation. It was made possible through Jesus' sinless life and selfless sacrifice. To be just, it was made free and unconditional, apart from the requirement that people repent of sin, believe on the gospel and accept Christ's atonement to receive that salvation. On that basis the power of sin is broken and a relationship with God reestablished.

4. The need to consciously and personally repent of sin and accept God's grace

"No, I say to you, But if you do not repent, you will all perish likewise." Luke 13:03 LITV

Bondage to sin and death are the default condition for rejecting God. Therefore, salvation by grace requires action to change the default. To change state from damned to saved, an individual must consciously choose salvation. Grace doesn't automatically provide immunity from the natural consequences of sin, only reestablishes the right relationship with God. Therefore the sin must stop, which is why repentance is a necessity. There is some tolerance with God for backsliding, but this is not defined and it is surely a temporary situation. Therefore it depends on God's sovereign judgment. Anyone who devalues grace by choosing to continue in sin risks losing it and incurring God's everlasting rejection. Genuine repentance includes becoming a partner in God in rectifying the consequences of sin by making restitution too. Restitution reminds us of the cost of sin, demonstrates God's love to the person we injured and pleases God.

5. The place of baptism by water in reconciliation to God

"The one believing and being baptized will be saved. And the one not believing will be condemned." Mark 16:16 LITV

In heaven, nothing is hidden. In God's earthly kingdom it will be the same. A change of heart from sinner to saint is apparent to God, but not necessarily to society. Baptism is an open declaration of belief in Jesus Christ as Savior and repentance of sins. The public declaration of baptism looks forward to the time when every deed and every thought will be apparent to all. God requires us to be public about our commitment to Him. Baptism is also patterned after the death and resurrection of Jesus and therefore should be full immersion rather than anointing or sprinkling. Circumstances vary from case to case and I presume God cares more about the state of the heart than the form of the rite. So, the nearest approximation to this should be performed. Baptism by proxy is permitted when the convert had no reasonable opportunity to be baptized between conversion and death, as in deathbed conversions or martyrs who profess the faith shortly before execution. Baptism of children below the age of accountability and of the mentally deficient is very difficult to justify. Baptism for deceased unbelievers has no precedent in scripture and lacks validity. Forced baptism is a great wrong. It does not impart salvation but rather resentment and resistance to the true faith in the one so violated. I believe it is safe to presume God will deal very strictly with those who abuse His ordinance of baptism and relatively leniently with exceptional cases.

6. The special purpose of the Holy Spirit as helper, comforter, guide and giver of spiritual gifts and the threefold nature of my relationship with Him, on me, in me and in my heart.

Due to the triune nature of God described above, Jesus the savior had to return to heaven so the Holy Spirit could come to earth as helper and comforter. Jesus came primarily as a teacher and as a sacrifice for sin. Though he encouraged, comforted, healed, cleansed and even resurrected, He could only do this on occasion with those he interacted with in person or by proxy. The Holy Spirit goes beyond this by entering us and becoming a part of us. Once in the believer, the Holy Spirit can not only help us, but help other through us by operating in the spiritual gifts God gives us. Unlike Christ, who manifested as an individual and interacted with individuals, the Holy Spirit can operate through the church as a whole. Therefore He can accomplish God's will on a scale limited only by those who are yielded to his will.

7. The baptism and gifts of the Holy Spirit

"Jesus answered, Truly, truly, I say to you, If one is not generated out of water and Spirit, he is not able to enter into the kingdom of God." John 3:5 LITV

"But when the kindness and love of God our Savior toward man appeared, not by works in righteousness which we had done, but according to His mercy, He saved us through the washing of regeneration and renewal of the Holy Spirit, whom He poured out on us richly through Jesus Christ, our Savior; that being justified by His grace, we should become heirs according to the hope of eternal life." Titus 3:4-7 LITV

The signs, which follow a true believer, include not only a changed character, but miraculous gifts and powers. Some churches teach that a person becomes a Christian by affirming a written creed and being publicly baptized in water. In the third chapter of the gospel of John, Jesus told Nicodemus that a true Christian is reborn of the Spirit. It is my own experience that a person cannot overcome sin or please God through ordinary efforts. Therefore, the Holy Spirit is our necessary helper to first resist the devil and second to serve God. He protects and guides us. The Holy Spirit is sovereign and is not bound by any conventions of man, so there is no formula for invoking Him. But the general pattern is that a person must prepare their heart through confession and repentance and then invite the Holy Spirit to come to them. When we have met His terms, he is pleased to respond. As awesomely terrible and powerful as He is, the Holy Spirit will not violate our God-given free will. Neither can we prevent Him from departing if we are disobedient or force Him to serve our purposes.

This is facilitated by the laying on of hands by a person already anointed with the Holy Spirit, but that is not necessary if the subject is receptive, willing and the Holy Spirit chooses to respond.

WARNING: There are apostate and occult-empowered ministers who will lay hands on the unwary and unready claiming to impart the Holy Spirit. The spirit they impart is a demonic counterfeit. Be very discerning and cautious about this matter. If it doesn't feel right, it probably is not right. If spiritual discernment is lacking in such cases, examine their conduct and reputation carefully. Seek confirmation from someone with discernment! Do not be hasty to receive such ministry. When in doubt, cast it out!

Once a person has received the Holy Spirit, they are under God's protection and may also receive spiritual gifts and power. However, the Holy Spirit is easily grieved by sin, and may depart a backslidden Christian. This is why salvation is not bestowed once on rebirth to become permanent, but must be upheld by our continuous selfless love for The Lord. The gifts remain, but may be neutralized by sin and do not operate effectively without the cooperation of the Holy Spirit. There is a terrible heresy commonly accepted that spiritual gifts "are for a season" and stop working when their purpose is fulfilled. Rather inoperative gifts are a symptom of a serious spiritual dysfunction that must be addressed.

8. The importance of dedicating one's life to God's purposes.

"Therefore, brothers, I call on you through the compassions of God to present your bodies a living sacrifice, holy, pleasing to God, which is your reasonable service." Romans 12:01 LITV

God has a purpose, even a detailed and specific plan for the life of every person. Yet He will not force us to follow that plan or give Him anything. We may follow our own heart and dispose of our talents and resources as we choose. However, that puts us squarely into the domain of the devil, who has no reservations about using every device at his disposal to exploit us for his purposes. Ultimately the devil and all who follow him are still controlled by God and serve His purposes, but in a very different way. They are but that which the children of God exercise themselves against as they progress in God's purposes. When the exercise is finished, the devil and all his followers will be summarily discarded with no thanks or reward and even the memory of them will be erased.

Also, while the devil can steal from a sinner, he cannot steal from God. A believer that gives over all that they are and all that they have to God (and is an obedient steward) cannot be robbed by the devil. Dedicating one's life to God not only aligns our lives with God's plan, but makes us God's property, which He will surely secure and defend! This is an excellent choice to make, because through it, God gives meaning, purpose and reward to all our thoughts and actions—even the "wrong" things we did, even our pre-Christian lives. Not dedicating our lives to God robs them of meaning and purpose and exposes us to exploitation by the enemy. Such a state makes us a partner with the devil by default. It is not an easy choice to make or an easy way to follow, for God expects us to serve Him diligently with all our heart to very high standards. But there is no mistake in living life to the fullest.

9. The fact that the Holy Spirit operates today in miraculous power through those gifts, including healing and personal prophesy.

"Tell of His glory among the nations, His wonders among all people." Psalm 96:03 LITV

Christianity is more than a way of life or a philosophy. It is a new life with a progressive transformation of our being from mundane mortality into divine immortality in the likeness of Christ. We are to become vessels for His Spirit and channels for His divine, life-giving power. God is a God of wonders and miracles. Manifestations of His power are not for entertainment or to awe the credulous. They are means to accomplishing God's purpose, which includes restoring life to this corrupt, dying world. The gifts and miracles are just a beginning that demonstrates and initiates the incredible wonders that are to come in His kingdom on earth and ultimately will be ours in heaven. Without these, a person can only make a pretense of serving God and can do nothing of truly eternal value. The enemy also works in occult power, and this can only be opposed in God's power. Occult power is power derived by exploiting unbelievers and careless believers and is used to control unbelievers and against the body of Christ. So, even if you don't mean to harm Christ, by not following God's plan explicitly you contribute to the battle against Him. We are also commanded to communicate to others the testimony of God's great works and miraculous nature.

10. That the devil, his demons and hell exist and are actively trying to destroy mankind.

Just as God, heaven and His angels are real, the devil, hell and his demons are real too. Though they are invisible to our natural senses, they interact with us subtly but persistently and deliberately. They are numerous, powerful, intelligent, capable, well organized and systematic in their attempts to exploit and destroy us—restrained only by God's intervention. The devil and his agents are our natural and implacable enemies. Tragically, many people partner with the enemy, some of these knowingly. These are either deceived or the very worst kind of traitors. There can be no agreement or compromise with them, but only determined resistance and strategic countermeasures in an unrelenting fight to victory.

11. The reality that Christians can be demonized and the importance of deliverance ministry.

Some teachers and ministers of the gospel have erroneously concluded that demons cannot directly attack, let alone inhabit, Spirit filled Christians. This is absolute heresy disproven by millions of counter examples. Typically such people are covering for the fact that they lack the ability to discern demons and expel them. To admit such a thing is to bring into question their credentials to minister at all, and more importantly their faith and personal relationship with Christ. So, rather than address the problem, they deny it exists. This is absolutely contemptible because it leaves their disciples unprotected and without remedy and therefore exposed to conditions that can compromise their salvation. Tragically, such leaders attract like-minded people who also want to believe they can be a Christian without being Christ-like.

The human body is a truly vast and complex vessel capable of containing not only the human soul, and designed to accommodate a variety of manifestations of the Holy Spirit, but also other spirits from God such as strength and courage. A Christian whose life is not fully yielded to God may open part or all of their being to demonization. Contrary to some teachings, their body can, at the same time, host the Holy Spirit, other divine spirits and innumerable demons of nearly all descriptions! Naturally the Holy Spirit is grieved by such a state and often withdraws from or reduces His presence in such cases. A demonized Christian cannot function fully for God. Left unchecked, demonization has the potential to destroy the believer and even make them an instrument of harm to others. A nearly universal consequence of demonization is the inability to discern God's voice or use spiritual gifts. Deliverance ministry is essential for any believer to fully realize their potential.

12. That our purpose in life is to develop into the likeness of Jesus Christ through resisting evil and responding constructively to suffering.

"But we know that to the ones loving God all things work together for good, to those being called according to purpose; because whom He foreknew, He also predestinated to be conformed to the image of His Son, for Him to be the First-born among many brothers." Romans 08:28-29 LITV

Resisting evil routinely brings a fierce response from the devil, often leading to suffering, rejection, loss, persecution and worse. Oddly, it does not appear to be explicitly stated in the scriptures, but suffering plays a good and necessary role in our lives. Responding positively, constructively, even thankfully to suffering helps us to become increasingly Christ-like. Jesus set us the standard. He didn't argue, accuse, judge or complain. He bore rejection and persecution obediently and patiently. However, Jesus was also ready to teach, correct, admonish and even fight when the occasion was right. In fighting He recognized that the enemy is not flesh, but spirit.

God has assured us that the devil cannot endure our resistance and we will prevail if we persist in God's principles. In the interim, the suffering we endure builds our character. There is no sorrow or suffering in heaven. Here and now we have the unique opportunity to advance ourselves and earn rich rewards for heaven. A key point is that we must maintain a good attitude through the trial and persevere through to the end. Our reward will be oneness with God and an elevated level of salvation.

An important point to understand here too is that partial credit is rare if found at all in God's tests. It is helpful to remember that the fundamental definition of sin is "missing the mark" or falling short of the expectation of God. Subsets of sin like "rebellion" (refusing to do good) and "transgression" (doing wrong) are merely extreme expressions of sin.

In short, if we do not know what God wants of us specifically (by word of knowledge or personal prophesy), and receive His provision (through the Holy Spirit), our best efforts will fail. Even the best Christian, who tries in their wisdom and strength to please God, will fail because

(1) They can only guess what is right, and are likely to guess wrong. Or even if they guess right, will not know how to accomplish it. Principle is necessary, but not sufficient.
(2) Human effort alone cannot achieve God's purposes. Without His Seven Spirits (Isaiah 11:2, Revelation 3:1), we, like Job, will find that our best and highest, no matter how noble or exceptional, are inadequate, even contemptible[1].

13. The central importance of selfless love

"And one of them, a lawyer, questioned Him, testing Him, and saying, Teacher, which is the great commandment in the Law? And Jesus said to him, 'You shall love the Lord your God with all your heart, and with all your soul, and with all your mind.' (Deut. 6:5) This is the first and great commandment. And the second is like it: 'You shall love your neighbor as yourself.' (Leviticus 19:18) On these two commandments all the Law and the Prophets hang." Matthew 22:35-40

In distinguishing between sin and righteousness, our motives mean as much or more than our words and deeds. The love a person gives and shares cannot be for the purpose of bettering our own situation. If it is not selfless, even love becomes a rejection of His purpose for us. Just as Christ showed that selfless love is the root answer to every question, so selfless love is the guiding principle for our purpose and relationship with God. From the principle of love, all other divine principles can be derived. Love is life. Without love there is death.

In the 13th chapter of his first epistle to the Corinthian believers[2], St. Paul eloquently explained that without love we and all we do and accomplish is meaningless. That doesn't mean if we don't feel love

---

[1] Isaiah_64:6

[2] Some well-versed Bible scholars may cite I Cor. 5:9, that, in fact, there was a previous letter to the Corinthians that is tragically lost and this references "II Cor." This text merely uses the conventional numbering of the Apostle's letters to avoid confusion for the general reader.

we should give up altogether. We need to start somewhere. The beginning of love is respect for God. If we respect God, we will obey Him. As we obey God and receive the fruits of obedience, the excellence of His way and the perfection of His person become apparent. Respect becomes obedience, obedience leads to closeness, closeness becomes intimacy, intimacy becomes love, and ultimately love transforms us into His likeness where love is normal and natural. Love for God flows back through us and becomes love for our fellow man. In this manner we may become the rivers of living waters Jesus spoke of in John 7:38.

To love selflessly requires sacrifice, with Christ's atonement on the cross being the ultimate expression of such love. It requires both action and inaction. Action involves expressing love in giving ourselves to others. Love expressed by inaction resists the natural inclination to selfishly reject those who offend and hurt us. That is, active love does what is right and inactive love restrains what is wrong. There is also wisdom in love, for it makes us vulnerable. Wisdom is necessary for those who love to avoid traps the devil sets to exploit and destroy them. It is a fine balance to walk in love where the protection and guidance of God are essential. Learning to balance life's priorities in love puts us in harmony with God and advances us into a state of oneness with Him.

The second journey was my near death experience where I received direct revelations of the nature of the demonic and the divine. From first-hand observations a number of important facts and principles can be derived. I am very grateful for these, because things that were matters of faith before are now known facts for me. In the interim, this knowledge has sustained me during trials that faith alone could not have endured. While I cannot impart the actual experience to others, they can be encouraged to know that someone has actually tested the theories and returned to communicate what they learned.

The account related first-hand knowledge of the following:

1. God exists and is accurately (but far from completely) portrayed in the Bible. He is a loving, holy, perfect being who possesses omniscience, omnipotence and omnipresence. Also, there is ultimately only one God. Other gods are the inventions of men or the counterfeits of the devil. The former are the things people choose to devote themselves to instead of God; and the latter are the evil spirits which make a pretense of being God, entice men to worship them and feed on that attention.

2. God is in control of everything to the minutest detail, both good and evil and offers us a choice of a purposeful life with spiritual growth or a purposeless life with spiritual disintegration, according to our free will. He has foreordained assigned roles for us that we have the option to fill. This includes the options to choose righteous or unrighteous roles. Our freedom is chiefly in terms of our attitude. For not choosing the righteous role only results in unrighteousness by default. The choices we make open or close opportunities to engage these options. Either direction accomplishes God's will, but there is a clearly preferred direction towards righteousness. God doesn't need us to choose evil to accomplish His purposes. The devil and his kind are quite adequate for that. But people may freely join that element too; though they shall share its fate as well. It should be a sobering thought that we can also choose roles where we play the part of God's opponent. Choose to lose? Not a good idea.

The right attitude will lead us to the roles God has prepared for us that serve the purpose of advancing our own development. These roles build on each other with good choices advancing us, and poor choices stopping or even regressing us. It has to be a constant effort so inaction doesn't become action against righteousness. Our advancement also aids others in their advancement too, especially when we lead the way. Faith, integrity, courage, strength, and love are all critical in making the right choices.

3. We, as human beings, are created in God's image, with an ultimate goal of oneness with Him, gained through opportunities He offers us for spiritual advancement and reward. We are children of God, made in His likeness. One of those characteristics is an uncompromising respect for free will. God gives us free will to choose to grow into His likeness or not. Eternal life is only possible on His terms, so to reject His ways leads to destruction. It is not as if God uses the promise of eternal life to compel us to be obedient to His will, it is not a bribe or a payoff. Conformity to God's nature is what makes eternal life possible. Any other nature has inherent flaws in it, which will ultimately lead to failure, degeneration and death. To have eternal life, we must adopt holiness as an intrinsic part of our nature. Eternal life without adopting all the characteristics of God is possible. But oneness with God requires acquiring all the characteristics of God through a full spectrum of continual spiritual growth. In contrast, attempting to control others against their will is totally contrary to God's nature and set us in opposition to Him and is purposes.

4. Heaven and hell are real. Heaven is a place of indescribable riches and opportunities for those that accept God and His ways. These riches are not material things such as gold, jewels, fancy houses or prestige, and any preacher who tells you otherwise is being untruthful and his own salvation should be called into question. True riches are developments to one's being in terms of capability, perfection, holiness and love that make a person more Christ-like. Hell, a place of torment and destruction, created to punish and destroy the devil and his angels, is real too. This is the eternal, unchangeable destination of those who reject God and adopt the devil's ways. It's not that if you don't follow God's plan you continue in the afterlife as you did in mortal life. No, a person's lack of love for God is an irrevocable ticket to hell. At death, our choice of destinations is determined unalterably. We may not be perfectly righteous or unrighteous at the moment of death, thus it is the direction we have chosen in life at that point that determines our direction for the rest of eternity. Of course, the aforementioned prerequisites must be met before a person may expect to continue on to heaven in the next life.

5. What matters most in this life is how we treat others and our relationship with God. Considering that the elect and God will ultimately become one, the distinction between how we treat God and how we treat others is really very fine.

6. I should add too, that while I did not directly observe heaven itself, but only experienced oneness with Jesus, there was no indication that we are, as some cults teach, destined to become other gods and goddesses, and create our own worlds with people of our own making. God offers us something far more wonderful than becoming provincial little godlets. His ultimate goal is to unite us once again with Himself where we will augment and share in His divinity. There has always been, is now and always will be only one God Most High. Those who believe and worse, teach such error, have only received a variation on the devil's original sin of wanting to "become like God" apart from God.

The obvious response should be to give ourselves to God's purpose in repentance and obedience. Once a person realizes they have divine purpose they should both take comfort in knowing that a loving God has their best interest at the heart of His plan for them, and take warning that deviating from that plan results in profound loss for them and others. Once a person has established a relationship with God through understanding His word and seeking His will, they must passionately seek to develop and exercise a love for Him and their fellow man. This is not the same as loyalty and obedience to an institutional church, though much can be done collectively that is difficult or impossible individually.

Ultimately we are personally responsible and accountable as individuals to God. We cannot depend on associations to family, friends, church or nation to commend us to God. On Judgment Day it will be too late for excuses or shifting blame. God will not accept excuses in any form. For He gives us everything we need to fulfill our purpose and His will. Selfishness, laziness and timidity are our common enemies and will lead us straight to hell! Ultimately it is a very simple matter. We make it complicated by trying to find our own ways around God's ways. Ask Him for wisdom—it is one thing He offers without restraint. Ask Him for help, that is why He gave us the Holy Spirit. And never, ever give up or compromise!

Lastly, when I have shared this story with others, some inevitably want to know what my list of questions was and what the answers are. So, for them and others like them I reproduce the list with my answers here. However, I make the disclaimer that, despite my near death experience, I am still a limited, fallible person. The only thing of real substance I was allowed to take away from the divine question-answer session was the ultimate question, which is all that really matters. That was the purpose of the exercise. I was not specifically given a command by God to share this revelation with others; the exercise was, as far as I can tell, for my benefit.

However, since the story appears to be helpful to others, I have written things down for their benefit too. Given the vast number of people who are going to hell, hopefully this will change the destiny of some. But in the timelines I saw, both past and future, there were no great future changes indicated in the proportions going to hell and heaven. So, I do not expect this testimony to make a profound impact. If telling this story means some take warning and act wisely, then it is well worth the effort to publish this account. For I do not wish anyone, no matter how evil a life they have lived, to suffer damnation—it is just too terrible and entirely unnecessary! But I do want to state clearly that the answers below are not divine revelation, but my own conclusions based on scripture, first-hand experience, research and some careful deduction and extrapolation. The best course to take in answering any such question is to inquire of the Holy Spirit. Providing answers is one of His roles.

Answers to questions on the list:

Jesus did not specifically answer any of the questions on my list. In light of answering the ultimate question, they were really not relevant. However, through my studies and experiences, I do recognize that others are interested in the answers and have answered these questions to my own satisfaction. Here, in brief form, are my own understandings. I do not represent them as divine revelation or even infallible doctrine, but only my own informed and considered opinions. The exercise of answering them has helped me settle certain troubling doubts. Perhaps these will be of similar value to others.

1. What is heaven like and do we continue to progress to higher orders of being after we get there?

Heaven, in the simplest terms, is being in the presence of God. God is triune in nature with three distinct persons: the Father, the Son and the Holy Spirit. The creation of a fourth person in the Godhead, the Bride of Christ, is the ultimate goal and purpose of the Church.[3] Between them flows a vast current of love. It is this exchange of love that generates life. From life springs everything else. God is alive and everything He creates is necessarily alive too. (This is at least initially true, for sin kills.) God is holy and nothing impure or imperfect can be in Him. Therefore heaven is pure and perfect and full of life and love. From life and love spring everything good.

Human beings are derived from very tiny fragments of God that He separates from Himself and endows with features and functions, power and ability to exist apart from Him and exercise free will on a limited scale. Heaven is an extension of God's core being in which He creates a multitude of environments and opportunities at multiple levels for us to grow and develop into His likeness. The goal of this is to reach a state where we are ready to reunite with Him in oneness with His core being that both preserves our identity and perfectly integrates it with His own. We are not a surprise to God, we have specific purposes elected by Him, if we choose to not follow the path of the righteous then we fall by the wayside only to be captured by Satan and devoured.

Heaven extends throughout everything, including multiple universes and even down to us on earth. It reaches to us when we are obedient to God. To be sure it is weaker here than virtually anywhere outside of

[3] Revelation 22:1, 9, 22:17

hell. (And it even reaches there to a degree.) But those of us who choose God's way will find that when we leave our mortal existence, that we come from and in reality never leave heaven.

St. Paul wrote:

"I know a man in Christ fourteen years before--whether in the body, I do not know, or out of the body, I do not know, God knows--such a one was caught up to the third Heaven." 2 Corinthians 12:02 LITV

In the New Testament the word οὐρανός, sky, (Strong's concordance G3772) is used generally for heaven with no distinction as to which level and no distinction between height, atmosphere or space. Some scholars say this refers to the terrestrial, telestial, and celestial heavens, or the atmosphere, space and heaven proper. In his book "Demons, an Eyewitness Account," Howard O. Pittman recounts a near death experience where he saw Satan and his demons in the second heaven (pg. 10).[xiii] In "Visions Given to Annie" (Schisler), R. Edward Miller confirms that the devil occupies, temporarily, the second heaven. He also writes that there are many levels to heaven. So, I would discount the sky, space, heaven theory.

I have not seen heaven nor been given a revelation about it. Based on available first-hand accounts, my best understanding of the given information is that heaven is multi-dimensional with many distinct levels. We are outside of heaven proper in one of many creations and are just below the least of these levels. Higher levels are like layers of an onion each successive level is greater than the one before it. However, their greatness in all degrees increases vastly from level to level. Whether the size and scope increases logarithmically or geometrically or otherwise I do not know. But the upper levels are so vast that the entire universe we know would be so microscopically small as to be irrelevant there.

According to others, such as Dr. Eby, earthly life mimics in a crude and warped way life in heaven. In heaven there are also people, animals and plants. Everything there is alive. Even things that are inanimate here (like rocks, clouds and streams) are alive. There are also many other living things there that have no counterpart here, like angelic beings. People dwell in buildings and there are gardens, cities, and other constructions. People and angels eat and drink as we do, though I presume it is not a dire necessity as it is here. According to Annie Schisler's visions, heaven is really an extension of God, which abounds with an endless variety of opportunities and environments for spiritual testing and development. There are also many places of creation and structures devised to give glory to God. It makes perfect sense that our journey to oneness is on-going and we must continue to grow in love for our Lord to travel into the higher realms of heaven.

2. What is the fate of the souls of people who die before they are born? Before they reach the age of accountability or who never develop sufficient mental faculties to know right from wrong?

The moment a human being is conceived, the body and soul are matched together. Whether the soul always fully enters the body I do not know. For some part of the soul may also reside in heaven while the rest abides in the body or a soul may reside exclusively in the body. But some portion of the soul unites with the body. A body cannot live long without the soul. It has been suggested by others that a fetus is viable in the womb without a soul because of its connection to the mother. I do not know if that is possible, but from the account of the Holy Spirit filling John the Baptist in the womb it is apparent that the normal and intended case is for the spirit to unite with the body before birth.

Until and unless a person reaches a state where they have sufficient mental capacity to choose right or wrong, to accept or reject God, they automatically return to heaven upon death. A soul that cannot reject God cannot be damned. That is the default state. The moment they make a decision to turn from selfless love and pursue a different path in life, they are on course for hell. Only a conscious decision to repent and an effort to make restitution and reconciliation can change that. The age of accountability is typically between the ages of 3 and 5, though mentally deficient persons may reach that state either later, or never. Full adulthood occurs at or around 20.[4]

An interesting note is that some people's souls are fragmented into multiple personalities by extreme trauma or occult rites. Unless reintegrated, each personality is separately accountable to God. So, one fragment of the same soul may ultimately go to heaven, while another fragment may ultimately perish in hell. The best course is for the personality to be reintegrated and accept the Christian faith. Then that person can wholly work towards the ultimate goal and purpose.

---

[4] Numbers 1:18

3. What is the fate of people who live and die without ever hearing the gospel?

Each person's situation is unique and ultimately only God can judge them. However, everyone who lives beyond the age of accountability is at some point in their life confronted by the Holy Spirit with a choice of righteousness or sin. Exposure to the gospel, while not necessary for accountability, precipitates it. Though the manner and depth of the experience may vary, there are no exceptions. The individual is responsible for their response. In the moments after death, God will reveal the whole matter and give some of those who have responded well to His Spirit an understanding of the true nature of things and the opportunity to accept His grace, as He has done with others and me. Those who have proved themselves lovers of iniquity will go directly to hell with no such opportunity.

4. Why do good people appear to suffer for no apparent reason, and why do evil people appear to escape the logical or natural consequences of their sins?

To properly understand this, a distinction must be made between purposeful suffering and purposeless suffering, earthly rewards and eternal rewards.

What makes this difficult to understand is the mindset that (1) this life is all there is to existence and (2) that suffering is undesirable. An evil person cannot participate in building the kingdom of heaven, only a righteous person can. But an evil person can be used of God to build the kingdom of Satan, which God uses to test and develop His saints. Evil people will have no heavenly reward, and receive all the reward they will have for serving God's purposes in this life. They will fully bear the consequences of their sin in hell. And if they should repent and change their ways, then Christ will have borne the consequences Himself.

For good people who suffer it is a different equation. Their reward is not in material things or earthly honors. Purposeful suffering in this life creates true riches that are character development and heavenly advancement and honors. There are only three things of value that can be taken from this life into the next:

a. Obedient service to God
b. Improvements to our person
c. Good things we do for others (those going to heaven)

An evil person who repents on their deathbed enters into eternal life bankrupt. One of the Elect who dies an anonymous pauper may be immensely rich and honored in heaven.

However, there are also good people who suffer for their ancestral and national sins because they have not repudiated these. For the nature of sin and righteousness are such that successive generations may inherit divine judgment against their ancestors, their race or nationality. Finally, people can suffer from the errors of other people or be directly attacked by the devil in opposition to God. These are people who have not taken care to protect themselves from both situations.

5. Why is the Biblical account of creation so vastly different from the scientific explanation for how the universe and life began, especially in terms of the time spans involved?

The Biblical account of creation is accurate and the timeline correct. The earth was created in 4003 B.C. The heavens were created during the seven literal days of creation afterwards. In 2347 B.C. the great flood occurred with a concurrent massive storm of ice created by subterranean water ejected high into the atmosphere and the collapse of a massive cloud that surrounded the earth covered the northern and southern hemispheres with a deep layer of ice. Massive qualities of rock and sediment were dislodged (largely from between the Americas, Europe and Africa as the once united continents broke up). This mixed with the waterborne remains of drowned plants and animals to create the fossil record. The fallen ice created the appearance of several ice ages as it partially melted.

At the same time as the flood, a spiritual veil was established around the world, partially separating it from the full presence of God. This resulted in a rapid attenuation in the divine life force that had previously fostered abundant life on the planet, resulting in the current, relatively barren conditions. This is illustrated in the exponential decline in the lifespans of the patriarchs between Noah (950), Shem (600), Eber (464), Jacob (147), Moses (120) and King David (69). Concurrent with this, the speed of light and other physical constants changed. The speed of light declined exponentially, with related changes in physical properties of matter. Essentially the earth went from a living planet to a (relatively) dead one. (The change in the speed of light is illustrated in Job 38:32 where it is clear that before the invention of the telescope, Job was able to discern the individual stars in and the unusual independent motions of the constellation Arcturus with the naked eye. Not so now.) The approximately ten-fold decrease in the speed of light accounts for the significant errors by physicists in formulating the age of the universe, for interpreting data like the rate of radioactive decay and the appearance of the stars and galaxies around us are vastly different because of this.

6. What is the nature of the soul—does it have structure and functions like the body? Can a soul be destroyed?

The human soul is multidimensional and co-exists both in our bodies on earth and, for believers, simultaneously extends through to the other "planes" of heavenly realms, much as a three-dimensional object exists in multiple two-dimensional planes. Its external shape can be altered at will and the human form is an adaptation specific for mortal life and only one of several possible variations. A sphere or cloud is the fundamental or natural shape of the human spirit. On each heavenly plane where God grants a person access, the soul may grow in size and functionality within the restrictions characteristic of that plane. Unlike a static three-dimensional object, which can manifest only in fixed ways on two-dimensional planes, a soul can have entirely different forms on different planes and each manifestation can engage in entirely independent activities on different planes. It is like having multiple bodies that can be used simultaneously for different purposes.

The soul has both external and internal structure with a significant number of analogies to the human body. However, the soul has a tremendous capacity to acquire and develop a multitude of functions and features beyond the basic ones necessary for independent existence that God imparts to the human soul upon initial formation. Many of these have no counterpart in the physical body. This would be like adding wings, RADAR, projectile weaponry or additional memory and processing capacity to a human body as has been proposed in some technical literature. The soul also can develop a nearly unlimited capacity for operating with intelligence and power. This, I think, is one of the central reasons why sinners must be destroyed in hell. Satan was among the sons of God, and the damage done by one of his kind gone wrong is beyond description. More beings like him is unthinkable!

As an aside, animals have souls too, and angelic beings are also spiritual entities that closely resemble humans in form and function. But while both of these are made from spirit derived from God, both of these lack the fragment of God's core essence He gives to humans and they also lack certain capacities for spiritual development, which are unique to humans.

The composition of man's spiritual being generally consists of three distinct parts: the heart, which is essentially a fragment of God about which He forms the rest; the soul, which contains the mind which is the seat of reason, will and memory; and the spirit, which contains the "support" functions for the senses, locomotion, nourishment, defense and etc. It is the heart, which will ultimately return to God when our course of divine development and perfection is complete. The soul and spirit may remain to provide a vessel in which we may manifest our person external to God and to interface with the body.

The soul and spirit of the damned are destroyed in hell, essentially erasing the personality. The heart, which is eternal and indestructible, returns to God. If this appears to put a finite limit on the suffering of the damned in hell, that is incorrect. They suffer for all of eternity, which is for all time. God exists outside of time though. From the perspective of the damned they suffer forever, even though from God's perspective it is over when time runs its course. Understandably, this is a difficult concept to grasp. I have been told by mathematicians that there are greater and lesser infinities. God outlasts time. It is something like that.

7. How did Jesus transmute water into wine and multiply the loaves and fishes?

Jesus was one with God, not separated by sin. He had repudiated the sins of his mortal ancestors and was Himself sinless. Therefore He had full access to love and receive love from God and therefore the power of life. He was an open channel and a fit and functional vessel for God's will to operate through. He did not do miracles in His own power, but acted as an instrument of God.

The material world was created by God (through Christ) and is responsive to God's will that is imparted through the words which God speaks. God's words are in fact derived from His own being and communicate His will to His creation. Jesus had learned the very important and critical ability to listen for and hear God's words and become responsive to them. (God speaks to all of us constantly at multiple levels, but we either cannot hear him or we refuse to listen.) As the sounding board of a musical instrument gathers and amplifies tones imparted to it, Jesus received, interpreted and amplified the words of God and then imparted them to their objective in the material world. The words of God convey with them information and power (they are essentially light, although there are other kinds of light than the photons science has identified). A material object, which receives the words of God in this fashion, must obey them.

In the case of the water, God's words provided the energy and information to rearrange the atomic structure and the molecules of water into a higher (more complex) state, namely wine. This could also theoretically be done by brute force in a very powerful and sophisticated nuclear reactor, but love peacefully and gently compels the subatomic particles to revise their "dance" into another pattern and the life from God gives them the energy and direction to do so. For obviously higher states of complexity in matter require higher states of energy. Energy is derived from life, not vice versa.

In contrast, science controls chemical reactions by force, leveraging the principles of physics to drive chemical reactions to produce a desired result. However, because man cannot create energy from nothing, to do so, it is required to transfer energy from one source to another. In any chemical reaction there are also typically losses and unwanted byproducts. Overall, all human effort apart from God results in an increase in entropy, or disorder because love is not involved.

The multiplication of the fishes and loaves described in Matthew's gospel Ch. 14 and Mark Ch. 6 is a variation on this. The fishes and loves already existed in alternate realities, parallel universes or other planes also created by God. Just as sin separates us from the words of God, it also separates us from the other realities He has created. For in heaven, a person may quite easily pass from one created reality to another, much as we use a corridor to go from room to room in a large building. In fact, from heaven, a person may enter ours or another reality at different points in time as well – like selecting different rows of seats in a large theater or stadium! In this case, in the act of blessing the loaves and fishes, Jesus removed that barrier and allowed a very small portion of the loaves and fishes that existed in an alternate creation into this creation. The implications of this are quite exciting when it is realized that, once barriers created by sin are removed, we may have limitless opportunities to travel between this and other parts of creation and other creations!

Jesus also said that by even a small faith, mountains could be relocated. Faith, or belief is a creative function. It is one of those "added" functions the human spirit can acquire in addition to the basic functions each of us are given when God first created us (and not everyone is created with exactly the same functions or capacities). This function allows us to make changes in the heavenly realm that are then manifested in the physical realm. For the physical realm is a shadowy reflection of what primarily exists in heaven. (Yes, heaven is far, far more real than the physical world! Contrary to perceptions, it is we who live in the ghost world, not the spirits.) Faith operates through our imaginations, especially visualization, to create or alter reality in heaven. We can will something to be created or altered in heaven—provided it agrees with God's will. Speaking things also manifests them in heaven and initiates the process by which they manifest here too. If the process is completed and sustained, the results will be manifested on earth.

8. Who or what is the Holy Spirit?

This one question I am still carefully considering. Error regarding the Holy Spirit is a very serious matter. So all I can safely say is that He is a distinct person in the triune God with male gender. As His title implies, He is Holy. If He has a name, it is not revealed to us yet. The scriptures also tell us that He acts as our helper, interpreter, teacher, guide and comforter. Believers may be baptized into the Holy Spirit, which may either come upon them or indwell them. He communicates things to us, including prophecies and memories. The Holy Spirit imparts spiritual gifts to us and is essential in developing spiritual fruit (growth and development). More I will not speculate.

9. What are demons and where do they come from?

Demons are not, as some assert, fallen angels. St. Peter and St. Jude both explain that fallen angels were already defeated and chained up in hell to await the Judgment Day.[5] Demons are not created by God. They are offspring of the devil through intimate, spiritual acts with people who, in the likeness of God, can engender other spirits. Since he lacks true generative/creative power, the devil must use living creatures in the process of creating demons. Therefore, they are a byproduct of illicit sex and worship (which are, for spiritual purposes,

---

[5] "For if God did not spare sinning angels, but delivered them to chains of darkness, thrust down into Tartarus, having been kept to judgment; "2 Peter_2:4 LITV
"And those angels not having kept their first place, but having deserted their dwelling-place, He has kept in everlasting chains under darkness for the judgment of a great Day;" Jude_1:6 LITV

interchangeable). Habitual sin causes them to be conceived[6] and nourished by a human or animal soul until they reach a state where they can exist independently of their host. This is another reason why sin is so evil—habitual sinners create an ever-growing host of demons that plague them and mankind in general.

Demons are illegitimate, unclean spirits and are therefore rejected by God and naturally gravitate to serving the devil. Essentially, they are bastard spirits without an origin in or relationship to God. Lacking the ability to obtain sustenance from God, they prey on living creatures, men, animals and plants. Because of their perverse origins they are incomplete and defective. That doesn't mean they are necessarily stupid, weak or particularly vulnerable. Demons may be extremely overdeveloped in a given function. They are all critically weak and vulnerable to the Holy Spirit though.

10. Why do we pray?

Prayer is not, as some assert, a mechanism by which people invoke God to do our will—though many try to misuse it in this manner. Prayer is the act of petitioning God to accomplish His will through us. Just as God's words convey information and power to transform His creation[7], our words also have power—both for good and evil. (The devil imparts power to the words spoken by his followers too!) The Lord's Prayer is a classic example of this. Really effective prayer is done in tandem with the Holy Spirit, following His lead in choosing the subject and content of our prayers. The first and foremost object of prayer is to transform the person praying into the likeness of our Lord. After that, prayer's dual purpose is to invoke God's will and oppose the devil's purposes. Speaking prayer without being empowered by His Spirit is no more effective than reading a book aloud. Praying in an ungodly spirit such as malevolence or greed is worse, for it serves the enemy's purposes. The strength of a given prayer is directly proportional to the true passion of and the love for God in the person's heart—not their sincerity or eloquence.

11. Where is hell? What are the criteria for being sent there?

The most basic definition of hell is the absence of God. It is characterized by qualities that are diametrically opposed to those of heaven. Therefore, wherever chaos, injustice, waste, hatred,

---

[6] Job 15:35, Psalm 7:4, Isaiah 59:4, James 1:13-15

[7] Amos 3:7

perversion and like things are present, in broad terms, hell is there too. God also created three places of confinement for the unredeemed dead, the devil and the angels that rebelled with him: Paradise (Sheol, Hades, the abode of the righteous dead), Abaddon (the place of destruction), and Gehenna or Tartarus (the pit, the deepest part of hell).

Paradise was where the righteous dead awaited Christ's death and resurrection. They were released from Paradise when Christ resurrected Himself from the dead and lead them into heaven. Abaddon is the place of confinement and torment for the devil, his angels and the damned. It is a temporary holding place until Judgment Day. Demons and the devil may come and go from there, but the fallen angels and the damned cannot leave their prisons. On Judgment Day the devil and all his followers, including the fallen angels and the damned, will be sent to Gehenna for truly terrible torment and destruction. I don't know the latitude or longitude or the depth beneath the earth of hell. A good guess would be near Mt. Sinai, since that is near where the earth swallowed up Dathan, Abiram and Korah and their men who fell directly into hell. Mary K Baxter in "A Divine Revelation of Hell Heaven" places it underground and describes its overall shape as that of a woman lying on her back.

The basic criterion for being sent to hell is rebellion against or rejection of God. At the most fundamental level, God is love and His will is for His creation to receive His love and return it back to Him freely. Listening expectantly for God's voice to reveal His will and obedience to that voice is the natural manifestation of that love. So, sin is responding to God's love with indifference or even hatred, which manifests as disobedience. The two commandments from which all other commandments are derived are to love God and love your neighbor. Therefore, anything that deviates from that is sin. Technically there are neutral actions that are not sin. And there are common, minor errors and sins that do not merit punishment in hell. However, anything that falls between total, selfless love and mortal sins are tragically missed opportunities to advance in God's purposes.

12. Is there a true church on earth that fully and accurately preaches and practices the gospel and properly represents God?

Not that I have found in institutional churches. But I believe I have met individuals from many variants of Christianity, independent as well as denominational, that do demonstrate the selfless love and obedience to God that defines the true church. House churches seem to have a disproportionate number of these. So it exists in the form of individual believers yielded and obedient to the Holy Spirit. If my estimate that 2% of the world population is saved, and approximately 1/3 of the global population is Christian, then only about 6% of Christians are genuine. This indicates an abysmal failure rate for any organized church. The organized church should exist for the primary purpose of teaching, prayer, praise and worship by true Christians. The true church will gather its own and exclude the rest. It will exist to serve God's purposes, not to exploit the believer to serve man's ambitions.

13. Why don't Christians manifest the miraculous powers recorded of Jesus and the saints in the scriptures?

"Christians" do not automatically manifest divine power because, in the first place, most people who call themselves Christians are not really Christ-like. Most of these are "cultural Christians" with no real spiritual involvement and a large majority of the rest is apostate or backslidden. Of those who have a meaningful, spiritual relationship with God, most have not unreservedly given themselves to God, fully repented of their sins, divested themselves of curses and learned to hear and obey the voice of God. It also helps to ask for the respective gifts and receive them by impartation from or have them activated by someone who already has them. But the latter point isn't absolutely necessary. In fact, true Christians do manifest the signs and miracles done by the saints in previous times. Someone who cannot manifest such things should carefully examine their beliefs and conduct.

Is there such a thing as reincarnation?

In a word, no. St. Paul wrote to the Jewish believers all that should be necessary to say:

"And as it is reserved to men once to die, and after this, Judgment;" Hebrews 09:27 LITV

Despite this, there is a huge body of literature purporting to provide evidence for reincarnation. Whole religions revolve around it. These are lies straight from the devil in hell.

Accounts of reincarnation are typically false memories manufactured by demons, which either invent them or derive them from the memories of individuals known to them. They then plant these ideas and false memories into the minds of impressionable individuals. Some accounts are the pure fantasies of gullible people. Others are maliciously contrived fables used to deceive and control the unwary and ignorant. The goal of this is to give people a false sense of security that causes them to be resigned to their role in life and ultimately leads them to delay preparing for eternity until it is too late.

The one possible exception in Scripture is John the Baptist.

"Behold, I am sending you Elijah the prophet before the coming of the great and dreadful day of Jehovah." Malachi 4:5 LITV

"And if you are willing to receive, he is Elijah, the one going to come. Matthew 11:14 LITV

Elijah didn't die, but went directly to heaven[8] like Enoch.[9] Thus, technically since he didn't die, Elijah could be reincarnated as John the Baptist. After the death of John the Baptist, Elijah manifested in the spirit with Moses[10]. This indicates he was now in the same class with Moses, the righteous dead.

The implication of this is quite interesting. Apparently we could reincarnate at least once, perhaps multiple times, as long as we never "died" but achieved the status of Enoch and Elijah and are simply "taken" back to God. I suspect that dying was never the real plan, but being raptured upon reaching spiritual maturity is. Nonetheless, the reincarnation of those who physically die is ruled out.

What is wrong with things like same-gender marriage, transgenders?

There is a very critical purpose in every part of God's creations where He has affirmed His will in the Scriptures. While a human soul does not have gender[11], we are assigned our gender according to His purpose and our destiny. We are made male or female because that is what we need to achieve His ultimate purposes. Living out those roles prepares us for our eternal destiny. To deny that negates the opportunity to achieve those purposes. The devil assigns perverse spirits (demons) to create things like same-gender attraction. Individuals who succumb to such temptation abandon their assignments for God and take up the devil's counter assignments.

---

[8] II Kings 2:11
[9] Genesis 5:24
[10] Luke 9:30
[11] Galatian 3:28

While having perverse feelings in not a sin, acting on same-gender attraction and other perverse sexual behavior negates the possibility of an individual becoming one with God, either in the body of Christ or His Bride. Perverse sexual desire is a symptom of a severe form of demonization. It is addressed in deliverance ministry. Conventional counseling and psychiatric treatment has limited effectiveness.

Accomodating individuals with perverse sexual desires does not help them. It only enables them to avoid dealing with the problem until ultimately death occurs and the devil can claim their soul for all eternity. Worse, those who accommodate sexual perverts are accomplices to their abominable sins and share the same fate.[12]

For example, the Scriptures tell us that the church is the Body and Bride of Christ[13]. It is inferred that our roles as men and women, male and female, prepare us for unique purposes in eternity. Those who live out theor purposes, especially those who are faithful in marriage, will enjoy a full measure of that destiny. Even if they inherit eternal life, those who pervert marriage, even by divorce in a heterosexual marriage, may not expect a full measure of their eternal purpose to be realized. It's not about being comfortable here, it's about preparing for our God-ordained purose there. Our souls are designed, even before birth, for development under certain conditions. To alter the process may well damage our spirit beings beyond repair or recovery.

Humans are really divinely created, eternally destined beings of great potential and complexity. The physical body is a vessel which the redeemed will exchange some day for a vastly improved version that will be incorruptible and deathless. Those individuals who have been granted the incredible opportunity of living in this realm are chosen for a great destiny we can't even imagine. Since evil cannot exist in heave, it is implied that we are here to accomplish things not possible in heaven. If we live our lives according to God's purposes, we will be developed in unique ways for that destiny. I believe that our intentions mean much more than our actual achievements. That is, circumstances and others' actions or inactions cannot rob us of our opportunities. However, if we live our lives independent of that purpose we will not develop as God intended and there may not be another opportunity to do so.

---

[12] Romans 1:32

[13] II Corinthian 11:2, Collosians 1:24

Chapter 20 – Epilogue

After my near death experience in 1995 there were three things foremost in my mind. The first was cleaning up the unrepented sin in my life. So, I contacted all of the people (or their heirs) that I could find that I had sinned against to offer my apologies and make restitution. There was a definite pattern I observed in this. Real Christians were glad to receive my apologies and arrange to receive restitution. The rest were either indifferent or hostile to my overtures. I spent more than two years searching down people and making monetary or in-kind restitution for my wrongs. I expected God to bless me financially to make this easier, but if anything, our family finances were tighter than normal. Yet I found that we could manage and make these sacrificial efforts. Although, I did have to make amends in installments sometimes. This showed me that there is really no excuse for not making restitution in addition to apologizing and asking forgiveness. This is also a strong argument for not putting such things off.

For restitution takes a good deal of time and effort to do properly. Proper Biblical restitution is full reparation of material damages plus a fifth part (20%)[14]. For pain and suffering a sincere apology should suffice, but more is recommended. Harm to a reputation must be repaired to the fullest extent reasonably possible. For example, if a person is viciously and wrongly maligned in a front-page article in the media, a single line retraction buried in an obscure section is entirely inadequate. In the case where restitution cannot be made to the victim or their heirs, it must be made to the Lord (Number 5:6-8).

Making amends to unbelievers was quite difficult. Even some close family members didn't want to forgive me and in certain cases were upset at even being reminded of past hurts. I was often disappointed at their indifference to my efforts and disbelief in my explanation for the source of my motivation. I can say even one such individual died of lung cancer adamantly refusing to believe me or accept my attempts at reconciliation. They even refused my prayers for their recovery! This caused me deep concern both for them and for me. This situation firmed my resolve to avoid making more mistakes with people, especially those who do not know Christ. In the few cases I could not get resolution on, I just had to give the matter over to God to work out.

---

[14] Numbers 5:5-8

The next thing that caught my attention was that I discovered a new sensitivity to people who also had a near death experience. When I was in their presence, I would feel a unique tingling sensation on the back of my head and a "feeling" that is difficult to describe told me they were like me. It was like RADAR or some advanced spiritual detection. As I learned to identify such people, I would try to elicit their stories from them. Not surprisingly, most were reluctant to tell me their stories. As I learned later, the common result of sharing such stories is disbelief, rejection and even hostility. People who have not had such experiences have great difficulty relating to them because of the implication that they need to change their ways and because it is so alien to their worldview. Not a few are inclined to attribute the whole experience to an unusual dream, altered states of consciousness or even mental illness. For that reason, those who shared my experience learned not to tell others. However, when they learned that I was sympathetic to them, they would relax and tell me amazing stories of the afterlife. What really surprised me was how common people who have either had a near death experience or a comparable visionary experience are. A rough guess based on my informal observations would put them at about 1-2% of the general population!

The third and most profound change was a deliverance from demonization and the activation of spiritual gifts. The feeling of an evil presence within and without me was wholly gone. I also began having vivid dreams of future events, some of which have been realized. When listening to sermons or reading the scriptures I found my discernment of spiritual truths was greatly heightened. Sometimes I would even find myself being prompted to read the very Bible passages during the week that the preacher would teach on in church on the next Lord's Day. This happened too frequently to be merely coincidence. Then there was the gift of healing. When I laid hands on, or even prayed over the telephone for sick or injured people, some were instantly healed. Some of the more profound cases involved stopping bleeding instantly, relief from paralysis due to a spinal cord cyst and in the most interesting case, an apparent cure from widespread, terminal cancer!

Strangely, most of the people I met who were ill refused my offer to pray for them, even fellow church members. They were so sure that God does not heal through prayer that they wouldn't even try. I suppose some of them were also reacting to the fact that it was I who offered to do so, and remembering my former conduct, rejected the idea that God would use me for such things. Others senselessly preferred to go under the surgeon's knife rather than seek healing on

God's terms of faith and repentance. The instances of disbelief and rejection, especially within the church, were very disappointing, even crushing to me. With each instance of rejection I could feel the power and the desire to heal diminish and the evil presence returned stronger with each rejection. Finally I stopped even looking for opportunities and offering to intervene. Over a period of about a year and a half the gift gradually diminished from disuse and eventually could only be summoned to service after much repentance, fasting and prayer, if at all.

Even when I did do this, I was surprised and disappointed that those who were healed were typically ungrateful and did not give glory to God. In such cases the illness that they were healed of returned with a vengeance! Fasting and prayer for days at a time are not things I enjoy and are difficult to arrange with family and professional responsibilities. So I concluded it wasn't even worth trying on people who would not repent their sins because divine healing didn't bring them closer to God and they didn't even care to make the necessary effort to retain and sustain their miracles. It astonished me that people would pay a physician great sums of money, often endure significant pain and inconvenience and diligently follow the physician's instructions to obtain healing in conventional ways. But when it was freely and miraculously given, they showed no thankfulness and little regard! Worse, at least one individual who was healed even denied it had ever happened! I still cannot understand how a person's mind works that they could forget such a thing. I eventually decided my time and effort was better spent on those who we willing to live on God's terms and show some thankfulness.

"And he said to him, If they will not hear Moses and the Prophets, they will not be persuaded even if one from the dead should rise." Luke 16:31 LITV

"Give not that which is holy unto the dogs, neither cast ye your pearls before swine, lest they trample them under their feet, and turn again and rend you." Matthew 7:6 LITV

The most difficult group to minister to was my own family, especially my children. It was no different trying to communicate the experience to them as with any other person who lacked a similar experience. For several years I struggled with trying to introduce them to the miraculous side of Christianity. We didn't find a means to do that in the denominational churches we attended near home.

It was in 2002 that an acquaintance told me about a prophetic ministry in Austin, Arise Christian Fellowship. There we found the first opportunity to witness Christians in a formal setting actually operating in the gifts of the Spirit, especially prophesy. There God gave prophetic words regarding the children that at least my daughters would fulfill His purposes for them. So, while I believe my decision to return to life for the children was the best one, the outcome will require some time and effort to be fully realized. It certainly hasn't been an easy choice; for they have often resisted my efforts to impart what I've learned. Yet I pray and continue to believe God for a good outcome. Meanwhile I use my additional time on earth for my own development and good works. For I know that God is in control and the best things are not the simplest or easiest. Moreover, I believe if God had a purpose for me returning, He had a plan for realizing it. I know He is in control and nothing can ultimately thwart His purposes in the lives of those obedient to Him.

A final word here to the reader is this. I have read many books on spiritual subjects and always found something helpful in each one. Yet in none of them, except the Bible, did I find something that really transformed me. I expect that in these words some people will find encouragement, warning and even good, practical advice. Yet my story is not a substitute for the plain truth of the scriptures. Nothing I relate should become the basis for a person's faith, or give them an excuse to diminish or reject the true and holy teachings of the prophets, apostles and Christ Himself.

There is no inerrant revelation in these pages that sheds any more light on the truth than the necessary revelation in scripture. If it appears that anything I write conflicts with the Bible, then I defer to the scriptures. It is my hope that what I write will direct the reader back to the scriptures and to the Holy Spirit. For in them are the same truths and more and better than presented here. Were it not for the situation that many of us are in need of such writings as this to direct us back to the true source, this book would be irrelevant and unnecessary. It is my hope that this will be the result and the reader will be encouraged and edified for having read my account. We are all expected to testify of the works God has done in our lives, and encourage each other to live for Him.

"How firm a foundation, ye saints of the Lord, Is laid for your faith in His excellent Word!"

From the lyrics, "How Firm A Foundation" by George Keith and Anne Steele

INDEX

Recommended Reading:

[i]Prayer, O. Hallesby, Augsburg Books, 1994, 208 pages
ISBN 145141529X, 9781451415292

[ii]C. S. Lewis:

Mere Christianity, Touchstone Books, 1996, 191 pages
ISBN13: 978-0684823782, ISBN10: 0684823780

Miracles
The Great Divorce, Touchstone Books, 1996, 125 pages.
ISBN 0-684-82376-4

The Abolition of Man, Touchstone Books, 1996, 109 pages
ISBN 10: 0684823713, ISBN 13: 9780684823713

The Problem of Pain, Touchstone Books, 1996, 144 pages.
ISBN 0-684-82383-7

The Screw Tape Letters, Touchstone Books, 1996, 128 pages.
ISBN: 0-684-83117-1, ISBN-13: 9780684831176

The Four Loves, Harcourt Brace Jovanovich, 1960, 192 pages.
ISBN 0-15-632930-1, ISBN 0-15-132915-X, LCCCN 60-10920

[iii] Caught Up Into Paradise, D.O. Richard E. Eby, Revell, 1978, 256 pages.
ISBN-10: 0800750667, ISBN-13: 9780800750664

[iv] Spiritual Hunger, The God-Men, Dr. John G. Lake, Gordon Lindsay, ed. Publisher: Christ for the Nations, 1987, 103 pages.
ISBN-10: 0899850200, ISBN-13: 978-0899850207

Complete Teachings, John G. Lake, Whitaker House, 2005, 992 pages.
ISBN-10: 088368568X, ISBN-13: 978-0883685686

[v] Smith Wigglesworth
On Healing, Paperback: Whitaker House, 1999, 208 pages.
ISBN-10: 0883684268, ISBN-13: 978-0883684269

On the Holy Spirit, Whitaker House, 1999, 224 pages
ISBN-10: 0883685442, ISBN-13: 978-0883685440

Greater Works, Whitaker House, 2000, 576 pages
ISBN-10: 0883685841, ISBN-13: 978-0883685846

Ever Increasing Faith, Empire Books, 2013, 138 pages
ISBN-10: 161949213X, ISBN-13: 978-1619492134

On The Power of Faith, Whitaker House, 2000, 544 pages
ISBN-10: 0883686082, ISBN-13: 978-0883686089

On The Power of Scripture, Whitaker House, 2009, 368 pages.
ISBN-10: 1603740945, ISBN-13: 978-1603740944

On the Anointing, Whitaker House, 2000, 768 pages
ISBN-10: 0883685302, ISBN-13: 978-0883685303

On Heaven, Whitaker House, 2003, 224 pages
ISBN-10: 0883689545, ISBN-13: 978-0883689547

[vi]Ivan Panin:

The Numeric English New Testament, CreateSpace Independent Publishing Platform, 2013, 270 pages.
ISBN-10: 1481836161, ISBN-13: 978-1481836166

Bible Chronology, The Association of the Covenant People, 192 pages
ASIN: B001P5NDIU

The Inspiration of the Scriptures Scientifically Demonstrated & Inspiration of the Hebrew Scriptures, Sacred Truth Ministries, 2008, 75 pages.
ISBN-10: 1588402525 ISBN-13: 9781588402523

[vii] E. W. Bullinger:

Number in Scripture, Publisher: Kessinger Publishing, LLC, 2010, 318 pages.
ISBN-10: 1162583673, ISBN-13: 978-1162583679

The Witness in the Stars, Ulan Press, 2012, 308 pages.
ASIN: B009X0OHWK

[viii] My Names Is Legion, Glenna Henderson, Bethany Fellowship, Minneapolis, Minnesota, 1972, 128 pages.
ISBN 10: 0871233746, ISBN 13: 9780871233745

[ix] The Handbook for Spiritual Warfare Handbook, Dr. Ed Murphy, Thomas Nelson, 2003. 640 pages
ISBN-10: 0785250263, ISBN-13: 978-0785250265

[x] Charles H. Kraft:
Confronting Powerless Christianity, Chosen Books, 2002, 256 pages
ISBN-10: 0800793145, ISBN-13: 978-0800793142

Culture, Communication and Christianity (2001), William Carey Library Pub., 2002, 504 pages
ISBN-10: 0878087842, ISBN-13: 978-0878087846

I Give You Authority (1997), Chosen Books; Revised edition 2012, 352 pages
ISBN-10: 0800795245, ISBN-13: 978-0800795245

Anthropology for Christian Witness, Orbis Books,1997, 493 pages
ISBN-10: 1570750858, ISBN-13: 978-1570750854

Deep Wounds, Deep Healing, Vine Books, 2004, 295 pages
ISBN-10: 0830734112, ASIN: B004E3XFAQ

Defeating Dark Angels (1992), Regal, 2011, 288 pages
ISBN-10: 0830747478, ISBN-13: 978-0830747474

Communication Theory for Christian Witness, Orbis Books; Rev Sub edition, 1991, 180 pages
ISBN-10: 0883447630, ISBN-13: 978-0883447635

Christianity in Culture, Orbis Books; 25th Annv edition 2005, 344 pages
ISBN-10: 1570755884, ISBN-13: 978-1570755880

[xi] Strongman's His Name, What's His Game, Dr.s Jerry & Carol Robeson, Whitaker House, 2000, 155 pages
ISBN-10: 0883686015, ISBN-13: 978-0883686010

[xii] Unbroken Curses, Rebecca Brown, and Daniel Yoder, Whitaker House, 1995, 175 pages.

ISBN-10: 0883683725, ISBN-13: 978-0883683729

[xiii] (Pg. 10) *Demons, An Eyewitness Account*, Howard O. Pittman, The Philadelphian Publishing House, 2010, 96 pages.

CPSIA information can be obtained
at www.ICGtesting.com
Printed in the USA
FSOW02n1352180516
20434FS

dime novel except that it is true. After fleeing to Europe Surratt enlisted in the Papal Zouaves. However, he was recognized by a fellow Zouave, Henry Ste. Marie, who reported his presence to the American minister, Rufus King. While the government was deciding what action it should take and conducting negotiations with the Papacy for Surratt's arrest, the Papal government took action on its own account to have him seized on November 7, 1866. While he was being transferred from the barracks at Veroli, he leaped over a precipice and escaped, with bullets flying past his head. The illustrated press and the dime novels popularized this rather dramatic flight. Finally making his way to Naples, he boarded a ship for Alexandria, Egypt. King was foiled in efforts to have Surratt apprehended along the route of his flight, but he was able to alert Consul Hale at Alexandria, who possessed full extraterritorial powers, and it was there that he was arrested on November 27. On December 21, he was sent back to the United States aboard the gunboat *Swatara* to stand trial.

On June 10, 1867, John Surratt was finally brought to trial before a civil jury for the murder of Abraham Lincoln. There was some difficulty in empanelling the jurors as both the prosecution and the defense wrangled over the jury's composition. In fact, Judge George P. Fisher set aside the initial panel at the prosecution's request. It was also not easy to find jurors who had not already formed an opinion about the case or else possessed views against capital punishment.

Among the most significant prosecution witnesses were Sergeant Joseph Dye, who testified that he had seen two men outside Ford's Theatre with Booth on the evening of April 14, calling out the time and engaging in other suspicious activities. While in 1865 Dye had seemed to indicate that the man resembled Spangler, he now claimed that it was John Surratt. He also added another detail, which he had not previously provided, that as he was returning to camp, a woman who he believed was Mrs. Surratt, had raised her window and inquired what was going on downtown. Numerous other witnesses, including John Lee, David C. Reed, Charles Wood, Susan Ann Jackson, and William Cleaver, also corroborated having seen John Surratt in Washington on the 14th.

Weichmann and Lloyd again told their stories without much change from 1865, although Weichmann did add some embellishments such as Anna Surratt's alleged statement at breakfast on the morning of April 15, that the death of Lincoln was no more than the death of any Negro in the army. When the defense attacked Lloyd's credibility, arguing that he was, himself, involved in the plot, the prosecution agreed, claiming that his reluctance to testify made his testimony all that more valuable.

Other prosecution testimony came from Dr. Lewis McMillan, Surgeon of the *Peruvian*, the ship which had carried Surratt to England, Henry Ste. Marie, and Charles Blinn. McMillan testified to having conversations with Surratt where he allegedly said that he hoped to live to see Andy Johnson served the way Lincoln had been. Ste. Marie testified that Surratt had told him he escaped from Washington on April 14. Blinn asserted that a handkerchief bearing the inscription John H. Surratt 2, had been found in the Burlington, Vermont, railroad depot on April 18, 1865.

Even Mrs. Surratt, who had been dead for two years, again became an issue during her son's trial. Defense counsel Joseph Bradley said that he hoped to do, "something in the way of vindicating the pure fame of (Surratt's) departed mother," while his colleague Richard Merrick added, "We have felt our blood run cold as the rustling of the garments from the grave swept by us." The defense apparently sensed that the public had come to doubt Mrs. Surratt's involvement and thought that invoking her memory might gain sympathy for her son. The prosecution, on the other hand, felt some obligation to justify the previous proceedings, because they were trying to convict the son on the same evidence.

When the prosecution rested its case, there was a fairly widespread belief that John Surratt would have difficulty in proving his innocence. Even the *New York World*, which was an implacable foe of the 1865 military trial, said, "If the testimony which has thus far been given is not shaken by counter-evidence, and is believed by the jury, it will go hard with the prisoner."

However, in 1867, just such counter-evidence was produced, which eventually cast a strong doubt over the prosecution's case. To counter Sergeant Dye, for example, the defense highlighted contradictions between his 1865 description of the men he had seen in front of the theater. The defense also made a persuasive case that the three men were not the conspirators but stage carpenter, James Gifford, actor C. B. Hess, and costumer Louis Carland, who was to sing a patriotic song. Hess, not wanting to be late for his performance, had called for the time and Carland had told him what it was. Mrs. Frederika Lambert, who was supported by her servant, testified that she had raised her window and asked a soldier what was going on downtown, undercutting the notion that Dye had encountered Mrs. Surratt.

Where the defense was most successful, however, was in creating doubt that John Surratt was even in Washington on April 14. Numerous witnesses placed Surratt in Elmira, New York, on April 13 and 14, and his signature appeared on the register of the Webster House in Canandaigua, New York, on April 15. Since the register had not been properly safeguarded for the past two years Judge Fisher would not allow it to be introduced.

The defense was so successful with this tactic, that the prosecution reversed itself and tried to make two basic changes in strategy. One shift in emphasis was to argue that if John Surratt was in New York he was still part of the conspiracy and was fulfilling his role from that location. The other was to produce transportation schedules to show that even if Surratt was in Elmira on April 13, he could still have made it back to Washington for April 14.

However, as far as the prosecution case was concerned, irrevocable damage had been done. Enough doubt had been cast about Surratt's presence in the nation's capital and it was almost an impossible task to show what role he might have been playing in a murder which was committed hundreds of miles away. As the *New York Tribune* said, "Morally, his presence or absence is not of the least consequence. If in the conspiracy what difference where he was at the moment of the blow? But, legally, it is vital." Even Prosecutor Edward Carrington admitted in 1889 that there had really been no good evidence that Surratt was in Washington on April 14. It thus became more and more evident that a conviction was unlikely.

1865 and 1867 Trials Not Analogous. Despite historians' attempts to equate the two trials, in many ways this is unfair. By 1867, the country was involved in other issues, such as the clash between Congress and the president over Reconstruction, and the congressional attempt to impeach Andrew Johnson. In fact, as preparations were occurring for the trial, there were rumors that John Surratt would be offered a deal if he would implicate Johnson. A House committee was also formed, with Benjamin Butler as chairman, which took some testimony from prisoners in the Dry Tortugas, although nothing new was elicited.

Johnson and the radical Republicans exchanged charges about plots and counterplots with the president claiming that the radicals were suborning perjury in order to strengthen their impeachment case.

By 1867, however, there was not the intense focus on Surratt's trial as there had previously been in 1865. Amidst the partisan wrangling over the jury's failure to reach a verdict, the *New York Times*, in an editorial, made one of the most perceptive comments about the differences between 1865 and 1867, "John H. Surratt was called to his account in a calmer state of public mind, after time had appeased its righteous anger and the passion for retribution had been allayed."

Near Duel Between Judge and Defense Lawyer. In fact, the hung jury was almost overshadowed by a dispute between Judge Fisher and defense attorney Joseph Bradley. The two had clashed on numerous occasions during the trial and on July 3 Bradley had followed the judge from the courtroom with the two almost coming to blows. Even the press got involved in the act with the *New York Herald* producing an editorial entitled "Bruiser Bradley."

At the end of the trial, Judge Fisher announced that he was disbarring Bradley from practicing before the Supreme Court of the District of Columbia. On the street, Bradley issued a challenge to a duel. There were shouts of "He's going to shoot," and armed partisans of both men appeared to be ready to enter the fray until the police arrived and restored order. On August 15, Bradley was arrested on a charge of violating the city's laws against dueling. He was released on a $1000 bail and never brought to trial, although in 1870 he accosted Fisher on the street and attempted to cane him. Needless to say, these events seemed to catch the public's fancy more than a case in which the jury could not reach a verdict.

Surratt Not Retried. While standard accounts usually state that Surratt was never retried, James Lange has discovered that it was not from lack of action on the part of the government. Edward C. Carrington, the United States attorney for the District of Columbia, did have Surratt indicted by two separate grand juries under the treason statute enacted in July of 1862. However, the District of Columbia had a two-year statute of limitations on every crime except fraud and murder and Judge Fisher dismissed the case. When Carrington appealed the decision to the Supreme Court of the District of Columbia, the full court upheld Judge Fisher's ruling. The second grand jury, aware of this ruling, chose to ignore the second indictment, thus ending government efforts to prosecute Surratt.

Lectures About Involvement. John Surratt, with the treason charges dismissed, in fact, lived a long life and even went on to lecture about his relationship with Booth, as he did in Rockville, Maryland, and elsewhere, in 1870. (*See Doc. No. 17.*) For the public there was a certain sense of closure, as well as relief, when Surratt went free, despite the rather ambiguous message sent by the jury's failure to agree and the government's failed efforts to bring additional charges. While the prosecutors had shown an interest in retrying Surratt, the public appeared content to leave to historians the unraveling of whatever mysteries still existed regarding Abraham Lincoln's assassination.

However, if they really believed that the assassination might be studied and analyzed like any other historical event, they were destined to be mistaken. For Abraham Lincoln, in dying at the hands of an assassin in the moment of triumph in the Civil War, had left the sphere of mortals and entered the realm of folk-myth and legend.

CHAPTER 4

ABRAHAM LINCOLN: FROM MAN OF CONTROVERSY TO AMERICAN FOLK HERO

Lincoln Becomes Folkmyth Figure. The Assassination of Abraham Lincoln by John Wilkes Booth, if it accomplished nothing else, vaulted the sixteenth president to the front ranks of American heroes and martyrs. The president's death, at the moment of Union triumph in the Civil War, has created a mythological figure of such enormous proportions that it is difficult, to this day, to separate the real man from the folkmyth legend which he has become.

Even the timing of Lincoln's murder, on Good Friday, was bound to evoke religious symbolism. Millions of Americans attended church services on Easter Sunday to hear clergymen attempt to explain and make sense of this calamity. One of the most common sermon themes preached was to equate the death of the president with that of Jesus. As one commentator said, "Jesus Christ died for the world, Abraham Lincoln died for his country."

Another strongly stated religious comparison was that of Lincoln to Moses. Similar to the leader of the Hebrews, Lincoln had reached the promised land but God had not allowed him to cross over to it. In fact, many people argued that the reason for this was that Lincoln was too tender and merciful for the task of Reconstruction. Lincoln's work was completed and Andrew Johnson, who upon assuming office was making statements about harsh treatment for former rebels, was seen as the right person for the task ahead. If Lincoln played the role of Moses, Johnson was clearly a sterner Joshua to deal with the defeated South.

Celebration and Feelings of Betrayal at End of Civil War. It would be naive to assume that if only Lincoln had lived that the problems of Reconstruction would have been negligible. However, the brief interval between the end of the war and the president's death unleashed a period of joyous celebration. At Harvard College, J. L. Sibley captured this mood when he jotted in his diary, "The people are wild with enthusiasm at the news of the surrender of the rebel General

Lee. It exceeds anything I have ever known. Another holiday in college. Illuminations, speeches, all round the country." In Washington, Secretary of War Stanton placed over his portico a clever arrangement of gas jets which spelled out "PEACE." In Philadelphia, a citizen summed up his feelings to the editor of the *Philadelphia Evening Bulletin* in the following manner: "It sounds like hell let loose, but it feels like paradise regained."

Although this initial outburst would certainly have dissipated as it came up against the real world problems of reconstructing the Southern states, the fact that it occurred seemed to make the president's death that much more horrible for the Northern public. It was as if the nation had briefly let down its guard, and, in that euphoric moment, the South had committed this last act of treachery. The chaos which occurred was well foreshadowed in the poem "The Martyr" by Herman Melville when he warned of the grief and anger which Lincoln's murder had engendered:

He lieth in his blood
The Father in his face;
They have killed him, the forgiver—
The Avenger takes his place.

There is sobbing of the strong,
And a pall upon the land;
But the people in their weeping
Bare the iron hand:
Beware the People weeping
When they barc the iron hand.

President's Martyrdom. Many contemporaries rapidly sensed that Lincoln was no longer simply a historical figure. A journalist captured this very perceptively when he wrote of the murder: "It has made it impossible to speak the truth of Abraham Lincoln hereafter." Or, as another commentator observed, "The most striking fact of our time, of a psychological kind, is the growth of Lincoln's fame since the earth closed over his remains." Perhaps it was inevitable that the Savior of the Union and the Great Emancipator would have become a folkhero in any case but the trend was accelerated by his martyrdom. The man whose election had precipitated secession and civil war entered the American Pantheon.

Assassination's Effect on Individuals. Many people who experienced John F. Kennedy's death still say they can remember exactly where they were the moment they heard the news and the impact of Abraham Lincoln's death was no less traumatic. Jane Addams of Hull House fame wrote: "To my amazement I found my father in tears, something I had never seen before. . . . The two flags, my father's tears and his impassioned statement that the greatest man in the world had died, constituted my initiation, my baptism, as it were, into the thrilling and solemn interests of a world lying quite outside the two white gate posts." Poet Katherine Lee Bates, who was five at the time and would later compose "America the Beautiful", would write:

> I heard it and hid me under the lilacs
> The mystery to prod.
> Lincoln! Lincoln! Abraham Lincoln!
> And not one angel to catch the bullet!
> What had become of God?

Even battle hardened General Joshua L. Chamberlain, the hero of Little Round Top, noted during the Grand Review of the Army on May 23, "But we miss the deep, sad eyes of Lincoln coming to review us after each sore trial. Something is lacking in our hearts now—even in this supreme hour."

Belief in Southern Responsibility. It is not difficult to understand how people who were affected in this manner came to the conclusion that the South was behind the president's murder. While this judgment has puzzled later historians, nothing was more natural. Occurring at the war's conclusion, the president's death appeared to be one more horrible statistic to cap the tragedy. Thousands of people, including government officials, could not help but believe that Booth worked for the Confederacy.

Therefore, very few Northerners, at least those who had supported the Union cause, had any trouble accepting President Johnson's May 2 proclamation that "the atrocious murder of the Late Pres. Abraham Lincoln and the attempted assassination of Hon. W. H. Seward Secretary of State were incited, concerted, and procured by and between Jefferson Davis, Clement C. Clay, Beverly Tucker, George Sanders, W. C. Cleary, and other rebels and traitors." This view certainly hardened many people's attitudes toward Reconstruction. If the defeated rebels had murdered Lincoln then they deserved no mercy at all.

Support for President Johnson. In fact, even though Johnson would later have bitter clashes with the radicals which would lead to his impeachment, in the aftermath of the murder, the public was convinced that Johnson was the proper man to carry the country forward. Senator Ben Wade said to the new president who was talking about hanging rebels and making treason odious, "Johnson, we have faith in you. By the Gods, there will be no trouble now in running the government." These words would become bitterly ironical a couple of years later but not in April, 1865.

Speculation About Johnson's Involvement. Interestingly, as previously noted, by 1867, there was some speculation that Johnson might have been involved in his predecessor's death. The enigmatic card which Booth left at the Kirkwood House "Don't wish to disturb you, are you at home?," which may not even have been meant for Johnson, led to speculation that, since Johnson had benefited the most from Lincoln's death he was behind it. Johnson's historical reputation has not been very good because of his clashes with the radical Republicans and his impeachment, even though he managed to avoid being removed from office. While his stature has been diminished, a fair number of contemporaries apparently could not erase the suspicion that Johnson was involved in his predecessor's murder.

Search For a Folk-Hero. While Johnson's stature with the public may have diminished, the growth of Abraham Lincoln as an American symbol knew no limits. It has been maintained that Americans were searching for just such a folk-hero as Lincoln became. As people of a revolutionary tradition, not only had we separated ourselves from our English heritage politically, but also culturally. Like other revolutionary peoples we had to reinvent our past.

Part of this was accomplished by glorifying the colonial and revolutionary periods. The *Mayflower*, Plymouth Rock, John Smith and Pocahontas, all became instant icons. So, too, did George Washington, who became both man and monument as the father of his country. Washington, however, was not an entirely satisfactory folk-hero. The first president was an Olympian folk-god, one who could be admired and worshipped from afar but who was not really approachable.

Abraham Lincoln thus became a folk-hero for the common man. Born in a log cabin, in humble circumstances, he rose to the highest office in the land, saved the Union, freed the slaves, and was struck down at the height of his glory. This is the stuff of which legends are made.

Rumors Booth Did Not Die. There are numerous illustrations of this mythology. Almost immediately after Booth's death and the secret burial of his body, there were rumors that the man killed in Garrett's barn was not the assassin. This was quickly followed by numerous alleged sightings of Booth who was encountered as often as a supposedly dead Elvis Presley has been in the twentieth century. Indeed, by 1929, Herbert Wells Fay, who was the custodian of the Lincoln tomb in Springfield, and who enjoyed keeping score, tallied at least twenty of these ghostly apparitions.

The peripatetic Booth was not only encountered often but also in a variety of locations. On January 12, 1867, James E. Campbell sent a letter to the *New York Times* claiming that, in Calcutta, India, William Martin Tolbert of the Confederate raider *Shenandoah* had offered to wager 500 pounds that he could prove that Booth was alive and well. Campbell obviously believed Tolbert's story must be true or why would a man wager so much money on something that was false. Similarly, the assassin was allegedly seen by Carroll Jackson Donelson in the Pelew Islands, telling Donelson that he had been in Mexico, South America, Africa, Turkey, Arabia, Italy, and China. If this account was correct, then it is no wonder that the sightings were so widespread, and Booth, rather than attempting to conceal his identity, always seemed eager to reveal who he was to those he met.

There were also people who apparently enjoyed the glamour and notoriety of being mistaken for Booth, including a Richmond minister, the Reverend James G. Armstrong. With his black hair, limp, dramatic preaching style, and interest in the theater, it was not long before whispers arose that he was John Wilkes Booth. Despite the fact that he was a clergyman, a profession which one might assume would encourage truthfulness, Reverend Armstrong did not seem particularly inclined to quell such rumors.

According to other legends, Booth, who was a dashing matinee idol and breaker of many a female heart, was also very active post-assassination on the marital front. There were numerous claimants to the role of the assassin's widow and children. Among the more vivid accounts was a book by Izola Forrester titled *This One Mad Act* (1937). Forrester claimed to be Booth's granddaughter and also asserted that her grandmother had journeyed to California to meet her very much alive husband in 1868.

The most far reaching account of Booth surviving Garrett's barn, however, was that by Finis L. Bates in his book *The Escape and Suicide of John Wilkes Booth* (1907). Bates, who was a lawyer, spun a tale about a client named John St. Helen, whom he had met in Granbury, Texas. One evening in 1877, St. Helen, who was gravely ill, and apparently thought he was dying, blurted out to Bates, "I am dying. My name is John Wilkes Booth, and I am the assassin of President Lincoln. Get the picture of myself from under the pillow. I leave it with you for my future identification. Notify my brother Edwin Booth, of New York City." St. Helen, however, did not die but recovered.

Bates also incorporated other myths into his account since St. Helen/Booth told him that he and Herold had visited Andrew Johnson on the afternoon of April 14 and the vice president had urged them to commit the murder. The reason that he was not killed was that he misplaced his diary and some personal papers in Garrett's barn when he left that location. Booth claimed that Colonel Samuel Cox's overseer Ruddy was sent to retrieve them and he died in the assassin's place.

Eventually, Bates moved to Memphis where he began to read what he could find about Lincoln's assassination. In the 1890s he even tried to interest the War Department in his evidence but with no success. This apparently only served to strengthen his conviction that there had been a conspiracy and cover-up.

In 1903, a drifter named David George died in Enid, Oklahoma. A minister from El Reno, where George had recently been living, the Reverend E. C. Harper, revealed that George had confessed to him that he was John Wilkes Booth. This news was picked up by the press and was seen by Bates in Memphis.

Sensing that this must be his old acquaintance, St. Helen, using an alias, Bates rushed to Enid to the undertaking establishment of W. B. Penniman. In his rather lurid prose Bates described his viewing of the body, "I knew him as instantly as men discern night from day, as the starlight from moonlight, or the moon from the light of day." The remains were embalmed and kept on display in Penniman's back room. Finally, the body was turned over to Bates on the understanding that he would provide it a decent burial.

Booth Mummy. However, there was another fate in store for the alleged Booth, whose remains had become virtually mummified by the amount of embalming fluid required to keep them in proper viewing condition. Bates, who saw a fine opportunity to make money, rented out the corpse to carnival side-shows where it toured for many years. Occasionally, the lawyer even sought a purchaser for his prized possession. One investigator claims that in 1937, long after Bates himself had died, the mummy earned in excess of $100,000. If true, this is four to five times what Booth, who was a well paid actor, made in yearly salary while he was alive.

Attempt to Exhume Remains. While Bates tale is bizarre enough in its own right, it has had an interesting recent revival. In October of 1994, a petition was filed in the Circuit Court for Baltimore City to exhume Booth's remains from Green Mount Cemetery. The petitioners, Lois Rathbun, a great-great-grand niece, and Virginia Kline, a first cousin twice removed, were supported by Arthur Ben Chitty of the University of the South and researcher Nathaniel Orlowek. The main evidence used to bolster their claim for exhumation was Bates's account.

In rebuttal, the cemetery, backed by a number of historians, contended that the Bates book was riddled with errors and inconsistencies and that there was no reason to doubt that it was Booth's remains which rest in Green Mount. The cemetery argued that it had a solemn obligation to protect the sanctity of those who were interred within its grounds unless there was an overwhelming reason to violate that trust which they did not believe existed in this case. In the end, Judge Joseph H. H. Kaplan agreed and in 1996 his decision was upheld by the Court of Special Appeals in Annapolis.

Boston Corbett A Mysterious Figure. In a similar fashion, the slayer of the assassin, Boston Corbett, also became a man of mystery. Corbett, whose religious fanaticism had caused him to be looked on as different even before the war, eventually returned to being a hatmaker, first in Boston, and later in Connecticut and New Jersey. It has been speculated by some authors that hat making, which was a very dangerous business because of the toxic chemicals used, including mercury, might have contributed to Corbett's later mental deterioration.

In 1878 he moved to Concordia, Kansas, where he lived in a crude dugout a few miles outside of town. He was reported to have given rambling religious lectures which were so disjointed and incoherent that he soon had trouble attracting an audience. In 1887, largely because of his celebrity status, he was appointed Assistant Doorkeeper of the Kansas House of Representatives. After overhearing a conversation mocking the legislature's opening prayer, he pulled out his revolver, threatening a number of legislators, and perhaps even firing some shots, although fortunately no one was injured. Corbett was arrested, found to be insane, and sent to the Topeka Asylum.

In May of 1888 Corbett escaped. He was last seen in Neodesha, Kansas, where he said he was heading for Mexico. Again stories abound about Corbett sightings including claims that he is buried in Minnesota. There is no definitive answer to this question but Lloyd Lewis noted one persistent story that Corbett was seen heading to Enid, Oklahoma, which was where David George died.

As already discussed in Chapter 3, there is no rational reason for stories like this to arise and no real grounds to doubt that Booth was killed in Garrett's barn. Every single tale to the contrary, when investigated, has turned out to be untrue. But, if that is the case, the question persists as to why these shadows have taken on a life of their own.

Slayer of Folk-God Survives. One author has provided an insightful suggestion. Lloyd Lewis in a very perceptive but underrated study, *Myths After Lincoln* (1929), argued that the belief that John Wilkes Booth survived Garrett's barn is not rooted in reality but in folkmyth. In traditional mythology the slayer of the folk-god could not die an easy death but had to wander the world alone and friendless to do penance for his sins. Perhaps, in the case of Corbett, the slayer of the slayer of the folk-god is destined to meet a similar fate.

Other Assassins and Western Outlaws. There are enough parallel cases to suggest that there might be some substance to the Lewis claim. Many books and articles have been written about Lee

Harvey Oswald doubles, and one author was so persistent in his claim that the "real" Oswald was not killed in Dallas that the body was exhumed after a messy legal battle between Oswald's brother and his widow, Marina. Jesse James's grave was also recently opened to an equal amount of fanfare in an attempt to prove that James had not been shot by Robert Ford. In both cases, the remains were positively identified, but this will probably not silence the true believers any more than people will cease to believe that Booth survived Garrett's barn.

Lincoln and Marfan's Syndrome. Lincoln, himself, became a historical figure who was treated like very few others. One of the recent debates that has raged about the sixteenth president is whether he had the disease Marfan's Syndrome and if bits of bone fragment should be used to generate DNA to test for this disease. Marfan's is a connective tissue disease, whose symptoms may include droopy eyes, sunken chest, deformities of fingers and toes, and which is often fatal. Eighty percent of the deaths are caused by a rupture of the aorta. Because it is hereditary and passed on through males in a family, it has also been suggested that this is the reason three of Lincoln's four sons died at an early age. If Lincoln did have Marfan's, some authors have argued that Booth's bullet might not have changed the course of history so dramatically, because the president would probably have died shortly anyway.

Even without DNA testing, historians, as well as medical doctors have demonstrated to a fair degree of probability that Lincoln did not have the disease. The president was in far too robust condition and, with the exception of his eyes, lacked all of the other symptoms. But that is not the point. With Lincoln we are insatiable to learn everything we can, even down to his genetic structure. It would be difficult to imagine such morbid curiosity about any other American president. And, even if Lincoln did suffer from the disease, it had no known impact on his presidency, in the manner that strokes and heart disease did on the presidencies of Wilson or Eisenhower.

Paradoxes Concerning Lincoln. Lincoln also became an enigmatic figure, with many groups claiming him as one of their own. Was Lincoln a true Christian, who accepted Jesus after Gettysburg and the death of his son Willie, or was he an atheist and skeptic as claimed by his law partner William Herndon? It is impossible to deny him his place as the Great Emancipator and yet, in the late nineteenth and early twentieth century, white racist groups combing his utterances adopted him as a kindred spirit. Similarly, prohibitionists have touted Lincoln as a teetotaler while pro-liquor forces have portrayed him as drinking wine, albeit in moderate amounts.

Lincoln Extremely Secretive. There are very few historical figures who can be seen as all things to all people in the manner in which Lincoln has been portrayed. One of the reasons for this ambivalence was Lincoln's reticence about his personal life and his inclination to secrecy. The consensus of many who knew him was that he was the most secretive man they had ever known. Historian Richard Hofstadter has argued that one of the creators of this Lincoln legend was Lincoln himself. Lincoln saw the virtue of the rags to riches myth in American politics and used it very effectively in his campaigns.

Many Assassination Books. Even the historiography of the assassination has mirrored some of the major trends in American history. Indeed, a cottage industry of Lincoln assassination books has grown up, the same way it has around the death of John Kennedy. As noted, at the end of the war, nothing was more natural than to assume that the South had been involved. People would have been incredulous if the authorities had announced that the South had no role in the president's death. After all, the Warren Commission did not put to rest the public's belief of conspiracy in the death of JFK.

Pioneer Historian David Dewitt. While it would take a fairly sizeable volume just to cover the historiography of the assassination, a look at the major historians who have exerted influence in the field is quite revealing. The first such author was David M. DeWitt who wrote *The Judicial Murder of Mary E. Surratt* (1895) and *The Assassination of Abraham Lincoln and Its Expiation* (1909). DeWitt was a lawyer and a member of the Democratic Party who had served in the House of Representatives in the 1870s and the New York Legislature in the 1890s.

Although DeWitt was a pioneer in the field, his work is marred by an extreme animus toward the military trial and particularly toward Edwin M. Stanton. DeWitt concluded that Stanton and Holt had railroaded an innocent Mary Surratt to the gallows, even speculating on some imaginary conversations that might have taken place, and concluding, "The execution of Mary E. Surratt is the foulest blot on the history of the United States."

His Chapter 3, "The Reign of Terror—Capture and Death of Booth," which appears in *The Assassination of Abraham Lincoln* is an excellent example of how he dealt with Stanton. By the severest standards, the pursuit of the conspirators could hardly be equated with the French Revolution's reign of terror, where thousands of people lost their lives.

The basic problem with DeWitt's work is that he apparently saw no connection between an assassination following the close of a bloody civil war and the seeming correctness of a military trial as it appeared to people in 1865. Rather he judged all events based on his legal training and his partisan politics whereby he saw most Republicans as evil and Reconstruction as an unmitigated disaster. The trial of the Lincoln conspirators was just a prelude to what these unprincipled radical Republicans had done over the next several decades. The public, however, ignored the partisan nature of DeWitt's work and his books came to be considered classics in the field.

Otto Eisenschiml's Questions. It was only a rather short step from the belief that the radical Republicans had used the murder to further their vindictive policies to attributing to them more sinister motives. Beginning with Otto Eisenschiml, authors began to hint that the radicals' hate was so strong that they had actually engineered the president's death. While Americans often tend to date mistrust of government to the assassination of John Kennedy, the Vietnam War, or Watergate, this belief that the president was betrayed by members of his administration predates our modern anxieties by several generations.

Eisenschiml published two influential but controversial works *Why Was Lincoln Murdered?* (1937) and *In The Shadow of Lincoln's Death* (1940). Although professional historians might have argued against Eisenschiml's hints that Stanton had masterminded Lincoln's murder, the general public was more than willing to accept such a conspiracy theory.

Eisenschiml used the very clever methodology of raising a series of provocative questions. Even though in many cases he was forced to admit that the orthodox answer was still correct until proven otherwise, he created unwarranted doubts. With this technique the question often becomes more important than the answer. It also allows the author to say that he merely asked the question without taking credit for the doubts he raises.

Eisenschiml argued that the protection provided for the president was criminally negligent. Among other charges against the War Secretary are those that he refused to allow Major Thomas Eckert, a very powerful man who could break pokers over his arm, to accompany Lincoln to the theater for protection. He also alleges that guard John Parker, despite his negligence, was not disciplined due to Stanton's intervention. Also, he muses, why General Grant did not accompany the Lincolns to the theater. The portrait that emerges is that the War Secretary knew what was going to happen and left the president to his fate.

In addition, he believed that the pursuit of the assassins was misdirected and that the only exit from Washington left unguarded was the one the murderers took. Eisenschiml also insinuates that detective Everton Conger might have shot Booth, not Boston Corbett, to keep Booth from revealing what he knew about the assassination plot. Finally, he speculates about the missing diary pages and even leaves the reader to believe that Booth might have escaped Garrett's barn.

Eisenschiml often uses his evidence in a dubious manner and his treatment of Grant's decision not to attend the theater with the Lincoln's is an excellent example. The reason that the general canceled the invitation was that his wife had recently been involved in an unpleasant incident with Mrs. Lincoln at City Point. Mrs. Grant informed her husband that she had no intention of spending an evening at the theater with Mrs. Lincoln, and the Grants then made excuses that they wished to visit their children in Philadelphia. Eisenschiml indicates that he is familiar with this traditional explanation but proceeds to ignore it anyway.

While Eisenschiml merely raised questions, sometimes refusing to take credit for the implied answers, others rushed in to fill in the blanks. There have been other allegations of elaborate plots involving Stanton or head of the National Detective police, Lafayette Baker. One book, *Mask for Treason* (1965) by Vaughan Shelton, even charged that Secretary Seward, who was attacked, was himself involved and that a co-plotter took advantage to try and eliminate him as well.

Sensational Book *The Lincoln Conspiracy*. One of the most sensational works ever done on the assassination was the 1977 book and movie *The Lincoln Conspiracy* by David Balsiger and Charles E. Sellier, Jr. produced by Schick-Sunn Classic Pictures. According to this account Booth was the head of several groups that were plotting to kidnap Lincoln for their own purposes. These included Maryland planters, Confederate agents in Canada, Northern businessmen involved in cotton speculation, and, of course, the radical Republicans who wished to seize power to carry out a vindictive Reconstruction. Booth, however, was so inept that he was removed from his position, and was warned by General Lafayette Baker and Colonel Everton Conger that if he and his conspirators did not stay out of the way that they would end up in the Potomac. He was then replaced by J. W. Boyd, a former Confederate soldier and spy, who just happened to bear a striking resemblance to the actor.

Boyd set the kidnapping plan in motion but Booth did not heed the warning. Instead, just as Boyd was about to kidnap Lincoln at Ford's Theatre, Booth shot and mortally wounded the president. By luck, the assassin was able to ride out of Washington over the same escape route that had been left open for Boyd. The governmental plotters were now in great fear that Booth might be taken alive and reveal their role in Lincoln's death. Therefore, detective and military forces were dispatched to Southern Maryland to scour the countryside. These included Boyd as well as David Herold, who had been involved with the Booth gang in the kidnapping, because it was believed they knew the countryside and could lead the pursuers to the assassin. Boyd and Herold, fearing they knew too much and might be killed once they had outlived their usefulness, slipped away from the detectives and, through a case of mistaken identity, were surrounded by government troops in Garrett's barn. Herold surrendered and Boyd was shot to death in the mistaken belief that he was Booth.

When Stanton learned of this error it was decided to act as if Booth had been killed. It was considered safer to have a dead Booth, even if it was the wrong one, to end the public's clamor. The real Booth escaped, living out the rest of his life in England and India, before returning to the United States to die in Enid, Oklahoma, in 1903. The book even has a photograph of the mummy which it says is in a private collection. Others who had knowledge of the plot were executed or imprisoned.

Impact of Sensational Books and Movies. The impact of a sensational book and movie should not be underestimated. For good or ill, far more people now get their history from movies, television, and videos, than from reading books. Recently, the enormously successful Oliver Stone movie *JFK*, gave new life to the very dubious thesis of New Orleans District Attorney, Jim Garrison, that American intelligence agencies killed John Kennedy because he threatened the goals of the military-industrial complex. Even the staid *American Historical Review*, caught up in the publicity, published a color photograph of Kevin Costner as Garrison, on the cover of its April, 1992, journal.

Historians Dubious About Conspiracy Theories. In general, historians no longer hold the views of DeWitt, Eisenschiml, and their followers in very high regard. DeWitt and Eisenschiml both based their work on the outmoded notion that the radical Republicans were evil men who wanted to bring down a reign of terror on the prostrate South. This view, fostered by Columbia University historian William Dunning, has been thoroughly discredited by modern scholarship which sees the radicals as the last of the nineteenth-century reformers, who stood for such noble causes as black civil rights. A number of authors now portray Lincoln as coming from that wing of the party. William Hanchett has also tarnished Eisenschiml's thesis, in detail, in *The Lincoln Murder Conspiracies* (1983) while William C. Davis in *Civil War Times Illustrated* (1977) demonstrated conclusively that Boyd did not die in Garrett's barn in 1865 but was alive in 1866. Although scholars may have highlighted the flaws in this previous work, it still resonates with large segments of the American public who see conspiracy around every corner.

Come Retribution. Recently, we have come full circle with William Tidwell, David Gaddy, and James Hall, arguing in *Come Retribution, the Confederate Secret Service and the Assassination of Lincoln* (1988), along with Tidwell's, *April '65* (1995), that Jefferson Davis and the Confederates actually were behind Booth's plot to kidnap Lincoln which eventually culminated in his murder. If Tidwell and his associates are correct then the public in 1865 had the answer to the crime all along.

The authors believe that early in the war, the Confederacy, at both the national and state levels, developed an extensive intelligence service in an attempt to overcome the Northern advantages in manpower and industrial base. Relying on agents within Washington and numerous operatives in Maryland and Virginia, messages, mail, and personnel could be rapidly transferred between North and South. The Confederates also turned to less conventional warfare, planting agents in Canada to plan raids on Northern soil, dabbling in the use of torpedoes and land mines, or trying to spread diseases such as yellow fever. Among the Confederates most important intelligence gatherers was General John Singleton Mosby who, despite his dashing and romantic reputation as the "Gray Ghost," commanded a regularly organized unit which, like most cavalry units, conveyed accurate intelligence information to the Confederate government and field commanders alike.

After the Kilpatrick-Dahlgren raid on Richmond, when papers found on the body of Ulrich Dahlgren allegedly revealed a plot to kill Davis and members of his government, the Confederates in retaliation developed a plan to capture Lincoln. The already established intelligence network was extended and action teams, including those of John Wilkes Booth, who was a Confederate agent, were assembled to carry out the plan. Ultimately in April, 1865, with the South on the verge of defeat, the Confederacy resorted to murder when Thomas Harney, a member of Mosby's command, was dispatched to blow up the White House. Harney was captured but Booth, who was aware of his plan, decided to duplicate it as best he could by killing the president and members of his cabinet.

It was no accident that Booth and Herold were aided in their flight by Confederate soldiers Ruggles, Bainbridge, and Jett, who were part of the forces which were on the lookout to help the conspirators even after the plot had turned to murder. When Booth died at Garrett's barn, however, the intelligence forces supposedly melted away and were disbanded, and naturally everyone kept quiet. Confederate envoy George Sanders, who had met Booth in Canada and perhaps even encouraged him to murder Lincoln, began a campaign to provide perjured testimony at the trial of Booth's alleged co-conspirators. When this testimony was discovered to be perjured it drew attention away from Confederate involvement in the murder.

Tidwell's thesis does deserve attention for, like Eisenschiml before him, while his arguments have not been readily accepted by academic historians, his views have begun to gain some ground with the general public. One of the things which has troubled critics is Tidwell's statement that from the time he first read about John Wilkes Booth he knew he was part of an intelligence operation. Reviewers of his work have pointed out that if you begin with this premise then you may be tempted to look for material to support your theory, ignoring, either intentionally or unintentionally, evidence of a contradictory nature.

Difference in Methodology. In fact, one of the major issues raised by Tidwell's work concerns methodology. David Gaddy, one of his co-authors, in a letter to the *Virginia Magazine of Biography and History* protesting what he perceived as an unfavorable review of *April '65*, made the point that he and General Tidwell, who both worked for the CIA, were writing, not from the historical but from the intelligence perspective. He claimed that critics had failed to appreciate their insights because they lacked the same expertise that working for an intelligence agency might provide. He went on to add that, unlike historians, intelligence operatives do not always require documented, written evidence.

No one would deny that intelligence officers must often act quickly and draw their conclusions from insights and experience, without always possessing complete evidence. When the tanks are approaching the forward line of troops, the commander requires the best information he can get and he needs it immediately. Historical methodology, however, is quite different. The historian cannot simply rely on insights into human nature to surmise what happened. He needs hard evidence and, if he cannot conclusively prove his theory, he, at least, has the luxury of being able to spend additional years pursuing more documentation, unlike the military commander whose lines will be overrun by the enemy. In the meantime, he should not make more claims than the evidence will support.

Tidwell, himself, admits that his thesis is based largely on circumstantial evidence and that there is no smoking gun. Critics also argue that his portrait of intelligence operations seems more firmly grounded in the twentieth century than the nineteenth. In fact, Tidwell's use of terms such as "action teams" and "safe houses" would have been incomprehensible to members of Civil War military intelligence units. As Mark Neely has noted, while no age has been completely free from barbarism, nations in the nineteenth century may have been as little likely to commit assassinations as in any age before or since. While capturing a chief executive was considered legitimate in time of war, Victorian gentlemen such as Jefferson Davis, are unlikely perpetrators of political murder. The enemy order of battle, that is how many troops the other side had and their disposition, could easily be gained by a man with binoculars on the top of a high hill. Other information could be gleaned by interrogating prisoners or even reading the newspapers. The type of strategic intelligence which military analysts specialize in now was undreamed of by nineteenth-century intelligence operatives. Even the CIA today employs far more Ph.D.'s with degrees in economics, history, political science, or languages than exotic field operatives, but the average person's view of intelligence has been colored by the many books and movies of the James Bond variety.

Rhetoric Versus Reality. In fact, one should also differentiate between political rhetoric and reality. Historians do not completely agree to this day as to whether the Civil War was or was not a total war. Again, Mark Neely, in a thoughtful article has argued that the Civil War would not fit into this total war category. He quotes Jefferson Davis's allegations that the North had devastated and laid waste Southern land, noting that this rhetoric occurred before the fighting in the war had even begun. In a similar fashion, historian William Harris has discovered that in anticipating the Hampton Roads Conference, where Lincoln and Seward met with three Southern envoys, Davis at first expressed grave misgivings when he believed that only Seward would be involved. He stated that if Lincoln was present a lot more could be accomplished since Lincoln could be trusted. Whatever his public utterances, this private statement certainly undercuts the idea that Davis was simultaneously contemplating Lincoln's murder, unless he was a lot more devious and unscrupulous than historians have portrayed him.

There have also been a number of other questions raised. It has been questioned whether Booth, who in this scenario was a Confederate super agent, would really have been chosen to be such a key player in Confederate intelligence. While his profession allowed him freedom of movement, Booth seemed to have a rather loose tongue and the actor's flair for the dramatic. When he killed Lincoln, even if he was only acting in conjunction with what he thought the Confederate authorities wanted, he ran a grave risk of capture and exposure of the plot.

Some Evidence Ignored. Also, some evidence is simply ignored. For example, the index to *April '65* does not even list Samuel Arnold, who was imprisoned in the Dry Tortugas and later left his recollections of events. Interestingly, when Booth recruited Arnold he did not tell him that the Confederate government was behind the plot, which would seem a logical thing to do if it was, since Arnold was dubious about the venture, but rather showed him bank statements to convince him that he had enough money to finance the abduction. John Surratt, in his Rockville Lecture also denied Confederate involvement although those who support Tidwell's thesis would counter that one would hardly expect a Confederate agent to admit to his government's complicity.

Despite Tidwell's claim that intelligence operations need to be supported by vast sums of money that can only come from outside sources, Booth was a wealthy actor who, while he had spent a lot of his fortune financing the capture plot, still had several thousand dollars in Union securities at the time of his death. Paradoxically, since some of his money was invested, he was at times cash poor and had borrowed $500 from Michael O'Laughlen. This act further undercuts the notion that he was receiving vast support from the Confederate government.

One Attempt to Capture Lincoln Fails. The one serious attempt to abduct the president on March 17 was a comic opera fiasco which produced no results. If the Confederates put all their hopes and investment into that scheme then they received little return. After that, Arnold was convinced that Booth had given up because when he asked him what he and O'Laughlen should do with their weapons, which Booth had purchased, the actor told him that they were his to keep. Arnold reached the logical conclusion that Booth had abandoned his plans. The Sam note, which Booth left in his trunk, sent by Arnold on March 27 and urging Booth to go and see how it would be taken at Richmond, also raises questions as to how deep Confederate involvement might have been. Why, two and a half weeks before the assassination was one of his major co-conspirators asking Booth to ascertain how the Confederate government might react to their scheme, if the Confederate government was really the driving force behind it?

Other Claims Require Verification. Paradoxically, in Tidwell's version of events the Southern intelligence agencies become so important that they overwhelm the real flesh and blood participants. If the kidnapping and murder were intelligence operations then the people who carried them out fade into the background.

The claim that Thomas Harney was going to blow up the White

House also needs to be examined more closely. How easy would it have been to enter the White House, plant explosives, and then hope the president and cabinet would all gather together at the right moment? Mosby partisans, who see the dashing Southern cavalry commander as being maligned, have countered that Harney had simply carried torpedoes to Mosby's command to replace artillery which had recently been lost in battle. In their view, when Harney was captured he was simply part of a normal raiding party and not on his way to participate in a quixotic scheme to blow up the White House.

Confederate Motivation. Additionally, one wonders what the Confederates really hoped to gain by their actions. Two presidents had died already in American history so this would not be the first time the nation had faced such an event although, admittedly, the other two had died in less chaotic times. There were clear Constitutional mechanisms for succession which would have taken effect. Also, the assumption is made that the North would have automatically freed tens of thousands of prisoners had Lincoln been abducted, but that is not necessarily the case. Abduction might simply have caused the North to fight with more fury and led to a harsh Reconstruction which would have lived up to its legend. Further, why would Northern officials have backed off claims that the South had murdered Lincoln once the war had ended? They were looking for grounds to try Davis as an assassination conspirator, and what better grounds could there have been than Davis's involvement in Lincoln's murder?

More Than Circumstantial Evidence Required. There have been enough questions raised about the Tidwell thesis that caution is in order. In cases such as this, the historian should demand more than circumstantial evidence. As noted, the reputation of Secretary of War Stanton was permanently tarnished by conspiracy charges against him. Michael Maione, the National Park Service Historian at Ford's Theatre, bemoans the fact that numerous visitors to that shrine are still convinced of Stanton's guilt largely based on some sort of exposure to the Eisenschiml thesis. Similarly, there should be a major reevaluation of Jefferson Davis if he resorted to political murder, no matter what the provocation. If such a reexamination is to occur it should be based on a very high standard of proof. The burden to sustain sensational charges is clearly on those who make them and not the other way around.

Tendency to See Conspiracy. In fact, given what we have observed about DeWitt and Eisenschiml, one might legitimately wonder whether Tidwell and his associates have not been equally influenced by events of the last several decades. Conspiracy theories are rampant in all areas of American life at the end of the twentieth century which may be part of what fuels conspiracy speculation about the death of Lincoln, as well as other American presidents. Conspiracies, in an odd sort of way, restore some sense of order to a world filled with random chaos and violence.

Historians' Full Circle. As regards the Lincoln assassination, perhaps we should not be surprised that we have come full circle. There are some figures in American history who have one or two standard biographies written about them and we are satisfied. This has never been the case with Abraham Lincoln. The secrecy of the man certainly contributed to this as well as the martyrdom he suffered. His assassination struck some deep psychological chord in the American psyche which has caused him to be reinterpreted from generation to generation for as Merrill Peterson writes in his conclusion to *Lincoln in American Memory* (1995), his highly acclaimed study of the mythmaking surrounding the sixteenth president:

> As everything about the war lived in memory, so did Lincoln. And his assassination in the hour of victory stabbed at the nation's heart. He was a man of mystery and paradox: raw and folksy, yet sturdy and dignified; a laughing friend, a melancholy stranger, "hard as rock and soft as drifting fog," as Sandburg said. There was so much of him, he seemed fated to remain forever unknown.

CONCLUSION

Professional Historians Begin to Research Assassinations. Despite the mythology surrounding Abraham Lincoln and his death, the assassination has begun to draw the historical attention which it deserves. Even as early as 1940, George S. Bryan's *The Great American Myth*, provided a balanced approach to assassination events, although it was somewhat eclipsed by Eisenschiml's sensational accounts which appeared in 1937 and 1940. William Hanchett's *The Lincoln Murder Conspiracies* (1983), is an excellent survey of assassination historiography, wherein Professor Hanchett totally discredits Eisenschiml as well as other past sensationalists. W. Emerson Reck in *A. Lincoln, His Last 24 Hours* (1987) provides a reliable account of the last day of the president's life. My own book, *Beware the People Weeping* (1982) is an attempt to place the pursuit and trials of the conspirators in the context of the times. Many other important studies, both articles and books, continue to appear in print. Even Tidwell, Gaddy, and Hall, while their views may be controversial, are not sensationalists but base their work on an extensive analysis of primary sources.

No Smoking Gun. Although this trend is a very positive one, those who continue to hope that the assassination may be "solved," in the same manner in which a murder mystery might be solved, are destined to be disappointed. The century which has passed, makes any new and definitive solution to the crime doubtful. It is unlikely that a smoking gun will surface even though there may still be new sources which will be discovered.

John F. Kennedy Case Unlikely to Be Solved. In a similar sense, the events of a more recent death, that of John Kennedy, appear destined to remain forever obscured by controversy. It remains virtually impossible to make complete sense out of all the sensational and contradictory evidence, although Gerald Posner in his recent book, *Case Closed* (1993), applying the same historical methodology which historians have used to study Lincoln's death, casts similar doubts about the validity of the wilder conspiracy theories.

Research Sheds Light on American Violence. Even if there will never be totally definitive answers to all of the mysteries, however, the quest to shed new light on American assassinations should and will continue. While there is much to admire in American history, there is also a much more somber side to our past, a side that we often tend to overlook. As a nation we like to hold ourselves up as a model to others, assuming that our experiences have been so different that they present a unique example to the world. While in some senses this may be true, there is at least one area in which our record is not so bright, and that involves the high levels of violence which have plagued us as a nation. Measured by almost any standard, the United States has the highest levels of violence of all modern industrial countries.

Numerous Public Officials Attacked. One of the manifestations of this violence has been four successful assassinations (Lincoln, Garfield, McKinley, and Kennedy), and six unsuccessful attempts (Jackson, Theodore Roosevelt, Franklin Roosevelt, Truman, Ford, and Reagan.) This list could be substantially broadened if it included non-presidential attacks on famous Americans such as Huey Long, Malcolm X, Martin Luther King, Robert Kennedy, or George Wallace. Nearly one in four of our chief executives have been subject to attack, a shockingly high percentage of those who have held the office. If any other modern industrial country had experienced so many assaults against its leaders, Americans would no doubt consider that nation on the verge of anarchy and chaos. Yet, in our own case, the alarming statistics are conveniently ignored.

The Darker Side of American History. In a very real sense, no matter what else it may have been or what other consequences his murder may have engendered, Abraham Lincoln really was one of the last Americans to die as a result of the Civil War. Whether we like to admit it or not, the United States has experienced levels of violence which are quite comparable to that of other nations. In that respect, our history is not so unique and the bloodshed between 1861–1865 is not the total aberration which we like to believe it is. All too often, our failure to confront this darker side of American life, and to stress our uniqueness, has led us to undue emphasis on the positive side of American history. Addressing our violent past in a more realistic manner, forces us to come to grips with other troubling aspects of the American dream.

PART II

DOCUMENTS

DOCUMENT NO. 1

BOOTH'S "TO WHOM IT MAY CONCERN" LETTER*

The "To Whom It May Concern" letter was written by Booth in November, 1864, probably shortly after Lincoln's reelection. The actor left the letter with his sister Asia in February of 1865, and it was published after the assassination on April 19 in the Philadelphia Inquirer. *The tone of the letter shows that Booth, rather than being a madman, considered himself a Southern patriot, who viewed Lincoln as a tyrant, trampling on Southern rights.*

γ γ γ

[No place]
[November?], 1864

My dear Sir,

You may use this, as you think best. But as *some* may wish to know *when, who and why* and know not *how* to direct, I give it (In the words of your master [Abraham Lincoln])

"To whom it may concern."

Right or wrong, God judge me, not man. For be my motive good or bad, of one thing I am sure, the lasting condemnation of the North.

I love peace more than life. Have loved the Union beyond expression. For four years have I waited, hoped and prayed, for the dark clouds to break, and for a restoration of our former sunshine. To wait longer would be a crime. All hope for peace is dead. My prayers have proved as idle as my hopes. God's will be done. I go to see, and share the bitter end.

I have ever held the South were right. The very nomination of Abraham Lincoln four years ago, spoke plainly, war—war upon Southern rights and institutions. His election proved it. "Await an overt act." Yes, until you are bound and plundered. What folly. The South were wise. Who

*Original in National Archives and Records Administration, Justice Department Files. Published in the *Philadelphia Inquirer*, April 19, 1865. For a modern transcription see John Rhodehamel and Louise Taper, eds., *"Right or Wrong God Judge Me:" The Writings of John Wilkes Booth* (Urbana: University of Illinois Press, 1997), 124–127.

thinks of argument or patience when the finger of his enemy presses on the trigger. In *a foreign war,* I too could say 'Country right or wrong,' but in a struggle *such as ours* (where the brother tries to pierce the brother's heart) for God's sake choose the right. When a country like this spurns *justice* from her side, she forfeits the allegiance of every honest freeman, and should leave him, untrammeled by any fealty soever, to act as his conscience may approve.

People of the North, to hate tyranny, to love liberty and justice, to strike at wrong and oppression, was the teaching of our fathers. The study of our early history will not let *me* forget it. And may it never.

This country was formed for the *white,* not for the black man. And looking upon *African slavery* from the same stand-point held by those noble framers of our Constitution, I for one have ever considered it one of the greatest blessings (both for themselves and us) that God ever bestowed upon a favored nation. Witness heretofore our wealth and power. Witness their elevation in happiness and enlightenment above their race elsewhere. I have lived among it most of my life and have seen *less* harsh treatment from master to man than I have beheld in the North from father to son. Yet, Heaven knows *no one* would be willing to do *more* for the negro race than I, could I but see a way to still *better their* condition. But Lincoln's policy is only preparing the way for their total annihilation.

The South *are not nor have they been fighting* for the continuance of slavery. The first battle of Bull-run did away with that idea. Their causes since for war have been as *noble,* and greater *far, than those that urged* our fathers *on. Even* should we allow they were *wrong* at the beginning of this contest, *cruelty and injustice* have made the wrong become the *right.* And they stand *now* (before the wonder and admiration of the *world*) as a noble band of patriotic heroes. Hereafter, reading of *their deeds,* Thermopylae will be forgotten.

When I aided in the capture and execution of John Brown (who was a murderer on our Western Border, and who was fairly *tried* and *convicted,*—before an impartial judge & jury—of treason—and who by the way has since been made a God—I was proud of my little share in the transaction, for I deemed it my duty and that I was helping our common country to perform an act of justice. But what was a crime in poor John Brown is now considered (by themselves) as the greatest and only virtue, of the whole Republican party. Strange transmigration. *Vice* to become a *virtue* simply because *more* indulge in it.

I thought then, *as now,* that the abolitionists *were the only* traitors in the land, and that the entire party deserved the fate of poor old Brown, not because they wish to abolish slavery, but on account of the means they have ever endeavored to use to effect that abolition. If Brown were living, I doubt if he himself would set slavery against the Union. Most, or many, in the North do, and openly curse the Union if the South are to return and retain a *single right* guaranteed them by every tie which we once *revered as sacred.* The South can make no choice. It is either extermination or slavery for *themselves* (worse than death) to draw from. I would know *my* choice.

I have, also, studied hard to discover upon what grounds the right of a state to secede has been denied, when our very name (United States) and our Declaration of Independence, *both* provide for secession. But there is no time for words. I write in haste.

I know how foolish I shall be deemed, for undertaking such a step as this, where on the one side I have many friends and everything to make me happy. Where my profession *alone* has gained me an income of *more than* twenty thousands dollars a year. And where my great personal ambition in my profession has such a great field for labor. On the other hand the South have never bestowed upon me one kind word; a place now where I have no friends except beneath the sod; a place where I must either become a private soldier or a beggar. To give up all of the *former* for the *latter,* besides my mother and sisters whom I love so dearly (although they so widely differ with me in opinion) seems insane. But God is my judge. I love *justice* more than I do a country that disowns it, more than fame and wealth, more (Heaven pardon me if wrong), more than a happy home.

I have never been upon a battle-field, but O my countrymen, could you all but see the *reality* or effects of this horrid war, as I have seen them (in *every state,* save Virginia) I know you would think like me and would pray the Almighty to create in the Northern mind a sense of *right* and *justice* (even should it possess no seasoning of mercy) and that he would dry up the sea of blood between us which is daily growing wider.

Alas, poor country, is she to meet her threatened doom. Four years ago I would have given a thousand lives to see her remain (as I had always known her) powerful and unbroken. And even now I would hold my life as naught to see her what she was. O my friends if the fearful scenes of the past four years had never been enacted, or if what has been had been but a frightful dream from which we could now awake, with what overflowing hearts could we bless our God and pray for his continued favor. How I have loved the *old flag* can never, now, be known. A few years since and the entire world could boast of *none so* pure and spotless. But I have of late been seeing and hearing of the *bloody deeds* of which she has *been made the emblem,* and would shudder to think how changed she had grown. O how I have longed to see her break from the mist of blood and death that circles round her folds, spoiling her beauty and tarnishing her honor. But no, day by day has she been draged [*sic*] deeper and deeper into cruelty and oppression, till now (in my eyes) her once bright red stripes look like *bloody gashes* on the face of Heaven. I look now upon my early admiration of her glories as a dream.

My love (as things stand today) is for the South alone. Nor do I deem it a dishonor, in attempting to make for her a prisoner of this man to whom she owes so much misery. If success attends me, I go penniless to her side. They say she has found *that* "last ditch" which the North have so long derided and been endeavoring to force her in, forgetting they are our brothers and that it's impolitic to goad an enemy to madness. Should I reach her in safety and find it true, I will proudly beg permission to triumph or die in that same "ditch" by her side.

A Confederate, ~~at present~~* doing duty upon his own responsibility.

J. Wilkes Booth

*Deleted in the original

DOCUMENT NO. 2

SAMUEL ARNOLD'S ACCOUNT OF HIS INVOLVEMENT IN THE CONSPIRACY TO CAPTURE ABRAHAM LINCOLN, *NEW YORK SUN*, DECEMBER 8, 1902*

This account of conspirator Samuel Arnold appeared in the Baltimore American *and the* New York Sun, *December 8, 1902. In this transcription from the* Sun, *which was based on a statement Arnold had made in the Dry Tortugas in 1867, he freely admitted his involvement in the capture plot, which he considred rather risky but, like Surratt, a worthwhile undertaking. At Gauthier's Restaurant on March 15, Arnold quarreled with Booth and the two threatened violence against each other. When the capture plot failed, on March 17th, due to Lincoln's failure to visit the Campbell Hospital, Arnold was convinced that Booth had abandoned his plans. Arnold was therefore upset that Booth left behind a letter that he had written to the actor, which linked him to the conspiracy.*

γ γ γ

ARNOLD'S EARLY CONFESSION.

It was in the latter part of August, or about the first part of September, A.D. 1864, that J. Wilkes Booth, hearing I was in town, sent word to me that he would like to see me at Barnum's Hotel in the City of Baltimore, at which place he was then stopping. I had not seen Booth since the year 1852, at which time we were fellow students at St. Timothy's Hall, Catonsville, Md., the Rev. L. Van Bokkelen being the President of said institute.

I called upon him and was kindly received as an old schoolmate and invited to his room. We conversed together seated by a table smoking a cigar, of past hours of youth, and the present war. He said he had heard I had been south, &c., when a tap at the door was given and O'Laughlin was ushered into the room. O'Laughlin was a former acquaintance of

**New York Sun* and *Baltimore American*, December 8, 1902. Also published as Samuel Bland Arnold, *Defense and Prison Experiences of a Lincoln Conspirator* (Hattiesburg, MS: The Book Farm, 1943) and Michael Kauffman, ed., *Memoirs of a Lincoln Conspirator* (Bowie, MD: Heritage Books, 1995).

Booths from boyhood up, so he informed me. I was introduced to him, and this was my first acquaintance with O'Laughlin.

In a short time wine was called for by Booth, and we drank and freely conversed together about the war, the present condition of the South and in regard to the non-exchange of prisoners.

Booth then spoke of the abduction or kidnapping of the President, saying if such could be accomplished and the President taken to Richmond and held as hostage, he thought it would bring about an exchange of prisoners. He said the President frequently went to the Soldiers' Home alone and unguarded, that he could be easily captured on one of these visits, and carried to the Potomac, boated across the river and conveyed to Richmond.

BOOTH THE MOVING SPIRIT.

These were the ideas advanced by Booth and he alone was the moving spirit. After a debate of some time and his pointing out its feasibility and being under the effects of some little of wine, we consented to join him in the enterprise. We alone comprised the entire party to the scheme at that time as far as my knowledge extends.

We separated that afternoon and I returned to my brother's home near Hookstown, Baltimore County, Md. Booth stating he would leave for New York the next day to wind up his affairs and make over his property to different members of his family, reserving enough to carry out his projected scheme and would soon return.

Booth said he would furnish all the necessary materials to carry out the project. He showed me the different entries in his diary of what his engagements paid him in his profession and I judged from what I have heard his income therefrom to be from $25,000 to $30,000. He also informed me he owned property in the oil regions of Pennsylvania and Boston. He was taken sick while at home, and upon his recovery he arranged his business and went to the oil regions from which place he wrote me enclosing twenty dollars for expenses, requesting me to look around and pick out a horse for him.

ARMS PURCHASED.

This is all the money I ever received from Booth or any other person in connection with this undertaking. He went from the oil regions to Canada and shipped his wardrobe to Nassau, as he afterwards informed me. Booth returned to Baltimore some time in November or December, 1864. He had purchased while North some arms to defend himself in case of pursuit, viz: two carbines, three pairs of revolvers, three knives and two pairs of handcuffs. Fearful that the weight of his trunk might attract attention, he asked me to take part of them, which I did and sent them to him by express to Washington.

A short time after his return from Canada to Baltimore he went to the lower counties of Maryland, bordering on the Potomac as he said for the purpose of purchasing horses and boats. I met him in Baltimore in January, I think at which time he purchased the horse that I had selected for him. He also purchased a buggy and harness and now said that all was completed and ready to work.

I informed my parents I was in the oil business with Booth, to prevent them from knowing the true cause of my association with Booth. O'Laughlin and I drove the buggy to Washington. This was sometime in the latter part of December 1864 or early part of January 1865.

THE EARLY PREPARATIONS.

We left the horse at Nailor's livery stable on the avenue near Thirteenth Street, and we went to Rullman's Hotel (kept by Lichau), on Pennsylvania Avenue. We remained there a few days and then went to Mitchell's Hotel, near Grover's Theatre, and remained a few days. We went from there and rented a room from Mrs. Van Tyne, 420 D Street and obtained our meals at the Franklin Hotel, at the corner of D & Eighth Streets. We remained there off and on, until March 20, 1865, during which time I frequently went to Baltimore-nearly every Saturday. O'Laughlin, as a general thing, always went and returned with me on these visits.

When in Baltimore I remained at my father's. When in Washington I spent most of my time at Rullman's Hotel (kept by Lichau), on Pennsylvania Avenue, at which place O'Laughlin and myself had acquaintances.

FIRST PLAN ABANDONED.

The President having ceased visiting the Soldiers' Home, Booth proposed a plan to abduct him from the theatre, by carrying him back off the stage by the back entrance, place him in a buggy which he was to have in attendance, and, during the confusion which would be produced by turning off the gas, make good our escape.

I objected to any such arrangement, and plainly pointed out its utter impracticability and told Booth it could not be accomplished. He would listen to no argument I could bring forth, and seemed resolved in carrying out this mad scheme. He endeavored to obtain a man from New York to turn off the gas. In this he failed, so he informed me.

This was in the latter part of January or the early part of February, 1865. Booth at that time was stopping at the National Hotel. About this time I called at his room, accompanied by O'Laughlin, and upon entering was introduced to Surratt under the name, I think, of Cole. This was about 10 or 11 o'clock in the morning and Booth was still in bed.

This was the first time I ever met Surratt. Surratt left a few moments after we came in, and Booth informed us he was one of the parties engaged in the abduction and his name was Surratt.

BOOTH'S MOTHER'S DREAMS.

About this time Booth told me he had received a letter from his mother in which she stated she had fearful dreams about him. She sent his brother Junius Brutus to Washington to persuade him to come home, so Booth told me.

Booth told me that he did not wish his brother to know how many horses he had as he knew that his brother would ask for an explanation as to why he kept so many. He asked me then to go down to Cleaver's Stable and I did so. He told Mr. Cleaver that I had purchased the horse, and he was turned over to me.

About a week afterward I went to the stable, paid the livery on the horse and rode him up to the corner of D and Eighth Streets and turned him over either to O'Laughlin or Booth. I never saw the horse afterward. Booth afterward repaid me for the board of the horse.

MEETING OF THE PLOTTERS.

Booth was absent from the city of Washington the best part of the month of February. On his return he stated he had been to New York.

On the night of March, 15, 1865 about 12 or 12.30 o'clock, O'Laughlin and myself were about leaving Rullman's Hotel, on our way to our room, when Booth sent a messenger (Herold) who at that time was unknown to me requesting us to accompany Herold to Gotier's eating saloon. (Herold, I learned from O'Laughlin, had been introduced to him that day by Booth during their buggy ride.)

We accordingly went up and were ushered into the room, where, seated around a table, were Booth, Surratt, Atzerodt, alias Port Tobacco, and Payne-alias Mosby, all of whom, with the exception of Booth and Surratt, I had never seen or heard of before. We were then formally introduced.

Oysters, liquors and cigars were obtained. Booth then remarked that those gathered were the parties engaged to assist in the abduction of the President. The plan of abducting him from the theatre was introduced and discoursed upon, Booth saying if it could not be done from the lower box, it could from the upper one.

THE PARTS ALLOTTED.

He set forth the part he wished each one to perform. He and Payne, alias Mosby, were to seize the President in the box, O'Laughin and Herold to put out the gas. I was to jump upon the stage and assist them as he was lowered down from the box, and Surratt and Atzerodt, alias Port Tobacco were to be on the other side of Eastern Branch bridge to act as pilots and to assist in conveying him to the boats which had been purchased by Booth. Booth said everything was in readiness.

The gist of the conversation during the meeting was whether it could or could not be accomplished in the manner proposed.

After listening to Booth and the others I firmly protested and objected to the whole scheme, and told them of its utter impracticability. I stated that prisoners were now being exchanged and that the object to be obtained by abduction had been accomplished; that patriotism was the motive that prompted me in joining the scheme, not ambition, and that I wanted a shadow of a chance for my life and that I intended having it.

BOOTH THREATENED BACKSLIDERS.

Then an angry discussion arose between Booth and myself, in which he threatened to shoot me. I told him that two could play at that game, and before them all expressed my firm determination to have nothing more to do with it after that week.

About 5 o'clock in the morning the meeting broke up and O'Laughlin and myself went to our room at Mrs. Van Tyne's.

The next day as I was standing in front of Rullman's Hotel, Pennsylvania Avenue, in company with O'Laughlin, Booth came riding by on horseback and stopped and called O'Laughlin. He conversed with him a short time and then O'Laughlin returned saying that Booth wanted to see me.

I went to the curb and met him. Booth apologized to me for the words he had used at the meeting, remarking that he thought that I must have been drunk in making the objections I did at the meeting in reference to his proposed plan of carrying out the abduction.

I told him no-drunkenness was on his and his party's part; that I was never more sober in my life and what I said the night before I meant, and that this week should end my connection with the affair.

ANOTHER PLAN HATCHED.

On March 17, 1865 about 2 o'clock, Booth and Herold met O'Laughlin and myself. Booth stated that he was told that the President was going to attend a theatrical performance out on Seventh Street at a soldiers' encampment or hospital at the outer edge of the city.

Booth had previously sent a small black box, containing two carbines, a monkey wrench, ammunition and four piece of rope, by the porter of the National Hotel to our room at Mrs. Van Tyne's. Not wishing it to remain in our room, O'Laughlin sent the box to an acquaintance of his in Washington. This box was sent to our room in the early part of March, I think, and was removed in about a week or ten days.

After Booth and Herold met O'Laughlin and myself and made arrangements to go out to the performance on Seventh Street, Booth, Herold, and O'Laughlin went for the box containing the two carbines &c.

The understanding was that Herold was to take the box with Booth's horse and buggy to either Surrattsville or T.B., and there meet us in case the abduction was successful. This was the last time I saw Herold until our trial.

O'Laughlin returned and we took our dinner at the Franklin Hotel, as usual. After dinner we met Booth and accompanied him to a livery stable near the Patent Office, at which place Booth obtained horses for us. O'Laughlin and I then rode to our room on D Street and made all our necessary arrangements, each arming himself. O'Laughlin and myself rode out to where the performance was to take place.

LINCOLN'S SECOND ESCAPE.

We stopped at a restaurant at the foot of the hill to await the arrival of the other parties. They not arriving as soon as we expected, we remounted our horses and rode out the road about a mile. We there returned and stopped at the same restaurant.

Whilst in there Atzerodt came in, having just arrived with Payne. A short time after, Booth and Surratt came in and we drank together. Booth made enquiries at the encampment where the performance was to be held, and learned that, the President was not there. After telling us this we separated, O'Laughlin, and myself riding back to the city together.

Surratt and Booth rode out the road toward the country. O'Laughlin and I left our horses back of the National Hotel, at a livery stable.

THE KIDNAPPING ABANDONED.

About 8 o'clock I met Booth and Surratt near the stable. This was the last time I ever saw Surratt, and I never saw Payne after we parted in our ride into the city until the day of our trial.

O'Laughlin and I left Washington on March 20 and went to Baltimore. Booth went to New York and thus I thought the whole affair abandoned. I then told my family I had ceased business in Washington and severed my connection with Booth. . . .

BOOTH's PERSISTENCE.

I went out to my brother's home at Hookstown, Baltimore county and I returned March 25 to Baltimore. I was informed at my father's that Booth had called to see me, and left a card requesting me to call upon him at Barnum's Hotel.

I found a letter there, also, from him for me, in which he stated he desired to give it another trial the week following, and if unsuccessful to abandon it forever. The letter found in Booth's trunk was in answer to the letter which I innocently wrote to prevent his undertaking it. . . .

SURRATT TOOK ANOTHER MISSION.

We saw Booth. During our conversation he told us that the President was not in Washington. He also said that Surratt had gone to Richmond, as he had understood through Weichman that a Mrs. Slater had arrived from Canada with despatches and that the party who had been in the habit of ferrying persons across the river had been arrested by the Government, in consequence of which Surratt offered his services to accompany her to Richmond.

I asked if he had received my letter of the 27th, and he replied that he had not. I asked him when the letter was received to destroy it. He told me he would.

This interview on March 31 took place in his room at the National Hotel. Booth O'Laughlin, and myself being present. In this conversation Booth stated that the enterprise was abandoned. He also stated that he intended to return to his profession.

It was at this interview that I asked Booth what I should do with the arms I had. He told me to keep them, to sell them, or do anything I desired with them. We left him at his room in the hotel about 2 o'clock in the afternoon and after that time I never received either a letter from him or any other communication, nor he from me, neither have I seen him since.

DOCUMENT NO. 3

EXCERPT FROM ABRAHAM LINCOLN'S LAST PUBLIC ADDRESS, APRIL 11, 1865*

Lincoln's last public address was delivered from the White House balcony on April 11, 1865. Booth and Lewis Powell were in the audience and when the president mentioned that he favored limited voting rights for blacks, the actor turned to his companion and muttered, "Now, by God, I'll put him through."

γ γ γ

Last Public Address
April 11, 1865

We meet this evening, not in sorrow, but in gladness of heart. The evacuation of Petersburg and Richmond, and the surrender of the principal insurgent army, give hope of a righteous and speedy peace whose joyous expression can not be restrained. In the midst of this, however, He, from Whom all blessings flow, must not be forgotten. A call for a national thanksgiving is being prepared, and will be duly promulgated. Nor must those whose harder part gives us the cause of rejoicing, be overlooked. Their honors must not be parcelled out with others. I myself, was near the front, and had the high pleasure of transmitting much of the good news to you; but no part of the honor, for plan or execution, is mine. To Gen. Grant, his skilful officers, and brave men, all belongs. The gallant Navy stood ready, but was not in reach to take active part. . . .

The amount of constituency, so to to (sic) speak, on which the new Louisiana government rests, would be more satisfactory to all, if it contained fifty, thirty or even twenty thousand, instead of only about twelve thousand, as it does. It is also unsatisfactory to some that the elective franchise is not given to the colored man. I would myself prefer that it were now conferred on the very intelligent, and on those who serve our cause as soldiers. Still the question is not whether the Louisiana gov-

*Roy P. Basler, Marion D. Pratt, and Lloyd A. Dunlop, eds., *The Collected Works of Abraham Lincoln*, (New Brunswick: New Jersey:Rutgers University Press, 1953), VIII, 399–405.

ernment, as it stands, is quite all that is desirable. The question is "Will it be wiser to take it as it is, and help to improve it; or to reject, and disperse it?" "Can Louisiana be brought into proper practical relation with the Union sooner by sustaining, or by discarding her new State Government?"

DOCUMENT NO. 4

NEW YORK TIMES, APRIL 16, 1865*

In the nineteenth century the American public received accounts of major events largely through the newspapers. This Sunday edition is typical as to how major newspapers, informed their readers about the president's murder.

γ γ γ

OUR GREAT LOSS

Death of President Lincoln.

The Songs of Victory Drowned in Sorrow.

CLOSING SCENES OF A NOBLE LIFE.

The Great Sorrow of an Afflicted Nation.

Party Differences Forgotten in Public Grief.

. . . .

Vice-President Johnson Inaugurated as Chief Executive.

MR. SEWARD WILL RECOVER.

John Wilkes Booth Believed to be the Assassin.

Manifestations of the People Throughout the Country.

OFFICIAL DISPATCHES.

War Department, Washington
April 15—4:10 A.M.

To Major-Gen. Dix:

The President continues insensible and is sinking.

Secretary Seward remains without change.

Frederick Seward's skull is fractured in two places, besides a severe cut upon the head.

**New York Times*, April 16, 1865.

The attendant is still alive, but hopeless. Maj. Seward's wound is not dangerous.

It is now ascertained with reasonable certainty that two assassins were engaged in this horrible crime, Wilkes Booth being the one that shot the President, and the other companion of his whose name is not known, but whose description is so clear that he can hardly escape. It appears from a letter found in Booth's trunk that the murder was planned before the 4th of March, but fell through then because the accomplice backed out until "Richmond could be heard from." Booth and his accomplice were at the livery stable at six o'clock last evening, and there left with their horses about ten o'clock, or shortly before that hour.

It would seem that they had for several days been seeking their chance, but for some unknown reason it was not carried into effect until last night.

One of them has evidently made his way to Baltimore — the other has not yet been traced.

Edwin M. Stanton
Secretary of War

War Department, Washington, April 15.

Major Gen. Dix:

Abraham Lincoln died this morning at twenty-two minutes after seven o'clock.

Edwin M. Stanton
Secretary of War

Major Gen. Dix, New York: War Department
Washington, April 15—3 p.m.

Official notice of the death of the late President, Abraham Lincoln, was given by the heads of departments this morning to Andrew Johnson, Vice-President, upon whom the constitution devolved the office of President. Mr. Johnson, upon receiving this notice, appeared before the Hon. Salmon P. Chase, Chief Justice of the United States, and took the oath of office, as President of the United States, assumed its duties and functions. At 12 o'clock the President met the heads of departments in cabinet meeting, at the Treasury Building, and among other business the following was transacted:

First — The arrangements for the funeral of the late President were referred to the several Secretaries, as far as relates to their respective departments.

Second — William Hunter, Esq., was appointed Acting Secretary of State during the disability of Mr. Seward, and his son Frederick Seward, the Assistant Secretary.

Third — The President formally announced that he desired to retain the present Secretaries of departments of his Cabinet, and they would go on and discharge their respective duties in the same manner as before the deplorable event that had changed the head of the government.

All business in the departments was suspended during the day.

The surgeons report that the condition of Mr. Seward remains unchanged. He is doing well.

No improvement in Mr. Frederick Seward.

The murderers have not yet been apprehended.

Edwin M. Stanton
Secretary of War.

THE ASSASSINATION.

Additional Details of the Lamentable Event.

Washington, Saturday, April 15.

The assassin of President Lincoln left behind him his hat and a spur.

The hat was picked up in the President's box and has been identified by parties to whom it has been shown as the one belonging to the suspected man, and accurately described as the one belonging to the suspected man by other parties, not allowed to see it before describing it.

The spur was dropped upon the stage, and that also has been identified as the one procured at a stable where the same man hired a horse in the evening.

Two gentlemen who went to the Secretary of War to apprize him of the attack on Mr. Lincoln met at the residence of the former a man muffled in a cloak, who, when accosted by them, hastened away.

It had been Mr. Stanton's intention to accompany Mr. Lincoln to the theatre, and occupy the same box, but the press of business prevented.

It therefore seems evident that the aim of the plotters was to paralyze the country by at once striking down the head, the heart and the arm of the country.

As soon as the dreadful events were announced in the streets, Superintendent Richards, and his assistants, were at work to discover the assassin.

In a few moments the telegraph had aroused the whole police force of the city.

Maj. Wallach and several members of the City Government were soon on the spot and every precaution was taken to preserve order and quiet in the city.

Every street in Washington was patrolled at the request of Mr. Richards.

Gen. Augur sent horses to mount the police.

Every road leading out of Washington was strongly picketed and every possible avenue of escape was thoroughly guarded.

Steamboats about to depart down the Potomac were stopped.

The Daily *Chronicle* says:

"As it is suspected that this conspiracy originated in Maryland, the telegraph flashed the mournful news to Baltimore and all the cavalry was immediately put upon active duty. Every road was picketed and every precaution taken to prevent the escape of the assassin. A preliminary examination was made by Messrs. Richards and his assistants. Several persons were called to testify and the evidence as elicited before an informal tribunal, and not under oath, was conclusive to this point. The murderer of President Lincoln was John Wilkes Booth. His hat was found in the private box, and identified by several persons who had seen him within the last two days, and the spur which he dropped by accident, after he jumped to the stage, was identified as one of those which he had obtained from the stable where he hired his horse.

This man Booth has played more than once at Ford's Theatre, and is, of course, acquainted with its exits and entrances, and the facility with which he escaped behind the scenes is well understood.

The person who assassinated Secretary Seward left behind him a slouched hat and an old rusty navy revolver. The chambers were broken loose from the barrel, as if done by striking. The loads were drawn from the chambers, one being but a rough piece of lead, and the other balls smaller than the chambers, wrapped in paper, as if to keep them from falling out.

CLOSING SCENES

Particulars of His Last Moments — Record of His Condition Before Death — His Death

Washington, Saturday, April 15—11 o'clock A.M.

The *Star* extra says:

"At 7:20 o'clock the President breathed his last, closing his eyes as if falling to sleep, and his countenance assuming an expression of perfect serenity. There were no indications of pain and it was not known that he was dead until the gradually decreasing respiration ceased altogether.

Rev. Dr. Gurley, of the New-York avenue Presbyterian Church, immediately on it being ascertained that life was extinct, knelt at the bedside and offered an impressive prayer, which was responded to by all present.

Dr. Gurley then proceeded to the front parlor, where Mrs. Lincoln, Capt. Robert Lincoln, Mrs.(sic) John Hay, the Private Secretary, and others, were waiting, where he again offered a prayer for the consolation of the family. . . .

Surrounding the death bed of the President were Secretaries Stanton, Welles, Usher, Attorney-General Speed, Postmaster-General Dennison, M.B. Field, Assistant Secretary of the Treasury; Judge Otto, Assistant Secretary of the Interior; Gen. Halleck, Gen. Meigs, Senator Sumner, R.F. Andrews, of New-York; Gen. Todd, of Dacotah; John Hay, Private Secretary; Gov. Oglesby, of Illinois; Gen Farnsworth, Mr. and Miss Kenney, Miss Harris, Capt. Robert Lincoln, son of the President, and Doctors E.W. Abbott, R.K. Stone, C.D. Gatch, Neal Hall, and Mr. Lieberman. Secretary McCulloch remained with the President until about 5 o'clock, and Chief Justice Chase, after several hours' attendance during the night, returned early this morning.

Immediately after the President's death a Cabinet meeting was called by Secretary Stanton, and held in the room in which the corpse lay. Secretaries Stanton, Welles and Usher, Postmaster-General Dennison, and Attorney-General Speed, were present. The results of the conference are as yet unknown. . . .

THE ASSASSINS.

Circumstances Tending to Inculpate G. H. (sic) Booth—Description of his Confederate in the Crime.

Washington, Saturday, April 15.

There is no confirmation of the report that the murderer of the President has been arrested.

Among the circumstances tending to fix a participation in the crime on Booth, were letters found in his trunk, one of which, apparently from a lady, supplicated him to desist from the perilous undertaking in which he was about to embark, as the time was inauspicious, the mine not yet being ready to be sprung.

The *Extra Intelligencer* says: "From the evidence obtained it is rendered highly probable that the man who stabbed Mr. Seward and his sons, is John Surratt, of Prince George County, Maryland. The horse he rode was hired at Naylor's stable, on Fourteenth-street. Surratt is a young man, with light hair and goatee. His father is said to have been postmaster of Prince George County."

About 11 o'clock last night two men crossed the Anacostia Bridge, one of whom gave his name as Booth, and the other as Smith. The latter is believed to be John Surratt.

Last night a riderless horse was found, which has been identified by the proprietor of one of the stables previously mentioned as having been hired from his establishment.

Accounts are conflicting as to whether Booth crossed the bridge on horseback or on foot; but as it is believed that he rode across it, it is presumed that he had exchanged his horse.

From information in the possession of the authorities it is evident that the scope of the plot was intended to be much more comprehensive.

The Vice-President and other prominent members of the Administration were particularly inquired for by suspected parties, and their precise localities accurately obtained, but providentially, in their cases, the scheme miscarried.

A boat was at once sent down the Potomac to notify the gunboats on the river of the awful crime, in order that all possible means should be taken for the arrest of the perpetrators.

The most ample precautions have been taken, and it is not believed the culprits will long succeed in evading the overtaking of justice.

The second extra of the *Evening Star* says:

"Col. Ingraham, Provost-Marshal of the defence north of the Potomac, is engaged in taking testimony to-day, all of which fixes the assassination upon H. (sic) Wilkes Booth.

Judge Olin, of the Supreme Court of the District of Columbia, and Justice Miller, are also engaged to-day, at the Police Headquarters, on Tenth-street, in taking the testimony of a large number of witnesses.

Lieut. Tyrell, of Col. Ingraham's staff, last night proceeded to the National Hotel, where Booth had been stopping, and took possession of his trunk, in which was found a Colonel's military dress-coat, two pairs of handcuffs, two boxes of cartridges and a package of letters, all of which are now in the possession of the military authorities.

One of these letters, bearing the date of Hookstown, Md., seems to implicate Booth. The writer speaks of "the mysterious affair in which you are engaged," and urges Booth to proceed to Richmond, and ascertain the views of the authorities there upon the subject. The writer of the letter endeavors to persuade Booth from carrying his designs into execution at that time, for the reason, as the writer alleges, that the government had its suspicions aroused. The writer of the letter seems to have been implicated with Booth in "the mysterious affair" referred to, as he informs Booth in the letter that he would prefer to express his views verbally; and then goes on to say that he was out of money, had no clothes, and would be compelled to leave home, as his family were desirous that he should dissolve his connection with Booth. This letter is written on note paper, in a small, neat hand, and simply bears the signature of "Sam."

At the Cabinet meeting yesterday, which lasted over two hours, the future policy of the government toward Virginia was discussed, the best feeling prevailed. It is stated that it was, determined to adopt a very liberal policy, as was recommended by the President. It is said that this meeting was the most harmonious held for over two years, the President exhibiting throughout that magnanimity and kindness of heart which has ever characterized his treatment of the rebellious States, and which has been so little requited on their part.

One of the members of the Cabinet remarked to a friend he met at the door, that "The government was to-day stronger than it had been for three years past." . . .

DOCUMENT NO. 5

EXAMINATION OF MRS. MARY SURRATT BY COLONEL H. S. OLCOTT, APRIL 28, 1865*

The examination of Mrs. Mary Surratt by Colonel H. S. Olcott took place at Carroll Prison on April 28, 1865. Suspicion fastened itself on Mrs. Surratt because she and her son were both acquainted with Booth, and many of Booth's co-conspirators met at her Washington boardinghouse. The arrival of Seward's assailant, Lewis Powell, at her doorstep when she was being arrested, also wove a strong web of circumstantial evidence around her.

γ γ γ

Carroll Prison, April 28th, 1865
Mrs. Mary E. Surratt
Examined by Col. Olcott

Q. I have been sent by the Govt. to examine you among others to see what statement you are willing to make about the circumstances of this murder. You are at liberty to decline answering, but you will understand any statement you make will be used in your trial. You are a woman of too good sense not to know that it is better to refuse to say anything, than not to tell the truth.

When was the last time you saw your son John H.?

A. Monday week previous to Mr. Lincoln being murdered he took dinner at home.

Q. Had he been living constantly at home before that?

A. We have been in Washt. some three or four months. Before that time all of our business was of course in Maryland where we came from. Sometimes he was a week at home and sometimes a week in the country. I thought it better for him to be in Maryland than here where there were restaurants and bad company. I thought this was not the place for a boy.

*National Archives and Records Administration, Microcopy-599, Roll 6, Frames 171–200.

Q. Up to the time when you last saw him he had not been a resident of your house?

A. He would come and stay a week and he would then go away and stay a week.

Q. Up to that Monday how long had he been here continuously?

A. That day he came from the country. He had been gone a week perhaps: a few days more I think. He left home Saturday week before the Monday he came home. He was only Monday to dinner. He went away after dinner.

Q. Where did he go?

A. He did not tell me where he was going. I expected the draft to come off and I wanted him to get money owing us and put whatever was necessary into the club there. When he came home I found he had not done so and I commenced to scold. He left the dinner table with Mr. Wieckman. He asked him to walk down the street and started out of the house. I had no idea that he was going away. When Mr. Wieckman came back I asked him where John was and he told me that he had bid him good evening and said that he was going away.

Q. You have never seen him since that time?

A. I have never seen him since.

Q. Do you know a man by the name of Atzerodt, or Port Tobacco?

A. Yes, sir. He came to my house to board. I had several rooms. I came from Maryland. I had no way of living except by renting the rooms and taking in a few boarders. I advertised in the "Star" several times that I had rooms to rent. I was down in the country and when I returned I found him there. He remained several days. I do not know how many days; he was not in the house but a few times. I found in his room bottles of liquor and when my son came home I told him that I did not want this man to board; that he kept bottles of liquor and I did not want him there. That is all of my acquaintance with "Port Tobacco."

Q. How long was he there altogether?

A. Three or four or five days; not exceeding that I am sure.

Q. How long before your son left?

A. That was several weeks ago. I could not say how long.

Q. Did he have a horse while he was there?

A. I think he did ride to the house on one or two occasions while he was there. Twice to my knowledge he rode a bay horse there.

Q. How many times did you go to the country a week or two previous to the murder?

A. Twice.

Q. Who went with you?

A. The gentleman who boarded with me, Mr. Wieckman,; he drove me down in a buggy.

Q. Where did you stop?

A. At Mr. Lloyd's who rents my place down there.

Q. What conversation did you have with Mr. Lloyd?

A. I do not remember any particular conversation. Mr. Lloyd was not at home when I was going to start.

Q. What time was that?

A. Friday evening.

Q. That is the day of the murder?

A. Yes, sir.

Q. About what time?

A. I did not start from home until after dinner. I had received a letter from Mr. Caldwell in relation to a piece of land. The parties wanted me to show my deed. I only wanted to say that the deed would be ready when the parties paid me the money. I got the letter that morning.

Q. What time do you drive?

A. Usually late after Mr. Wieckman comes from the office.

Q. What time did you get dinner that day?

A. Only took a lunch about one o'clock.

Q. After one o'clock you started?

A. Yes, sir.

Q. How long does it take to drive down there?

A. About an hour and a half.

Q. How long did you stop at Lloyds?

A. I do not remember.

Q. About how long?

A. I think we started from there about 5 o'clock to the best of my knowledge. When I got there I learned that Mr. Knothe, the man I had business with, had gone to Marlboro. I remained there as long as I could to see whether he would return. In this I had a letter written to Mr. Knothe stating what he could do. It was directed to the care of Captain Gwin. Just as I was about to start the Captain drove up. I told him my business and left the letter also.

Q. How long a conversation did you have with Mr. Lloyd?

A. Only a few minutes conversation. I did not not sit down. I only met him as I was going home.

Q. Where was Mr. Wieckman?

A. He was there.

Q. He heard the conversation?

A. I presume he did. I do not remember.

Q. What did the conversation relate to?

A. He spoke of having fish and oysters. He asked me whether I had been to dinner, I said he could give me fish and oysters. Mr. Wieckman said that he would return home as he was in need of his bread and butter.

Q. What did you say about any shooting iron or carbines?

A. I said nothing about them.

Q. Any conversation of that kind? Did you not tell him to have the shooting irons ready, that there would be some people there that night?

A. To my knowledge no conversation of that kind passed.

Q. Did you know any shooting irons were there?

A. No sir, I did not.

Q. Where about is Mr. Wieckman?

A. I do not know. I have been here ever since. He went away from the house with a detective by the name of Mc.Donough, or something like that.

Q. Where were they going?

A. I do not know. They came in Sunday morning and went away together.

Q. What time did you see Mr. Wieckman?

A. Sunday morning about 10 o'clock.

Q. Did he pass Saturday night at your house?

A. No sir.

Q. Where did he stay?

A. I do not know. He was with this gentleman. He left the house with him. I never saw him anymore.

Q. You mentioned the other day to Colonel Foster you had a man by the name of Wood, a Baptist minister, at your house.

A. Yes sir. He remained there for a few days. He came there to board and on Monday evening he left, saying he was going to preach there on Sunday.

Q. Where did he come from?

A. I do not know.

Q. How did he happen to come to your house?

A. I advertised those rooms and he came to board.

Q. What time did he come?

A. I do not remember. It was several weeks ago.

Q. Was it before the Inauguration?

A. I think it was in February. I do not remember and would not like to state it.

Q. You could tell by the advertisement in the paper?

A. Yes, sir. He said he saw we had rooms to rent, and he wanted to get rooms and board. He was a stranger to me. I had never seen him before.

Q. What sort of a man was he?

A. Stout, black hair and eyes. He was a short stout man of few words. He did not seem inclined to talk. He seemed to be a young man, twenty years and odd.

Q. Did your son have any acquaintance with him?

A. Not that I knew of.

Q. What did he state his name was?

A. He said that his name was Wood.

Q. Did he give his full name?

A. No, sir. He said he came from Baltimore and that he was returning there to preach on Sunday. He said that he was a Baptist Minister.

Q. How long did he stay?

A. A few days. He came some day during that week and left on Friday for Baltimore. He remained in his room most of the time.

Q. What was he doing?

A. I never go into the boarders rooms any more than if I were not there.

Q. Do you recollect the man who came to your house at the time of your arrest?

A. I do not. I thought he was someone calling for the gentlemen there. I never noticed him.

Q. You did not look to see whether it was this man Wood?

A. I only saw a stranger. I never saw him before. I never thought it was the Wood who was at our house.

Q. When did you get acquainted with Mr. Booth?

A. Some three months ago.

Q. Who brought him to the house?

A. He came to the house and asked whether my son was in. We always found him pleasant. His visits were short. I never knew anything about his private matters at all.

Q. Were his visits always visits of courtesy?

A. Yes, sir.

Q. No business, discussed.

A. No, sir. No political affairs. I do not think that his longest stay was over one hour.

Q. What part of the day did he used to come?

A. Sometimes in the day and sometimes in the evening.

Q. Did not an attachment spring up between him and your daughter?

A. Not particularly I should suppose. Not that I knew of.

Q. He was a handsome man?

A. He was a handsome man and gentlemanly; that is all we knew of him. I did not suppose he had the devil-he certainly possessed in his heart.

Q. I should suppose from the papers and letters that Miss Surratt thought favorably of him.

A. If so, she kept it to herself. She never corresponded with him.

Q. Did he pay particular attention to any one of the young ladies?

A. No particular attention. We were in the parlor together, and he did not pay particular attention to any one.

Q. How long has your son known him?

A. Ever since he came to the house. I do not know whether he knew him before, or why he came there. I only know Mr. Wieckman was with my son when they met at some hotel, the National I presume, and there made his acquaintance.

Q. Mr. Wieckman was well acquainted with Mr. Booth before they came together?

A. I do not know. I think Mr. Wieckman was with my son when he was introduced.

Q. Your son never went to college with Mr. Booth?

A. No, sir. He went with Mr. Wiechman to St. Charles Ellicott's (illegible) some three or four years.

Q. The night of the murder who was at your house?

A. No one except our own family. A gentleman I did not know called for some newspapers for a niece of mine. He did not come in and I don't think I saw him. The little servant girl took the paper.

Q. No one else?

A. No, sir.

Q. When did you first know of the President's murder?

A. When a gentleman called at my house next morning.

Q. What time?

A. Just about day.

Q. A few hours after the assassination?

A. I suppose so.

Q. Who were there Saturday or Saturday night besides the detective police?

A. I do not remember anyone but the detectives.

Q. Who came there Saturday night?

A. I do not know anyone but Mr. Kirby.

Q. Who is he?

A. He lives in Washt. and is employed in the Government service. Wm. Wallace Kirby:he lives on H street between 4th and 5th.

Q. What did he come there for?

A. He generally calls upon us. He married a connection. I do not remember whether he called before or after dark. He was alone. He was the one person who called, but I am not sure of it. If there was any other I do not recollect it.

Q. Did three men call there on Saturday or Sunday night, talking about your son and other friends who had disappeared?

A. I do not remember anyone speaking to me except Mr. Wieckman, this detective and Mr. Holahan. I cannot say what the conversation was about.

Q. When was that?

A. Sunday morning when Mr. Wieckman came and changed his clothes.

Q. Did Mr. Wieckman have a lead colored suit of clothes in the room over the parlor, or was the one he wore that of Mr. Holahan?

A. I do not remember.

Q. Did Mr. Wieckman wear light or dark clothes?

A. Sometimes he wore light and sometimes he wore dark clothes.

Q. Is Holahan a larger man than Wieckman?

A. I think they are nearly about one size.

Q. I am speaking of the visit of three more men to your house on Saturday or Sunday evening when you had a conversation with them?

A. I do not remember. There was no one there but detectives.

Q. Where did you have your conversation with the detectives?

A. In the front parlor.

Q. No conversation with them in the back parlor?

A. No, sir.

Q. The back parlor is the dining room?

A. The dining room is downstairs in the basement.

Q. Did you, or not, have a conversation with three men in the dining room about your son, asking whether they had seen your son and his friends and receiving the information they had seen them but did not speak to them there were so many people about?

A. No such conversation, nothing of the kind occurred.

Q. Have you a relative in the Confederate army with the rank of general?

A. No, sir.

Q. What is your son's rank?

A. I have no son in the Confederate army that I know of. The day of Mr. Lincoln's inauguration he went to Texas, & the last I heard of him he was in Matamoros, Mexico. I have no knowledge there are any of my relatives in the army on either side. My husband had a Captain Surratt in this army and a Captain Surratt in the rebel army but I never saw either of them.

Q. (Page torn) my son or Mr. Booth or Port Tobacco tell me they had engaged in a plot to kill the President!

A. Never in the world if it was the last I have ever to utter.

DOCUMENT NO. 6

STATEMENT OF DR. SAMUEL A. MUDD, UNDATED*

The undated statement of Dr. Samuel Mudd is in Mudd's own handwriting. Controversy has swirled around the guilt or innocence of the doctor. Defenders have accepted his claims to the authorities that he did not recognize that the man who came to his house was Booth, and that he simply did his duty as a physician in setting a stranger's broken leg. Critics have countered that Booth and Mudd were well acquainted, making it impossible for him not to recognize the actor. In their view, while he may not have known about the murder in advance, he was involved in the capture operation, and was an accessory after the fact in Booth's escape.

γ γ γ

STATEMENT OF SAMUEL A. MUDD VOLUNTARY STATEMENT, UNDATED, IN MUDD's OWN HANDWRITING.

I reside in Charles County, Maryland, near Bryantown, about 25 miles from Washington. My house is, I suppose, between 18 & 20 miles from the nearest point on the Potomac river, and about 60 or 70 miles from the west shore of the Chesapeake. I am a physician by profession, and have been practicing some 9 years, having graduated in 1856 in Baltimore.

I first heard of the assassination of President Lincoln on Saturday afternoon (April 15) about two or three o'clock in the afternoon.

There are two or three physicians besides myself living in that immediate neighborhood. The village in which I live is a very small one, having only some 8 or 10 houses in it.

About 4 o'clock on Saturday morning, the 15th, two persons came to my house and commenced rapping very loudly at the door. I was very much alarmed at this, fearing it might be somebody who had come there not for any good purpose, and hesitated at first about going down. On

*National Archives and Records Administration, Microcopy-599, Roll 5, Frames 227–239.

their knocking very heavily the second time, I aroused my wife, and we conferred with one another a moment as to who should go to the door. She thought she had better go as it might be some one who came there with an evil intent. Knowing her nervous nature, however, I determined it would be better for me to go. I, therefore, concluded to do so. Before opening the door, however, I inquired who was there. They told me two strangers from St. Marys Co. who were on their way to Washington; but that the horse *of* one of them had fallen, and broken the rider's leg. Satisfying myself of the correctness of the statement of one of them having received an injury, by going to a window & seeing one of them in distress, I went and opened the door.

I took them into the parlor, and laid the injured man on the sofa, until I could get a light, when I took him upstairs. His friend urged me to attend to his leg as soon as possible, as they were very anxious to get to Washington; and then it is my impression he enquired (sic) if they could not reach some point on the Potomac where they could get a boat to Washington.

I examined the injured leg, but did not give it a very thorough examination owing to the parties wanting it attended to in such haste. My examination was sufficiently thorough, however, to enable me to discover that there was one bone broken about two inches above the ankle joint—what we call a "direct fracture." In setting the limb, having no splinters, or anything of that sort at hand, I was compelled to cut up an old band-box and use it. I do not remember of their having assigned any reason for their great haste-other than that they had made an early start and were anxious to get to Washington as soon as possible.

As regard the personal appearance *of* these two men, one was a very small one. I should call him a well grown boy. He looked to be about 17 or 18—to be a boy who had never yet shaved. The other was a man of medium size, with black hair. He had whiskers, and also a moustache.

A photograph of Booth was afterwards shown me by a detective, but I did not observe any resemblance between the two men, though I must say that I have very often been shown likenesses of intimate friends, and failed to recognize them by their pictures. The last man I have described had a black streak down the side of his face.

These men remained at my house until 4 & 5 o'clock in the afternoon. I never saw either of the parties before, nor can I conceive who sent them to my house. They themselves gave me no intimation on the subject.

The man whose leg was broken had on a dark suit but I cannot tell whether he had on pants, coat & vest of the same material and color, or not. The injured man had very little to say. He had a heavy shawl which he kept around him; and he seemed to be laboring under considerable nervousness, or pain.

I was at home pretty much all day, and was in the room where they were at short intervals. The reason I took them upstairs was because I had no room downstairs. Including the entry recently built between the house and the kitchen, and the kitchen itself, there are five rooms on the lower floor, which is occupied by myself and wife.

I had very little conversation with these men during the day, though one (the smaller) seemed to be quite communicative, and well acquainted through out the whole neighborhood. Nothing was said by them leading me to infer that they had been engaged in any such deed as this assassination.

The small one also had on a dark suit, with black hair.

After the injured man had got off of his horse, the other one asked me if I could not have the two horses stabled, as one of them would not suffer herself to be hitched. I went after the boy, and he held them until the boy came.

I did not see the parties when they left in the afternoon. The small one said he would not need any one to assist him in putting the injured man on the horse as he had before put him on at the time he broke his leg; so I did not go out. . . .

They requested me to have a pair of crutches made after I set the leg when I got two arm pieces and whittled them out as best I could. I afterwards gave them to the old man who works on the farm to put a stick in.

They paid me $25 for my services, which they rather pressed me to accept. I told them a small fee would answer.

Before they left they inquired the way to the Rev. Wilmer's, an acquaintance of mine, who resides not far from Beantown. His house is about five miles from mine, round the road, and about 4 directly across. I think they took the road across as they inquired for the nearest road. He is regarded by neighbors as a Union man. I have always called myself a Union man, though I have never voted with the administration party. I have never heard any expression from my neighbors as to what they thought of me in that respect.

I do not think any of my neighbors saw these men at my house. I think

I first communicated the fact of these men stopping at my house under these circumstances to Mr. John F. Hardy, and Frances Farrell. It was on Saturday evening when I did so if my memory serves me right.

This injured man had boots on, but whether he had spurs on or not I dismember. I had to cut the boot from the injured limb. This boot he left, and it is now in possession of the military authorities.

The names given by these parties—the young man Henson, and the other Tyson or Tyser. There are some Hansons down in our neighborhood who are regularly called Hensons.

I only saw one of these horses. That one was a small bay mare, with a natural tail as far as I could observe. I did not notice any white scars, or spots about him. This horse was a very lively one.

The older of these men I should judge to be about 30 or 35 years of age.

I first heard of the assassination of President Lincoln at Bryantown.

The injured man after having his leg set seemed to suffer a good deal of pain, and said he did not think he would be able to travel on horseback, and desired to get a carriage, buggy, or something of the sort that he might be enabled to continue his journey. I told him I had nothing of the sort, but that perhaps, he might get an old carriage from my father, and that as I was going to ride out that afternoon, the young man might go over there with me, and see if he could do so. After dinner, the young man ordered the bay mare, and then we rode over to my father's together. We found my father out, but saw my brother who was getting his horse ready to go to the Post Office, or to church. I asked him if he could lend a carriage. He said the carriage he had was old & very much out of repair, and unfit to travel in, any distance. While I was holding this conversation with my brother this young man stood just behind a house in front of the shed where I was engaged in talking.

My brother not being willing to take the responsibility of lending this carriage, the young man said he would go to Bryantown, and endeavor to get a conveyance there. He started off at a pretty fair gallop and I after him. He soon got a good distance ahead of me as his horse was quite a sprightly one, while mine was a very dull one. When he got a mile and a half beyond my father's house, he abruptly turned round and came back, meeting me as he did so. He seemed to be engaged in deep thought. As he passed me he observed, "I believe I will get my friend to go to Rev. Dr. Wilmer's on horseback." He, therefore, did not go to Bryantown—at least with me. My object in going there was to purchase some articles which were needed by the family; and I thought I would at the same time see about some nails that were intended for immediate use. I purchased at Mr. Beans some calico & some pepper, for which I paid him. I got back to the house between 4 & 5 o'clock. The two men were just getting ready to start when I got back. It was about 12 o'clock when we had dinner. One of the men, the young one, ate dinner with me. The other one had his dinner sent to him.

I was not where I could see these men mount their horses at the time of their departure. I was down at the front of my place below the swamp. In describing the way to Rev. Wilmer's I told them that in going across this swamp there would be but one fence to pull down between that place and the barn, which would lead them to the place where they desired to go.

No suspicion was aroused in my mind of anything being wrong with regard to these men. After I had heard of the assassination, and began to have suspicion as to these two men being in some way connected with it, a little circumstance occurred to me as confirmatory of such suspicions & which I had not thought of before. It was this. After breakfast the older one asked for a razor and some soap; which he got; and on my giving him the articles which I had prepared, a short time afterward, I noticed that his moustache had disappeared.

The pantaloons of this man were covered with mud in many places; and the appearance of his clothes would in other respects indicate that he had been riding very rapidly.

I mentioned my suspicion of these men, and the circumstance of the moustache being removed, the next morning to a "brother" physician, a relative of mine, Dr. Geo. Mudd and I think also to Mr. Wm. Mudd and Mr. T. L. Gardiner.

The injured man had a belt with two revolvers in it concealed under his clothing, which I discovered when he got into bed after having his wound dressed. I did not discover whether the other one was armed or not.

DOCUMENT NO. 7

BOOTH'S "DIARY"*

Booth's "Diary," which was actually an appointment book, was found on his body when he was shot and killed in Garrett's barn on April 26, 1865. In the diary Booth described his act and his motives for the murder. This slim volume has remained controversial, partially because it was not introduced at the 1865 conspiracy trials, as well as claims, which are completely erroneous, that there are missing pages which show a government cover-up.

γ γ γ

April 13th 14 Friday the Ides

Until today nothing was ever thought of sacrificing to our country's wrongs. For six months we had worked to capture. But our cause being almost lost, something decisive & great must be done. But its failure was owing to others, who did not strike for their country with a heart. I struck boldly, and not as the papers say. I walked with a firm step through a thousand of his friends, was stopped, but pushed on. A Col- was at his side. I shouted Sic semper before I fired. In jumping broke my leg. I passed all his pickets, rode sixty miles that night with the bone of my leg tearing the flesh at every jump. I can never repent it, though we hated to kill: Our country owed all her troubles to him, and God simply made me the instrument of his punishment. The country is not what it was. This forced Union is not what I have loved. I care not what becomes of me. I have no desire to out-live my country. This night (before the deed), I wrote a long article and left it for one of the Editors of the National Intelligencer, in which I fully set forth our reasons for our proceedings. He or the Govmt

Friday 21-

After being hunted like a dog through swamps, woods, and last night being chased by gunboats till I was forced to return wet cold and starv-

*Original in Ford's Theatre. For modern transcriptions see William Hanchett, "Booth's Diary," *Journal of the Illinois State Historical Society* (February, 1979): 39–56 and John Rhodehamel and Louise Tapers, eds., *"Right or Wrong God Judge Me:" The Writings of John Wilkes Booth* (Urbana: University of Illinois Press, 1997), 154–155.

ing, with every man's hand against me, I am here in despair. And why; For doing what Brutus was honored for, what made Tell a hero. And yet I for striking down a greater tyrant than they ever knew am looked upon as a common cutthroat. My action was purer than either of theirs. One, hoped to be great himself. The other had not only his countrys but his own wrongs to avenge. I hoped for no gain. I knew no private wrong. I struck for my country and that alone. A country groaned beneath this tyranny and prayed for this end. Yet now behold the cold hand they extend to me. God cannot pardon me if I have done wrong. Yet I cannot see my wrong except in serving a degenerate people. The little, the very little I left behind to clear my name, the Govmt will not allow to be printed. So ends all. For my country I have given up all that makes life sweet and Holy, brought misery upon my family, and am sure there is no pardon in the Heaven for me, since man condemns me so. I have only heard of what has been done (except what I did myself) and it fills me with horror. God, try and forgive me, and bless my mother. To night I will once more try the river with the intent to cross, though I have a greater desire and almost a mind to return to Washington and in a measure clear my name which I feel I can do. I do not repent the blow I struck. I may before my God but not to man.

I think I have done well, though I am abandoned, with the curse of Cain upon me. When if the world knew my heart, that one blow would have made me great, though I did desire no greatness.

To night I try to escape these bloodhounds once more. Who who can read his fate. God's will be done.

I have too great a soul to die like a criminal. Oh may he, may he spare me that, and let me die bravely.

I bless the entire world. Have never hated or wronged anyone. This last was not a wrong, unless God deems it so. And its with him, to damn or bless me. As for this brave boy with me, who often prays (yes before and since) with a true and sincere heart, was it crime in him if so why can he pray the same I do not wish to shed a drop of blood, but "I must fight the course." Tis all that's left to me.

DOCUMENT NO. 8

EXAMINATION OF CHARLES M. COLLINS, APRIL 27, 1865*

This examination of Charles M. Collins, on board the Monitor Montauk, *April 27, 1865, was an attempt to positively identify the person killed in Garrett's barn as John Wilkes Booth.*

γ γ γ

Examination of *Charles M. Collins*, taken by Hon. John A. Bingham, Special Judge Advocate, United States Army, on board the Monitor "Montauk." Washington, D.C. April 27th, 1865.

Question.__What is your name and what your occupation?

Answer.__My name is Charles M. Collins. I am Captain's Clerk and Signal Officer on board the "Montauk."

Question.__Are you personally acquainted with J. Wilkes Booth, and how long have you known him?

Answer.__I have known him personally about six weeks. I have known him by sight since 1862.

Question.__State if you have examined the dead body lying on the deck of this vessel?

Answer.__I have.

Question.__State whether in your judgment or opinion, it is the body of J. Wilkes Booth?

Answer.__I have not the least doubt that it is the body of J. Wilkes Booth.

Question.__State whether you judge it to be his body from the general appearance of the countenance, or from any particular marks?

*National Archives and Records Administration, Microcopy-599, Roll 4, Frames 351–352.

Answer.__From the general appearance, having been well acquainted with him. I notice no particular marks.

Question.__State when you last saw J. Wilkes Booth in life, where and what he said, if anything?

Answer.__I met him at the National Hotel, at the office, about half past six o'clock, April 14th, 1865. He bade me good evening. I returned the compliment, shook hands with him, and asked him where he had been. His answer was that he

(Last page missing from the record)

DOCUMENT NO. 9

EXAMINATION OF CHARLES DAWSON, APRIL 27, 1865*

This examination of Charles Dawson on board the Montauk, *April 27, 1865, was an attempt to identify the person killed in Garrett's barn as John Wilkes Booth.*

γ γ γ

Examination of *Charles Dawson*, taken by Brigadier General Joseph Holt, Judge Advocate General, United States Army, on board the Monitor "Montauk." Washington, D.C. April 27th, 1865.

Question.__What is your name, and what your occupation?

Answer.__My name is Charles Dawson. I am clerk in the National Hotel, Washington, and have charge of the office of that establishment.

Question.__Will you state if you are acquainted with J. Wilkes Booth and how intimately?

Answer.__I have been acquainted with him since October, 1863—merely as intimately as I would be with any guest in the hotel.

Question.__Have you just examined the dead body, which is claimed to be that of J. Wilkes Booth, on board of this vessel?

Answer.__I have.

Question.__Will you state whether or not in your judgment it is the body of J. Wilkes Booth?

Answer.__I distinctly recognize it as the body of J. Wilkes Booth—first, from the India-ink letters: "J.W.B." on his wrist, which I have very frequently noticed, and then by a scar on the neck. I also recognize the vest as that of J. Wilkes Booth.

Question.__On which hand or wrist are the India-ink initials referred to.

Answer.__On the left.

*National Archives and Records Administration, Microcopy-599, Roll 4, Frames 354–355.

DOCUMENT NO. 10

EXAMINATION OF SEATON MUNROE, APRIL 27, 1865*

The examination of Seaton Munroe on board the Montauk, *April 27, 1865, was an attempt to identify the person killed in Garrett's barn as John Wilkes Booth.*

γ γ γ

Examination of *Seaton Munroe*, taken by Brigadier General Joseph Holt, Judge Advocate General, United States Army, on board the Monitor "Montauk." Washington, D.C. April 27th 1865

Question._What is your name and what your occupation?

Answer._My name is Seaton Munroe and I am an Attorney-at-law in Washington.

Question._Will you state whether you knew J. Wilkes Booth, how long you have known him and how intimately?

Answer._I have known him by sight for over two or three years. About two months ago I met him one evening at a "bar" at the National Hotel, in this city, was introduced to him, and conversed with him a short time. I never have been intimate with him, nor knew him more than that. I am very familiar with his face and distinctly recognize it.

Question._Have you examined carefully the dead body claimed to be that of J. Wilkes Booth and now on board of this vessel?

Answer._Only by close inspection of the features several times this morning.

Question._What is your opinion as to it being the dead body of J. Wilkes Booth?

Answer._I am confident that it is the dead body of J. Wilkes Booth.

*National Archives and Records Administration, Microcopy-599, Roll 4, Frames 357–359.

Question.__Are there any special marks which enable you to recognize it?

Answer.__I recognize it only from the general appearance, in which I do not think I can be mistaken.

DOCUMENT NO. 11

EXAMINATION OF JOHN FREDERICK MAY, APRIL 27, 1865*

The examination of John Frederick May on board the Montauk, *April 27, 1865, was an attempt to identify the person killed in Garrett's barn as John Wilkes Booth.*

γ γ γ

Examination of *John Frederick May*, taken by Brigadier General Joseph Holt, Judge Advocate General, United States Army, on board the Monitor "Montauk." Washington, D.C. April 27th, 1865.

Question.__What is your name and what your occupation?

Answer.__My name is John Frederick May. I am a physician, residing in this city.

Question.__Were you acquainted with J. Wilkes Booth, if so, how long and under what circumstances?

Answer.__I was acquainted with him. I cannot with exactness give the date but, I should say eighteen months or two years ago. I could specify the time by reference to my books. He came to my house about that time and desired me to cut a tumor from the back of his neck. He was then playing an engagement, and desired to know if the removal would prevent him from fulfilling that engagement. I told him if he would be careful not to make any violent efforts, he would not. He then agreed to have the operation performed. I took the tumor out, and united the wound very closely. The union was a very close one. Booth played his engagement, and came regularly to my office for some two weeks afterwards to have the wound dressed. He came some four or five days after the wound had united, with it all torn open, stating that in some part of a play, in which he said Miss Cushman (who he remarked was a stong, powerful woman,) for a part, she had either to throw her arms around his neck or to strike him—perhaps to strike him a blow; and

*National Archives and Records Administration, Microcopy-599, Roll 4, Frames 361–365.

that she struck him on the tender cicatrix, tearing it completely open, and making a gaping wound, which had to fill up by the process of granulation. I told the Surgeon General these facts this morning, before I looked at the cicatrix at all, and said that he would probably find a large ugly looking scar, instead of a neat line. He said it corresponded exactly with my description. The scar looks as much like the effect of a burn as the cicatrix from a surgical operation.

Question.__Have you, since you came on board this vessel, examined the dead body which is alleged to be that of J. Wilkes Booth?

Answer.__I have Sir.

Question.__Will you state whether, in your opinion, it is the body of J. Wilkes Booth?

Answer.__I believe it to be sir; I have no doubt that it is. I believe I have only seen Booth once since the time to which I have referred.

Question.__Do you recognize the body as that of J. Wilkes Booth from its general appearance, and also from the particular appearance of the scar?

Answer.__I do recognize it, though it is very much altered since I saw Booth. It looks to me much older, and in appearance much more freckled than he was. I do not recollect that he was at all freckled. I have no doubt it is his body. I recognize the features. When he came to my office, he had no beard excepting a moustache.

Question.__From the nature of this wound, even apart from the general appearance, you could not be mistaken as to the identity of the body?

Answer.__From the scar, also in connection with the recognition of the features, which though much changed and altered, still have the same appearance, I think I cannot be mistaken. I recognize the likeness. I have no doubt that it is the person from whom I took the tumor, and that it is the body of J. Wilkes Booth.

DOCUMENT NO. 12

EXAMINATION OF WILLIAM WALLACH CROWNINSHIELD, APRIL 27, 1865*

The examination of William Wallach Crowninshield, on board the Montauk, *April 27, 1865, was an attempt to identify the person killed in Garett's barn as John Wilkes Booth.*

γ γ γ

Examination of Acting Master *William Wallach Crowninshield,* taken by Brigadier General Joseph Holt, Judge Advocate General, United States Army, on board the Monitor "Montauk." Washington, D.C. April 27th, 1865.

Question.__What is your name, and what your occupation?

Answer.__My name is William Wallach Crowninshield, and I am Acting Master in the United States Navy.

Question.__Are you acquainted with J. Wilkes Booth?

Answer.__Yes Sir.

Question.__How long have you known him?

Answer.__About a month and a half. I have been introduced to him on two different occasions.

Question.__Have you a distinct knowledge of his features and personal appearance?

Answer.__In figure he was a man not quite so high as myself. He was about five feet nine and three-quarters inches high, and was what I should call a very genteel and graceful figure.

Question.__Have you any knowledge of his appearance. of his features?

Answer.__Yes Sir.

*National Archives and Records Administration, Microcopy-599, Roll 4, Frames 367–369.

Question.__Have you examined the dead body on board of this vessel, which is alleged to be that of J. Wilkes Booth?

Answer.__I have sir.

Question.__What is your opinion as to whether or not it is his body?

Answer.__I feel satisfied that it is the body of J. Wilkes Booth.

Question.__Are there any special marks which enable you so to declare, or do you form your opinion from your knowledge of his general appearance?

Answer.__From my knowledge of his general appearance.

Question.__Have you seen him frequently?

Answer.__Yes Sir.

Question.__Do you feel you cannot be mistaken?

Answer.__I cannot be mistaken.

DOCUMENT NO. 13

TESTIMONY OF MAJOR H. W. SMITH, MAY 19, 1865*

Testimony of Major H. W. Smith given on May 19, 1865, and compiled by court stenographer Benn Pitman. Smith who arrived with other officers to arrest Mrs. Surratt described the arrival of Lewis Powell at her doorstep, as she was about to be arrested, and her denials that she knew him. Defenders have blamed her age, poor eyesight, and poor lighting, for her failure to recognize a man who had boarded at her home. Critics have found her reactions to be as suspicious as Mudd's alleged failure to recognize Booth.

γ γ γ

MAJOR H. W. SMITH.

For the Prosecution.—May 19.

I was in charge of the party that took possession of Mrs. Surratt's house, 541 H Street, on the night of the 17th of April, and arrested Mrs. Surratt, Miss Surratt, Miss Fitzpatrick, and Miss Jenkins. When I went up the steps, and rang the bell of the house, Mrs. Surratt came to the window, and said "Is that you, Mr. Kirby?" The reply was that it was not Mr. Kirby, and to open the door. She opened the door, and I asked, "Are you Mrs. Surratt?" She said, "I am the widow of John H. Surratt." And I added, "The mother of John H. Surratt, jr.?" She replied, "I am." I then said, "I come to arrest you and all in your house, and take you for examination to General Augur's head-quarters." No inquiry whatever was made as to the cause of the arrest. While we were there, Payne came to the house. I questioned him in regard to his occupation, and what business he had at the house that time of night. He stated that he was a laborer, and had come there to dig a gutter at the request of Mrs. Surratt. I went to the parlor door, and said, "Mrs. Surratt, will you step

*Benn Pitman, *The Assassination of President Lincoln and the Trials of the Conspirators*, (New York: Moore, Wilstach and Baldwin, 1865), reprinted in a facsimile edition with an introduction by Philip Van Doren Stern (New York: Funk and Wagnalls, 1954), 121–122.

here a minute?" She came out, and I asked her, "Do you know this man, and did you hire him to come and dig a gutter for you?" She answered, raising her right hand, "Before God, sir, I do not know this man, and have never seen him, and I did not hire him to dig a gutter for me." Payne said nothing. I then placed him under arrest, and told him he was so suspicious a character that I should send him to Colonel Wells, at General Augur's headquarters, for further examination. Payne was standing in full view of Mrs. Surratt, and within three paces of her, when she denied knowing him.

Cross-examined by Mr. AIKEN.

A variety of photographs were found in a photograph-album and in various parts of Mrs. Surratt's house.

Payne was dressed that night in a gray coat, black pantaloons, and rather a fine pair of boots. He had on his head a gray shirt sleeve, hanging over at the side. His pantaloons were rolled up over the tops of his boots; on one leg only, I believe.

I have known some loyal people who had in their possession photographs of the leaders of the rebellion. I can not say that I have seen on exhibition at bookstores, or advertised by newspaper dealers and keepers of photographs, cartes-de-visite of the leaders of the rebellion. I have seen photographs of Booth, but only since this trial.

Re-examined by the JUDGE ADVOCATE.
[Joseph Holt, Judge Advocate General].

Payne was dressed at the time in a gray coat and black pantaloons.

[Exhibiting to the witness a brown and white mixed coat.]

That is the coat Payne wore, to the best of my belief.

By MR. DOSTER.
(William E. Doster, Defense Counsel for George Atzerodt and Lewis Powell).

I am certain that this is the coat; I remember it by its color and general look. As near as I could judge by the light that was in the hall at the time, that was the coat.

[Submitting to the witness a dark gray coat.]

The coat now shown me is the one worn by Payne on the night of his arrest. I recognize it by the buttons. All that was wanting in the other coat was the buttons, but it was difficult in the light in which I was standing to tell. The coat just shown me is the one.

[The gray coat was offered in evidence.]

By MR. AIKEN.

I think, if I saw a gentleman dressed in black, with a white neck-cloth, representing himself as a Baptist preacher, and two months afterward I met the same person, with a shirt-sleeve on his head, an old gray coat, his pantaloons stuffed into his boots, with a pickaxe on his shoulder, presenting himself as a laborer, and in the night-time, I think that, were I very familiar with his countenance, I should recognize him as the same person.

DOCUMENT NO. 14

REPORT OF LIEUTENANT ALEXANDER LOVETT TO MAJOR JAMES O'BEIRNE, APRIL 29, 1865*

This report of Lieutenant Alexander Lovett was made to Major James R. O'Beirne, April 29, 1865. In this report Lieutenant Lovett detailed his role in the arrest of Dr. Samuel Mudd.

γ γ γ

Washington DC, April 29, 1865.
Major James R. O'Beirne
Provost marshal DC

Major

I have the honor to submit the following report of service in pursuit and detection of the assassin of the President, and persons implicated in the assassination.

In accordance with your order I started on the night of Monday the 17th inst. with officers Simon Gavacan and William Williams and 9 mounted men of Provisional Cavalry and proceeded to Surattsville (*sic*) Prince Georges Co. Md. for the purpose of arresting any parties implicated in the late assassination. At this place we were joined by Officers Lloyd and Cottingham, left the latter at Surattsville (*sic*) and proceeded toward Newport Tuesday morning the 18th. Having ascertained that John M. Lloyd a resident in the vicinity, was suspected of being in complicity with the assassination, I arranged his arrest which was accomplished on Tuesday P.M. on the road between Newport and T. B. about 2 miles beyond the latter place. After his arrest, he made a partial confession to me in private of his implication in the crime, stating that he knew the whole party and to save himself would "come out" on all of them, and that though he supposed he might be hung, he would not hesitate to tell all he knew of the affair. He said he was acquainted with Booth and Harrold (sic), who had frequently visited his home before the

*National Archives and Records Administration, Microcopy-619, Roll 456, Frames 0488–0490.

murder, and had had their arms concealed in his (house) for a week or ten days before it was committed.

On Friday morning the 14th inst. Mrs. Sarrat (*sic*) called at his house and told him that the party engaged in the plot would be along that night requesting him to furnish them with the arms (secreted) with him. Booth and Harrold (*sic*) came along and stopped at his house between 12 and 1 o'clock that night and took the arms secreted there with him, with the exception of one piece a seven shooter carbine which Booth could not carry on account of sickness resulting from a fractured leg. His confession was much confused as he was very agitated and frightened and cried most of the time. He was left in confinement at Roby's P. O. under charge of Officer Cottingham.

We then proceeded on Wednesday the 19th to Bryantown where we obtained information which led us to suppose that Booth had his leg dressed by Dr. Samuel Mudd who resided about 4 1/2 miles distant. We started for his residence where we arrested the said Dr. Mudd. He stated that two men came to his house about daybreak on Saturday morning, April 15th, one mounted on a bay horse, and the other on a roan. One of them was assisted into his house, and requested to have his leg set, which he said had been broken by his horse falling upon him. Booth seemed very much excited and declined any further explanation of the accident. After the operation of setting the leg, the patient asked for a razor and soap and water with which he shaved off his moustache. He then asked if he could obtain a buggy anywhere in the neighborhood. Dr. Mudd tried to get a buggy from his father, but did not suceed (sic). They remained until about 3 or 4 o'clock P. M. during which time he had a pair of crutches made for the injured man. When he was helped upon his horse and in company with his accomplice was piloted through the swamp by Dr. Mudd himself. The doctor said he left them after passing through the swamp and that was the last he saw of them. Before being asked if he knew Booth, he at first denied that he did, but afterwards acknowledged that he did, having been around the neighborhood with him last fall, and in introducing to different parties, that he was with him when he purchased a horse from Squire Gardiner and that he was satisfied the injured man was Booth when he set his leg. I obtained a boot which was cut from Booth's foot in order to set his leg. Inside was the name "J. Wilkes." I took the prisoner to Bryantown and turned him over to Col. Wells commanding at that place.

I am Major Very

Respectfully

your obt. Sevt.

Alexander Lovett (signed)

1st Lt. 14th Co. 2 Bat. VRC

DOCUMENT NO. 15

TESTIMONY OF JOHN M. LLOYD, MAY 13, 1865*

Testimony of John M. Lloyd, given on May 13, 1865 and compiled by court stenographer Benn Pitman. Lloyd was one of the most damaging witnesses against Mrs. Surratt, with his assertions that she carried a set of field glasses for Booth to the tavern which he operated in Surrattsville as well as his claim that she asked him to have the "shooting irons" ready as there would be parties to call for them. Booth and Herold stopped at the tavern during their flight through the Maryland countryside.

γ γ γ

JOHN M. LLOYD.

For the Prosecution.—May 13.

I reside at Mrs. Surratt's tavern, Surrattsville, and am engaged in hotel-keeping and farming. Some five or six weeks before the assassination of the President, John H. Surratt, David E. Herold, and G. A. Atzerodt came to my house. Atzerodt and Surratt drove up to my house in the morning first, and went toward T. B., a post-office about five miles below there. They had not been gone more than half an hour, when they returned with Herold. All three, when they came into the bar-room, drank, I think. John Surratt then called me into the front parlor, and on the sofa were two carbines, with ammunition; also a rope from sixteen to twenty feet in length, and a monkey-wrench. Surratt asked me to take care of these things, and to conceal the carbines. I told him there was no place to conceal them, and I did not wish to keep such things. He then took me to a room I had never been in, immediately above the store-room, in the back part of the building. He showed me where I could put them underneath the joists of the second floor of the main building. I put them in there according to his directions.

I stated to Colonel Wells that Surratt put them there, but I carried

*Benn Pitman, *The Assassination of President Lincoln and the Trial of the Conspirators* (New York: Moore, Wilstach and Baldwin, 1865), reprinted in a facsimile version with an introduction by Philip Van Doren Stern (New York: Funk and Wagnalls, 1954), 85–87.

the arms up and put them in there myself. There was also one cartridge-box of ammunition. Surratt said he just wanted these articles to stay for a few days, and he would call for them. On the Tuesday before the assassination of the President, I was coming to Washington, and I met Mrs. Surratt, on the road, at Uniontown. When she first broached the subject to me about the articles at my place, I did not know what she had reference to. Then she came out plainer, and asked me about the "shooting-irons." I had myself forgotten about them being there. I told her they were hid away far back, and that I was afraid the house might be searched. She told me to get them out ready; that they would be wanted soon. I do not recollect distinctly the first question she put to me. Her language was indistinct, as if she wanted to draw my attention to something, so that no one else would understand. Finally she came out bolder with it, and said they would be wanted soon. I told her that I had an idea of having them buried; that I was very uneasy about having them there.

On the 14th of April I went to Marlboro to attend a trial there; and in the evening, when I got home, which I should judge was about 5 o'clock, I found Mrs. Surratt there. She met me out by the wood-pile as I drove in with some fish and oysters in my buggy. She told me to have those shooting-irons ready that night, there would be some parties who would call for them. She gave me something wrapped in a piece of paper, which I took up stairs, and found to be a field-glass. She told me to get two bottles of whisky ready, and that these things were to be called for that night.

Just about midnight on Friday, Herold came into the house and said, "Lloyd, for God's sake, make haste and get those things." I did not make any reply, but went straight and got the carbines, supposing they were the parties Mrs. Surratt had referred to, though she didn't mention any names. From the way he spoke he must have been apprised that I already knew what I was to give him. Mrs. Surratt told me to give the carbines, whisky, and field-glass. I did not give them the rope and monkey-wrench. Booth didn't come in. I did not know him; he was a stranger to me. He remained on his horse. Herold, I think, drank some out of the glass before he went out.

I do not think they remained over five minutes. They only took one of the carbines. Booth said he could not take his, because his leg was broken.

Just as they were about leaving, the man who was with Herold said,

"I will tell you some news, if you want to hear it," or something to that effect. I said, "I am not particular; use your own pleasure about telling it." "Well, said he, "I am pretty certain that we have assassinated the President and Secretary Seward." I think that was his language, as well as I can recollect. Whether Herold was present at the time he said that, or whether he was across the street, I am not positive; I was much excited and unnerved at the time.

The moon was shining when the men came. The man whose leg was broken was on a light-colored horse; I supposed it to be a gray horse, in the moonlight. It was a large horse, I suppose some sixteen hands high; the other, ridden by Herold, was a bay, and not so large.

Between 8 and 9 o'clock the next morning the news was received of the assassination of the President, and I think the name of Booth was spoken of as the assassin.

I have heard Atzerodt called by the nickname of "Port Tobacco." I used to call him "Miserable." And then I called him, for a long time, "Stranger." I do not think I had been acquainted with him over two months before the assassination.

[Two carbines, Spencer rifles, were exhibited to the witness.]

The carbines were brought in covers. The cover that is on this one looks like the cover in which it was brought to me. I took the cover off one, and the peculiar kind of breech attracted my attention, never having seen one like it before. They look like the carbines that were brought to my place.

Cross-examined by MR. AIKEN.

[Frederick Aiken, Defense Counsel for Mary Surratt]

I rented Mrs. Surratt's house at Surrattsville, about the first of December last, and Mrs. Surratt frequently came there after that. When I met Mrs. Surratt on the Tuesday preceding the assassination, I was coming to Washington, and she was going to my place, I supposed. I stopped, and so did she. I then got out and went to her buggy. It had been raining, and was very muddy. I do not know that the word "carbine" was mentioned. She spoke about those shooting-irons. It was a very quick and hasty conversation. I am confident that she named the shooting-irons on both occasions; not so positive about the first as I am about the last; I know she did on the last occasion. On the Friday I do not think Mrs. Surratt was there over ten minutes.

When I first drove up to the wood-yard, Mrs. Surratt came out to where I was. The first thing she said to me was, "Talk about the devil, and his imps will appear," or something to that effect. I said, "I was not aware that I was a devil before." "Well," said she, "Mr. Lloyd, I want you to have those shooting-irons ready; there will be parties here to-night who will call for them." At the same time she gave me something wrapped up in a newspaper, which I did not undo until I got up stairs.

The conversation I had with Mrs. Surratt about the shooting-irons was while I was carrying the fish and oysters into the house. Mrs. Surratt then requested me to fix her buggy for her. The front spring bolts were broken; the spring had become detached from the axle. I tied them with some cord; that was the only fixing I could give them. Mrs. Offutt, my sister-in-law, was, I believe, in the yard; but whether she heard the conversation or not, I do not know.

The first information I gave of this occurrence was to Lieutenant Lovett and Captain Cottingham, some time about the middle of the week; but I did not detail all the circumstances. I told these officers that it was through the Surratts that I had got myself into the difficulty. If they had never brought me on there, I never would have got myself into difficulty or words to that effect; and I gave full information of the particulars to Colonel Wells, on the Saturday week following.

When Booth and Herold left my house, they took the road toward T. B. Herold came up toward the stable between me and the other man, who was on the light-colored horse, and they rode off at a pretty rapid gait. When Herold brought back the bottle from which Booth had drank the whisky, he remarked to me, "I owe you a couple of dollars;" and said he, "Here." With that he offered me a note, which next morning I found to be one dollar, which just about paid for the bottle of liquor they had just pretty nearly drank.

I think I told Mrs. Offutt, after Mrs. Surratt went away, that it was a field-glass she had brought. She did not tell me that Mrs. Surratt gave her a package.

DOCUMENT NO. 16

EXCERPT FROM THE TESTIMONY OF LOUIS J. WEICHMANN, MAY 13, 1865*

The testimony of Louis J. Weichmann was given on May 13, 1865 and compiled by court stenographer, Benn Pitman. The testimony of Weichmann, who was one of her boarders, was also very damaging to Mrs. Surratt. He portrayed the boarding house as a meeting place for the conspirators and described private conversations between Booth and both Mary and John Surratt. His revelations that he was present at meetings between Dr. Mudd, John Surratt and Booth, were equally devastating for the doctor. There have been persistent allegations that Weichmann might have been one of the plotters, and that he turned state's evidence to save himself.

γ γ γ

LOUIS J. WEICHMANN.

For the Prosecution.—May 13.

I have been a clerk in the office of General Hoffman, Commissary-General of prisoners, since January 9, 1864.

My acquaintance with John H. Surratt commenced in the fall of 1859, at St. Charles College, Maryland. We left college together in the summer of 1862, and I renewed my acquaintance with him in January, 1863, in this city. On the 1st of November, 1864, I went to board at the house of his mother, Mrs. Surratt, the prisoner, No. 541 H Street between Sixth and Seventh, and boarded there up to the time of the assassination.

On the 2d of April, Mrs. Surratt asked me to see J. Wilkes Booth, and say that she wished to see him on "private business." I conveyed the message, and Booth said he would come to the house in the evening, as soon as he could; and he came.

On the Tuesday previous to the Friday of the assassination, I was sent by Mrs. Surratt to the National Hotel to see Booth, for the purpose of

*Benn Pitman, *The Assassination of President Lincoln and the Trial of the Conspirators* (New York: Moore, Wilstach and Baldwin, 1865), reprinted in a facsimile version with an introduction by Philip Van Doren Stern (New York: Funk and Wagnalls, 1954), 113–119.

getting his buggy. She wished me to drive her into the country on that day. Booth said that he had sold his buggy, but that he would give me $10 instead, that I might hire one. He gave me the $10, and I drove Mrs. Surratt to Surrattsville on that day, leaving this city about 9 and reaching Surrattsville about half-past 12 o'clock. We remained at Surrattsville half an hour, or probably not so long. Mrs. Surratt stated that she went there for the purpose of seeing Mr. Nothe, who owed her some money.

On Friday, the day of the assassination, I went to Howard's stable, about half-past 2 o'clock, having been sent there by Mrs. Surratt for the purpose of hiring a buggy. She herself gave me the money on that occasion, a ten-dollar note, and I paid $6 for the buggy. I drove her to Surrattsville the same day, arriving there about half-past 4. We stopped at the house of Mr. Lloyd, who keeps a tavern there. Mrs. Surratt went into the parlor. I remained outside a portion of the time, and went into the bar-room a part of the time, until Mrs. Surratt sent for me. We left about half-past 6. Surrattsville is about a two-hours' drive to the city, and is about ten miles from the Navy Yard bridge.

Just before leaving the city, as I was going to the door, I saw Mr. Booth in the parlor, and Mrs. Surratt was speaking with him. They were alone. He did not remain in the parlor more than three or four minutes; and immediately after he left, Mrs. Surratt and I started.

I saw the prisoner, Atzerodt, at Howard's stable, when I went to hire the buggy that afternoon. I asked him what he wanted, and he said he was going to hire a horse, but Brook Stabler told him he could not have one.

I remember going with John H. Surratt to the Herndon House, about the 19th of March, for the purpose of renting a room. He inquired for Mrs. Mary Murray, who kept the house; and when she came, Surratt said that he wished to have a private interview with her. She did not seem to comprehend; when he said, "Perhaps Miss Anna Ward has spoken to you about this room. Did she not speak to you about engaging a room for a delicate gentleman, who was to have his meals sent up to his room?" Then Mrs. Murray recollected, and Mr. Surratt said he would like to have the room the following Monday, I think, the 27th of March, when the gentleman would take possession of it. No name was mentioned. I afterward heard that the prisoner, Payne, was at the Herndon House. One day I met Atzerodt on the street, and asked him where he was going. He said he was going to see Payne. I then asked, "Is it Payne who is at the Herndon House?" He said, "Yes." That was after the visit John H. Surratt had made to engage the room. . . .

Surratt returned from Richmond on the 3d of April, the day the news of the fall of Richmond was received. I had some conversation with him about the fall of Richmond and he seemed incredulous. He told me he did not believe it; that he had seen Benjamin and Davis in Richmond, and they had told him that Richmond would not be evacuated.

Surratt only remained in the house about an hour, when he told me he was going to Montreal, and asked me to walk down the street with him and take some oysters. He left that evening, saying he was going to Montreal, and I have not seen him since.

I saw nine or eleven $20 gold pieces in his possession, and $50 in greenbacks, when he came back from Richmond; and just before leaving for Canada, he exchanged $40 of gold for $60 in greenbacks, with Mr. Holahan.

I afterward learned in Montreal that Surratt arrived there on the 6th of April, and left on the 12th for the States; returned on the 18th, and engaged rooms at the St. Lawrence Hall, and left again that night, and was seen to leave the house of a Mr. Porterfield, in company with three others, in a wagon. I arrived at Montreal on the 19th, and my knowledge was derived from the register of St. Lawrence Hall.

I saw a letter from John Surratt to his mother, dated St. Lawrence Hall, Montreal, April 12th, which was received here on the 14th; I also saw another letter from him in Canada to Miss Ward, but that was prior to the letter to his mother.

About the 15th of January last I was passing down Seventh Street, in company with John H. Surratt, and when opposite Odd Fellows' Hall, some one called "Surratt, Surratt;" and turning round, he recognized an old acquaintance of his, Dr. Samuel A. Mudd, of Charles County, Md.; the gentleman there [pointing to the accused, Samuel A. Mudd.] He and John Wilkes Booth were walking together. Surratt introduced Dr. Mudd to me, and Dr. Mudd introduced Booth to both of us. They were coming down Seventh Street, and we were going up. Booth invited us to his room at the National Hotel. When we arrived there, he told us to be seated, and ordered cigars and wines for four. Dr. Mudd then went out into a passage and called Booth out, and had a private conversation with him. When they returned, Booth called Surratt, and all three went out together and had a private conversation, leaving me alone. I did not hear the conversation; I was seated on a lounge near the window. On returning to the room the last time Dr. Mudd apologized to me for his private conversation, and stated that Booth and he had some private business; that Booth wished to purchase his farm, but that he did not care about selling, as Booth was not willing to give him enough. Booth also apologized, and stated to me that he wished to purchase Dr. Mudd's farm. Afterward they were seated round the center-table, when Booth took out an envelope, and on the back of it made marks with a pencil. I should not consider it writing, but from the motion of the pencil it was more like roads or lines.

After this interview at the National Hotel Booth called at Mrs. Surratt's frequently, generally asking for Mr. John H. Surratt, and in his absence for Mrs. Surratt. Their interviews were always apart from other persons. I have been in the parlor in company with Booth, when Booth has taken Surratt up stairs to engage in private conversation. Sometimes, when engaged in general conversation, Booth would say, "John, can you go up stairs and spare me a word?" They would then go up stairs and engage in private conversation, which would sometimes last two or three hours. The same thing would sometimes occur with Mrs. Surratt.

When I saw Booth at the National Hotel on the Tuesday previous to the assassination, to obtain his buggy for Mrs. Surratt, he spoke about the horses that he kept at Howard's stable, and I remarked, "Why, I thought they were Surratt's horses." He said, "No, they are mine."

John H. Surratt had stated to me that he had two horses, which he kept at Howard's stable, on G Street.

Some time in March last, I think, a man calling himself Wood came to Mrs. Surratt's and inquired for John H. Surratt. I went to the door and told him Mr. Surratt was not at home; he thereupon expressed a desire to see Mrs. Surratt, and I introduced him, having first asked his name. That is the man [pointing to Lewis Payne, one of the accused.] He stopped at the house all night. He had supper served up to him in my room; I took it to him from the kitchen. He brought no baggage; he had a black overcoat on, a black dress-coat, and gray pants. He remained till the next morning, leaving by the earliest train for Baltimore. About three weeks afterward he called again, and I again went to the door. I had forgotten his name, and, asking him, he gave the name of Payne. I ushered him into the parlor, where were Mrs. Surratt, Miss Surratt, and Miss Honora Fitzpatrick. He remained three days that time. He represented himself as a Baptist preacher; and said that he had been in prison for about a week; that he had taken the oath of allegiance, and was now going to become a good and loyal citizen. . . .

I met the prisoner, David E. Herold, at Mrs. Surratt's on one occasion; I also met him when we visited the theater when Booth played Pescara; and I met him at Mrs. Surratt's, in the country, in the spring of 1863, when I first made Mrs. Surratt's acquaintance. I met him again in the summer of 1864, at Piscataway Church. These are the only times, to my recollection, I ever met him. I do not know either of the prisoners, Arnold or O'Laughlin. I recognize the prisoner Atzerodt. He first came to Mrs. Surratt's house, as near as I can remember, about three weeks after I formed the acquaintance of Booth, and inquired for John H. Surratt, or Mrs. Surratt, as he said. Since then he must have been at the house ten or fifteen times. The young ladies of the house, not comprehending the name that he gave, and understanding that he came from Port Tobacco, in the lower portion of Maryland, gave him the nickname of "Port Tobacco." I never saw him in the house with Booth.

At the time Booth played the part of Pescara, in the "Apostate," he gave Surratt two complimentary tickets, and as Surratt and I were going to the theater, we met Atzerodt at the corner of Seventh Street and Pennsylvania Avenue, and told him where we were going. He said he was going there, too; and at the theater we met David E. Herold [pointing to the accused, David E. Herold, who smiled and nodded in recognition.] We also met Mr. Holahan, who boarded at Mrs. Surratt's.

After the play was over, all five of us left the theater together—Mr. Surratt, Holahan, and myself, in company. We went as far as the corner of Tenth and E Streets, when Surratt, turning round, noticed that Atzerodt and Herold were not following, and desired me to go after them. When I went back, I found Atzerodt and Herold in the restaurant adjoining the theater, talking confidentially with Booth. On my approach they separated, and Booth said, "Mr. Weichmann, will you not come and take a drink?" which I did. We then left the restaurant, and joined the other two gentlemen on E Street; went to Kloman's and had some oysters; after that we separated—Surratt, Holahan, and myself going home, and the others going down Seventh Street.

Cross-examined by HON. REVERDY JOHNSON.
(Defense Counsel for Mary Surratt).

When I went to board with Mrs. Surratt, in November, 1864, she rented her farm at Surrattsville to Mr. Lloyd, and removed to this city. Her house is on H Street, and contains eight rooms—six large and two small. Mrs. Surratt rented her rooms and furnished board. Persons were in the habit of coming from the country and stopping at her house. Mrs. Surratt was always very hospitable, and had a great many acquaintances, and they could remain as long as they chose. During the whole time I have known her, her character, as far as I could judge, was exemplary and lady-like in every particular; and her conduct, in a religious and moral sense, altogether exemplary. She was a member of the Catholic Church, and a regular attendant on its services. I generally accompanied her to church on Sunday. She went to her religious duties at least every two weeks, sometimes early in the morning and sometimes at late mass, and was apparently doing all her duties to God and man up to the time of the assassination. I visited Mrs. Surratt several times during '63 and '64 while she lived in the country. I made her acquaintance through her son, who had been a college mate of mine for three years. . . .

He never intimated to me, nor to any one else to my knowledge, that there was a purpose to assassinate the President. He stated to me, in the presence of his sister, shortly after he made the acquaintance of Booth, that he was going to Europe on a cotton speculation; that $3,000 had been advanced to him by an elderly gentleman, whose name he did not mention, residing somewhere in the neighborhood; that he would go to Liverpool, and remain there probably only two weeks to transact his business; then would go to Nassau; from Nassau to Matamoras, Mexico, and find his brother Isaac, who had been in Magruder's army in Texas since 1861. . . .

On the occasion of Mrs. Surratt's visit to Surrattsville, on the 11th of April, she told me she had business with Mr. Nothe; that he owed her a sum of money, $479, and the interest on it, for thirteen years. On arriving there, about half-past 12, she told Mr. Nott, the bar-keeper, to send a messenger immediately to Mr. Nothe. In the mean time, Mrs. Surratt and myself went to Captain Gwynn's place, three miles lower down, took dinner there, and remained about two hours. At Mrs. Surratt's desire, Captain Gwynn returned with us to Lloyd's. When we arrived there, Mr. Nott said that Mr. Nothe was in the parlor. They went in and transacted their business; but I did not go in, and did not see Mr. Nothe.

Mrs. Surratt's second visit to Surrattsville was on the afternoon of the 14th of April. She rapped at my room-door on that afternoon, and told me she had received a letter from Mr. Charles Calvert in regard to that money that Mr. Nothe owed her, and that she was again compelled to go to Surrattsville, and asked me to take her down. Of course I consented. I did not see the letter. We took with us only two packages; one was a package of papers about her property at Surrattsville; and another package, done up in paper, about six inches, I should think, in diameter. It looked to me like perhaps two or three saucers wrapped up. This package was deposited in the bottom of the buggy, and taken out by Mrs. Surratt when we arrived at Surrattsville. We returned to Washington about half-past 8 or 9. About ten minutes after we got back, some one rang the front-door bell. It was answered by Mrs. Surratt, and I heard footsteps go into the parlor, immediately go out again, and down the steps. I was taking supper at the time. . . .

By MR. EWING.
(Thomas Ewing, Defense Counsel for Samuel Mudd).

Dr. Mudd introduced Booth to John H. Surratt and myself about the 15th of January. I could fix the exact date, if reference could be had to the register of the Pennsylvania House, where Dr. Mudd had a room at the time. I am sure it was after the 1st of January, and before the 1st of February. It was immediately after the recess of Congress. The room that was occupied by Booth at the National Hotel had been previously occupied, so Booth said, by a member of Congress. Booth, I remember, walked round the room, put his hand on the shelf, and took down some Congressional documents, and remarked, "What a good read I shall have when I am left to myself." It was the first day of Booth's arrival in the city, and of his taking possession of the room, I understood. Most of the Congressmen had returned; Congress was in session at the time.

When Booth and Dr. Mudd met Surratt and myself, on Seventh Street, Surratt first introduced Dr. Mudd to me, and then Dr. Mudd introduced Booth to both of us. Booth then invited us down to his room at the National Hotel. As we walked down Seventh Street, Mr. Surratt took Dr. Mudd's arm, and I walked with Booth. The conversation at the National lasted, I suppose, three-quarters of an hour. When Booth took the envelope out of his pocket, and with a pencil drew lines, as it were, on the back of this envelope, Mr. Surratt and Dr. Mudd were looking on. All the while he was doing it they were engaged in deep private conversation, which was scarcely audible. I was sitting about eight feet from them and could hear nothing of it. When Booth went out of the room with Dr. Mudd, they remained not more than five or eight minutes. They went into a dark passage, and I judge they remained there, as I heard no retreating footsteps, and they did not take their hats.

Almost immediately after their return Surratt went out, and all three staid out about the same length of time as at the first interview.

After their return to the room, we remained probably twenty minutes; then left the National Hotel and went to the Pennsylvania House, where Dr. Mudd had rooms. We all went into the sitting-room, and Dr. Mudd came and sat down by me; and we talked about the war. He expressed the opinion that the war would soon come to an end, and spoke like a Union man. Booth was speaking to Surratt. At about half-past 10, Booth bade us good night, and went out; Surratt and I then bade Dr. Mudd good night. He said he was going to leave next morning.

I had never seen Dr. Mudd before that day. I had heard the name of Mudd mentioned in Mrs. Surratt's house, but whether it was this Dr. Samuel Mudd I can not say. I have heard of Dr. George Mudd and Dr. Samuel Mudd. . . .

By MR. CLAMPITT.

(John W. Clampitt, Defense Counsel for Mary Surratt).

There was nothing in the conversation between Dr. Mudd, Booth, and Surratt, at the National Hotel, that led me to believe there was any thing like a conspiracy going on between them.

When Mrs. Surratt sent me to Booth, and he offered me the ten dollars, I thought at the time that it was nothing more than an act of friendship. I said to Booth, "I am come with an order for that buggy that Mrs. Surratt asked you for last evening." He said, "I have sold my buggy, but here are ten dollars, and you go and hire one." I never told Mrs. Surratt that.

Mrs. Surratt would sometimes leave the parlor on being asked by Booth to spare him a word. She would then go into the passage and talk with him. These conversations would not, generally, occupy more than five or eight minutes. . . .

By MR. DOSTER.

(Defense Counsel for George Atzerodt and Lewis Powell).

Atzerodt has been frequently to Mrs. Surratt's house, and had interviews with John H. Surratt in the parlor. I knew nothing of what took place between them. On the occasion of Payne's last visit to the house, Atzerodt came to see Surratt, and I saw Payne and Atzerodt together, talking in my room. I do not know of any conversation that passed between Atzerodt and Booth, or Atzerodt and Payne, having reference to a conspiracy.

Surratt was continually speaking about cotton speculations, and of going to Europe, and I heard Atzerodt once remark that he also was going to Europe, but he was going on horseback; from that remark I concluded he was going South.

At half-past two o'clock, on the afternoon of the 14th, I saw Atzerodt at the livery-stable, trying to get a horse. The stable-keeper, in my presence, refused to let him have one. I asked Atzerodt where he was going, and he said he was going to ride in the country, and said he was going to get a horse and send for Payne. I met Atzerodt one day on Seventh Street, and asked him where he was going. He said he was going to see Payne. I asked him if it was Payne who was at the Herndon House. He said, "Yes." When Payne visited the Surratts, his business appeared to be with Mr. Surratt. On the occasion of his first visit, I was in the parlor during the whole time. I did not notice any other disguise than the false moustache spoken of, nor any thing else to show that Payne wanted to disguise himself. He appeared to be kindly treated by Mr. Surratt, as if he was an old acquaintance.

I do not know whether the Surratt family regarded him as a man in disguise or as a Baptist minister. One of the young ladies looked at him, and remarked that he was a queer-looking Baptist preacher, and that he would not convert many souls.

Recalled for the Prosecution.—May 18.

[A telegraphic dispatch was handed to the witness.]

I received this dispatch and delivered it to John H. Surratt on the same day. I can not say that I received it on the 23d of March, but it was after the 17th of March.

New York, March 23, 1865.

To Weichmann, Esq., 541 H Street:

Tell John to telegraph number and street at once.

[Signed] J. BOOTH.

[The original of the above dispatch was offered in evidence.]

This is in Booth's handwriting. I have seen Booth's handwriting, and recognize his autograph. When I delivered the message to John Surratt, I asked him what particular number and street was meant, and he said, "Don't be so damned inquisitive."

During Payne's second visit to Mrs. Surratt's house, some time after the 4th of March, I returned from my office one day at half-past 4 o'clock. I went to my room, and ringing the bell for Dan, the negro servant, told him to bring me some water, and inquired at the same time where John had gone. He told me Massa John had left the front of the house, with six others, on horseback, about half-past 2 o'clock. On going down to dinner, I found Mrs. Surratt in the passage. She was weeping bitterly, and I endeavored to console her. She said, "John is gone away; go down to dinner, and make the best of your dinner you can." After dinner, I went to my room, sat down, and commenced reading, and about half-past 6 o'clock Surratt came in very much excited—in fact, rushed into the room. He had a revolver in his hand—one of Sharpe's revolvers, a four-barreled revolver, a small one, you could carry it in your vest-pocket. He appeared to be very much excited. I said "John, what is the matter; why are you so much excited?" He replied, "I will shoot any one that comes into this room; my prospect is gone, my hopes are blighted; I want something to do; can you get me a clerkship?" In about ten minutes after, the prisoner, Payne, came into the room. He was also very much excited, and I noticed he had a pistol. About fifteen minutes afterward, Booth came into the room, and Booth was so excited that he walked around the room three or four times very frantically, and did not notice me. He had a whip in his hand. I spoke to him, and, recognizing me, he said, "I did not see you." The three then went up stairs into the back room, in the third story, and must have remained there about thirty minutes, when they left the house together. On Surratt's returning home, I asked him where he had left his friend Payne. He said, "Payne had gone to Baltimore." I asked him where Booth had gone; he said Booth had gone to New York. Some two weeks after, Surratt, when passing the post-office inquired for a letter that was sent to him under the name of James Sturdey. I asked him why a letter was sent to him under a false name; he said he had particular reasons for it.

The letter was signed "Wood," and the substance of it was, that the writer was at the Revere House in New York, and was looking for something to do; that he would probably go to some boarding-house on West Grand Street, I think. This must have been before the 20th of March.

When I asked the negro servant to tell me who the seven men were that had gone out riding that afternoon, he said one was Massa John, and Booth, and Port Tobacco, and that man who was stopping at the house, whom I recognized as Payne. Though they were very much excited when they came into the room, they were very guarded indeed. Payne made no remark at all. Those excited remarks by Surratt were the only ones made. . . .

DOCUMENT NO. 17

EXCERPT FROM JOHN H. SURRATT'S "ROCKVILLE LECTURE," DECEMBER 6, 1870*

John Surratt's Rockville lecture was delivered December 6, 1870, in Rockville, Maryland. Adults paid 50 cents and children 25 cents to hear Surratt discuss his involvement with Booth in the plot to capture Lincoln, which he called a noble plan, that any young man in the North might just as readily have undertaken against Jefferson Davis. Surratt denied any involvement in the murder, stating that he was in upstate New York on a mission for the Confederate government. This account appeared in the December 7, 1870 edition of the Washington Evening Star.

γ γ γ

Ladies and gentlemen: - Upon entering that door a few moments ago the impression on my mind was so strong as to vividly recall scenes of three years ago. I am not unacquainted with court room audiences. (Sensation.) I have stood before them before; true, not in the character of a lecturer, but as a prisoner at the bar, arraigned for the high crime of murder. In contrasting the two positions I must confess I felt more ease as the prisoner at the bar than I do as a lecturer. Then I felt confident of success; now I do not. Then I had gentlemen of known ability to do all my talking for me; now, unfortunately, I have to do it for myself, and I feel illy capable of performing the task; still I hope you will all judge me kindly. I am not here to surprise you by any oratorical effort-not at all-but only to tell a simple tale. I feel that some explanation, perhaps, indeed an apology is due you for my appearance here this evening. In presenting this lecture before the public I do it in no spirit of self-justification. In a trial of sixty-one days I made my defense to the world, and I have no need or desire to rehearse it; nor do I appear for self-glorification. On the contrary, I dislike notoriety, and leave my solitude and obscurity unwillingly. Neither is it an itching for notoriety or fame. My object is merely to present a simple narrative of events as they occurred. I stand here through the force of that which has obliged many other men to do things quite as distasteful-pecuniary necessity, for the supply of which no more available channel presented itself. This is a rea-

* *Washington Evening Star*, December 7, 1870.

son easily appreciated. So you will take it kindly, I trust, and the ground we will have to go over together will guarantee sufficient interest to repay your kind attention. In this my first lecture I will speak of my introduction to J. Wilkes Booth, his plan-its failure-our final separation-my trip from Richmond, and thence to Canada-then my orders to Elmira-what was done there-the first intimation I had of Mr. Lincoln's death, my return to Canada and concealment there, and final departure for Europe. At the breaking out of the war I was a student at St. Charles College, in Maryland, but did not remain long there after that important event. I left in July, 1861, and returning home commenced to take an active part in the stirring events of that period. I was not more than eighteen years of age, and was mostly engaged in sending information regarding the movements of the United States army stationed in Washington and elsewhere, and carrying dispatches to the Confederate boats on the Potomac. We had a regular established line from Washington to the Potomac, and I being the only unmarried man on the route, I had most of the hard riding to do. (Laughter.) I devised various ways to carry the dispatches -sometimes in the heel of my boots, sometimes between the planks of the buggy. I confess that never in my life did I come across a more stupid set of detectives than those generally employed by the U.S. government. They seemed to have no idea whatever on how to search men. In 1864 my family left Maryland and moved to Washington, where I took a still more active part in the stirring events of that period. It was a fascinating life to me. It seemed as if I could not do too much or run too great a risk.

In the fall of 1864 I was introduced to John Wilkes Booth, who, I was given to understand, wished to know something about the main avenues leading from Washington to the Potomac. We met several times, but as he seemed to be very reticent with regard to his purposes, and very anxious to get all the information out of me he could, I refused to tell him anything at all. At last I said to him, "It is useless for you, Mr. Booth, to seek any information from me at all; I know who you are and what are your intentions." He hesitated some time, but finally said he would make known his views to me provided I would promise secrecy. I replied, "I will do nothing of the kind. You know well I am a Southern man. If you cannot trust me we will separate." He then said, "I will confide my plans to you; but before doing so I will make known to you the motives that actuate me. In the Northern prisons are many thousands of our men whom the United States Government refuses to exchange. You know as well as I the efforts that have been made to bring about that much desired exchange. Aside from the great suffering they are compelled to undergo, we are sadly in want of them as soldiers. We cannot spare one man, whereas the United States Government is willing to let their own soldiers remain in our prisons because she has no need of the men. I have a proposition to submit to you, which I think if we can carry out will bring about the desired exchange." There was a long and ominous silence which I at last was compelled to break by asking, "Well, Sir, what is your proposition?" He sat quiet for an instant, and then,before answering me, arose and looked under the bed, into the wardrobe, in the doorway and the passage, and then said, "We will have to be careful; walls have ears." He then drew his chair close to me and in a whisper said, "It is to kidnap President Lincoln, and carry him off to Richmond!" "Kidnap President Lincoln!" I said. I confess that I stood aghast at the proposition, and looked upon it as a foolhardy undertaking. To think of successfully seizing Mr. Lincoln in the capital of the United States surrounded by thousands of his soldiers, and carrying him off to Richmond, looked to me like a foolish idea. I told him as much. He went on to tell with what facility he could be seized in various places in and about Washington. As for example in his various rides to and from the Soldiers' Home, his summer residence. He entered into the minute details of the proposed capture, and even the various parts to be performed by the actors in the performance. I was amazed-thunderstruck- and in fact, I might also say, frightened at the unparalleled audacity of this scheme. After two days' reflection I told him I was willing to try it. I believed it practicable at that time, though I now regard it as a foolhardy undertaking. I hope you will not blame me for going thus far. I honestly thought an exchange of prisoners could be brought about could we have once obtained possession of Mr. Lincoln's person. And now reverse the case. Where is there a young man in the North with one spark of patriotism in his heart who would not have with enthusiastic ardor joined in any undertaking for the capture of Jefferson Davis and brought him to Washington? There is not one who would not have done so. And so I was led on by a sincere desire to assist the South in gaining her independence. I had no hesitation in taking part in anything honorable that might tend toward the accomplishment of that object. (Tremendous applause.) Such a thing as the assassination of Mr. Lincoln I never heard spoken of by any of the party. Never! (Sensation.) Upon one occasion, I remember, we had called a meeting in

Washington for the purpose of discussing matters in general, as we had understood that the government had received information that there was a plot of some kind on hand. They had even commenced to build a stockade and gates on the navy yard bridge; gates opening towards the south as though they expected danger from within, and not from without. At this meeting I explained the construction of the gates, etc., and stated I was confident the government had wind of our movement, and the best thing we could do would be to throw up the whole project. Everyone seemed to coincide in my opinion, except Booth, who sat silent and abstracted. Arising at last and bringing his fist upon the table he said, "Well, gentlemen, if the worst comes to the worst, I shall know what to do."

Some hard words and even threats then passed between him and some of the party. Four of us then arose, one saying, "If I understand you to intimate anything more than the capture of Mr. Lincoln I for one will bid you goodbye." Everyone expressed the same opinion. We all arose and commenced putting our hats on. Booth perceiving probably that he had gone too far, asked pardon saying that he "had drank too much champagne." After some difficulty everything was amicably arranged and we separated at 5 o'clock in the morning. Days, weeks and months passed by without an opportunity presenting itself for us to attempt the capture. We seldom saw one another owing to the many rumors afloat that a conspiracy of some kind was being concocted in Washington. We had all the arrangements perfected from Washington for the purpose. Boats were in readiness to carry us across the river. One day we received information that the President would visit the Seventh Street Hospital for the purpose of being present at an entertainment to be given for the benefit of the wounded soldiers. The report only reached us about three quarters of an hour before the time appointed, but so perfect was our communication that we were instantly in our saddles on the way to the hospital. This was between one and two o'clock in the afternoon. It was our intention to seize the carriage, which was drawn by a splendid pair of horses, and to have one of our men mount the box and drive direct for southern Maryland via Benning's bridge. We felt confident that all the cavalry in the city could never overhaul us. We were all mounted on swift horses, besides having a thorough knowledge of the country, it was determined to abandon the carriage after passing the city limits. Upon the suddenness of the blow and the celerity of our movements we depended for success. By the time the alarm could have been given and horses saddled, we would have been on our way through southern Maryland towards the Potomac river. To our great disappointment, however, the President was not there but one of the government officials-Mr. [Salmon P.] Chase, if I mistake not. We did not disturb him, as we wanted a bigger chase (Laughter) than he could have afforded us. It was certainly a bitter disappointment, but yet I think a most fortunate one for us. It was our last attempt. We soon after this became convinced that we could not remain much longer undiscovered, and that we must abandon our enterprise. Accordingly, a separation finally took place, and I never saw any of the party except one, and that was when I was on my way from Richmond to Canada on business of quite a different nature-about which, presently. Such is the story of our abduction plot.

Rash, perhaps foolish, but honorable I maintain in its means and ends; actuated by such motives as would under similar circumstances be a sufficient inducement to thousands of southern young men to have embarked in a similar enterprise. Shortly after our abandonment of the abduction scheme, some dispatches came to me which I was compelled to see through to Richmond. They were foreign ones, and had no reference whatever to this affair. I accordingly left home for Richmond, and arrived there safely on the Friday evening before the evacuation of that city. On my arrival I went to [the] Spotswood Hotel, where I was told that Mr. Benjamin, the then Secretary of War of the Confederate States, wanted to see me. I accordingly sought his presence. He asked me if I would carry some dispatches to Canada for him. I replied "yes." That evening he gave me the dispatches and $200 in gold with which to pay my way to Canada. That was the only money I ever received from the Confederate government or any of its agents. It may be well to remark here that this scheme of abduction was concocted without the knowledge or the assistance of the Confederate government in any shape or form. Booth and I often consulted together as to whether it would not be well to acquaint the authorities in Richmond with our plan, as we were sadly in want of money, our expenses being very heavy. In fact the question arose among us as to whether, after getting Mr. Lincoln, if we succeeded in our plan, the Confederate authorities would not surrender us to the United States again, because of doing this thing without their knowledge or consent. But we never acquainted them with the plan, and they never had anything in the wide world to do with it. In fact, we were jealous of our undertaking and wanted no outside help. I have not made this statement to defend the officers of the Confederate government. They are perfectly able to defend themselves. What I have done myself I am not ashamed to let the world know. I left Richmond on Saturday morning before the evacuation of that place, and reached Washington the following Monday at 4 o'clock P.M., April 3d, 1865. As soon as I reached the Maryland shore I understood that the detectives knew of my trip South and were on the lookout for me. I had been South several times before for the secret service but had never been caught. At that time I was carrying the dispatches Mr. Benjamin gave me: in a book entitled "The Life of John Brown." During my trip, and while reading that book, I learned, to my utter amazement, that John Brown was a martyr sitting at the right hand of God. (Uproarius laughter.) I succeeded in reaching Washington safely, and in passing up Seventh street met one of our party, who inquired what had become of Booth. I told him where I had been; that I was then on my way to Canada, and that I had not seen or heard anything of Booth since our separation. In view of the fact that Richmond had fallen, and that all hopes of the abduction of the President had been given up, I advised him to go home and go to work. That was the last time I saw any of the party. I went to a hotel and stopped over that night, as a detective had been to my house inquiring of the servant my whereabouts. In the early train next morning, Tuesday, April 4, 1865, I left for New York, and that was the last time I was ever in Washington until brought there by the U.S. Government a captive in irons, all reports to the contrary notwithstanding.

The United States, as you will remember, tried to prove my presence in Washington on the 15th of April, the day on which Mr. Lincoln met his death. Upon arriving in New York, I called at Booth's house, and was told by the servant that he had left that morning suddenly, on the ground of going to Boston to fulfill an engagement at the theater. In the evening of the same day I took the cars for Montreal, arriving there the next day. I put up at the St. Lawrence Hotel, registering myself as "John Harrison" such being my first two names. Shortly afterwards I saw General Edward G. Lee, to whom the dispatches were directed, and delivered them to him. Those dispatches we tried to introduce as evidence on my trial, but his Honor Judge Fisher ruled them out, despite of the fact that the government had tried to prove that they had relation to the conspiracy to kill Mr. Lincoln. They were only accounts of some money transactions-nothing more or less. A week or so after my arrival there, General Lee came to my room, and told me he had a plan on foot to release the Confederate prisoners then in Elmira, N.Y. He said he had sent many parties there, but they always got frightened, and only half executed their orders. He asked me if I would go there and take a sketch of the prison, find out the number of prisoners, also minor details in regard to the number of soldiers on guard, cannon, small arms, etc. I readily accepted these new labors, owing to the fact that I could not return to Washington for fear of the detectives. The news of the evacuation of Richmond did not seem to disturb the General much in his plan, as he doubtless thought then that the Confederacy wanted men more than ever, no one dreaming that it was virtually at an end. I was much amused at one expression made use of by an ex-reb with regard to the suddenness of its demise: "D—-n the thing, it didn't even flicker, went right out." (Laughter and applause.) In accordance with Gen. Lee's order, I went to Elmira, arriving there on Wednesday, two days before Mr. Lincoln's death, and registered at the Brainard House, as usual as "John Harrison." The following day I went to work, and made a complete sketch of the prison and surroundings. About ten o'clock on Friday night I retired, little thinking that on that night a blow would be struck which would forever blast my hopes, and make me a wanderer in a foreign land. I slept the night through, and came down the next morning little dreaming of the storm then brewing around my head. When I took my seat at the table around 9 o'clock A.M., a gentleman to my left remarked: "Have you heard the news?" "No, I've not," I replied. "What is it?" "Why President Lincoln and Secretary Seward have been assassinated." I really put so little faith in what the man said that I made a remark that it was too early in the morning to get off such jokes as that. "It's so," he said, at the same time drawing out a paper and showing it to me. Sure enough, there I saw an account of what he told me, but as no names were mentioned, it never occurred to me for an instant that it could have been Booth or any of the party, for the simple reason that I never had heard anything regarding assassination spoken of during my intercourse with them. I had good reason to believe that there was another conspiracy afloat in Washington, in fact we all knew it. One evening, as I was partially lying down in the reading-room of the Metropolitan Hotel, two or three gentlemen came in and looked around as if to make sure that no one was around. They then commenced to talk about what had been done, the best means for the expedition, etc. It being about dusk, and no gas light, and partially concealed behind a writing desk, I was an unwilling listener of what occurred. I told Booth of this afterward, and he said he had heard something to the same effect. It only made us all the more eager to carry out our plans at an early day for fear some one should get ahead of us. We didn't know what they were after exactly, but we were well satisfied that their object was very much the same as ours. Arising from the table I thought over who the party could be, for at that time no names had been telegraphed. I was pretty sure it was none of the old party. I approached the telegraph office in the main hall of the hotel for the purpose of ascertaining if J. Wilkes Booth was in New York. I picked up a blank and wrote "John Wilkes Booth," giving the number of the house. I hesitated a moment, and then tore the paper up, and then wrote one "J.W.B.," with directions, which I was led to do from the fact that during our whole connection we rarely wrote or telegraphed under our proper names, but always in such a manner that no one could understand but ourselves. One way of Booth's was to send letters to me under cover to my quondam friend, Louis J. Weichman.

Doubtless you all know who Louis J. Weichman is. They were sent to him because he knew of the plot to abduct President Lincoln. I proclaim it here and before the world that Louis J. Weichman was a party to the plan to abduct President Lincoln. He had been told all about it, and was constantly importuning me to let him become an active member. I refused, for the simple reason that I told him that he could neither ride a horse nor shoot a pistol, which was a fact. (Laughter.) These were two necessary accomplishments for us. My refusal nettled him some; so he went off, as it afterwards appeared by his testimony, and told some government clerk [Captain Gleason] that he had a vague idea that there was a plan of some kind on hand to abduct President Lincoln. This he says himself: that he could have spotted every man on the party. Why didn't he do it? Booth was sometimes rather suspicious of him, and asked me if I thought he could be trusted. Said I, "Certainly he can. Weichman is a Southern man," and I always believed it until I had good reason to believe otherwise, because he had furnished information for the Confederate government, besides allowing me access to the government records after office hours. I have very little to say of Louis J. Weichman. But I do pronounce him a base-born perjurer; a murderer of the meanest hue! Give me a man who can strike his victim dead, but save me from a man who, through perjury, will cause the death of an innocent person. Double murderer!!!! Hell possesses no worse fiend than a character of that kind. (Applause.) Away with such a character. I leave him in the pit of infamy, which he has dug for himself, a prey to the lights of his guilty conscience. (Applause.) . . .

BIBLIOGRAPHY

Abbott, Martin, "Southern Reaction to Lincoln's Assassination," *Abraham Lincoln Quarterly* 7 (Sept., 1952):111–127.

Alford, Terry, ed., *John Wilkes Booth, A Sister's Memoir*, (Jackson: University Press of Mississippi, 1996).

Arnold, Samuel Bland, *Defence and Prison Experiences of a Lincoln Conspirator*. (Hattiesburg, MS: The Book Farm, 1943).

Balsiger, David and Sellier, Charles, *The Lincoln Conspiracy*. (Los Angeles: Schick Sun Classic Books, 1977).

Bates, Finis L., *Escape and Suicide of John Wilkes Booth, Assassin of President Lincoln*. (Memphis, TN: Pilcher Printing Co., 1907).

Bishop, James, *The Day Lincoln Was Shot*. (New York: Harper & Row, 1955).

Bryan, George S., *The Great American Myth*. (New York: Carrick and Evans, 1940). Reprint (Chicago: Americana House, 1990). Introduction by William Hanchett.

Campbell, Helen J., *The Case For Mrs. Surratt*. (New York: G. P. Putnam's Sons, 1943).

Chamlee, Roy, *Lincoln's Assassins*. (New York: McFarland and Company, 1990)

Chesebrough, David, *"No Sorrow Like Our Sorrow," Northern Protestant Ministers and the Assassination of Lincoln*. (Kent, Ohio: Kent State University Press, 1994).

Clark, Champ, *The Assassination*. (Alexandria, VA: Time-Life Books, 1987).

Clarke, Asia B., *The Unlocked Book, A Memoir of John Wilkes Booth by His Sister Asia Booth Clarke*. Foreword by Eleanor Farejon (New York: G. P. Putnam's Sons, 1938).

Clarke, James W., *American Assassins, The Darker Side of Politics*. (Princeton, NJ: Princeton University Press, 1982).

Davis, William C., "Behind the Lines: Caveat Emptor," *Civil War Times Illustrated* (August, 1977), 33–37.

———. "Behind the Lines: 'The Lincoln Conspiracy'—Hoax?" *Civil War Times Illustrated* (November, 1977): 47–49.

DeWitt, David Miller, *The Assassination of Abraham Lincoln and Its Expiation*. (Freeport, NY: Books for Libraries Press, 1909).

———. *The Judicial Murder of Mary E. Surratt*. (Baltimore: John Murphy, 1893).

Eisenschiml, Otto, *In the Shadow of Lincoln's Death*. (New York: Wilfred Funk, 1940).

———. *Why Was Lincoln Murdered?* (Boston: Little, Brown, 1937).

Ferguson, William, *I Saw Booth Shoot Lincoln*. (Boston: Houghton Mifflin, 1930).

Forrester, Izola, *This One Mad Act*. (Boston: Hale, Cushman, and Flint, 1937).

Fowler, Robert H., *Album of the Lincoln Murder*. (Harrisburg: Stackpole Books, 1965).

Gaddy, James, "Letter to the Editor", *The Virginia Magazine of History and Biography* (Summer, 1996):416–418.

Garson, Barbara, *MacBird*. (New York: Grove Press, 1966).

George, Joseph, Jr., "Who is Buried in Booth's Tomb?", *Lincoln Herald* (Winter, 1994): 27–32.

Good, Timothy, *We Saw Lincoln Shot: One Hundred Eyewitness Accounts* (Jackson: University Press of Mississippi, 1995).

Hanchett, William, *The Lincoln Murder Conspiracies*. (Urbana: University of Illinois Press, 1983).

Harrell, Carolyn, *When the Bells Tolled For Lincoln*. (Macon: Mercer University Press, 1997).

Harris, Thomas M., *Assassination of Lincoln*. (Boston: American Citizen Company, 1892).

Higdon, Hal, *The Union vs. Dr. Mudd*. (Chicago: Follett, 1964).

Jones, John Paul, ed., *Dr. Mudd and the Lincoln Assassination, The Case Reopened*. (Conshocken, PA: Combined Books, 1995).

Jones, Thomas A., *J. Wilkes Booth, An Account of His Sojourn in Southern Maryland after the Assassination of Abraham Lincoln, His Passage Across the Potomac, and His Death in Virginia*. (Chicago: Laird and Lee, 1893).

Kauffman, Michael W., ed., *Memoirs of a Lincoln Conspirator*. (Bowie, MD: Heritage Books, 1995).

Kimmel, Stanley, *The Mad Booths of Maryland*. (Indianapolis: Bobbs-Merrill, 1940).

Kirkham, James F., Levy, Sheldon G., and Crotty, William, *Assassination and Political Violence: A Report to the National Commission on the Causes and Prevention of Violence*. (New York: Praeger, 1970).

Kunhardt, Dorothy, and Philip Kunhardt, *Twenty Days*. (North Hollywood, CA: Newcastle, 1985).

Laughlin, Clara, *The Death of Lincoln*. (New York: Doubleday, 1909).

Leale, Charles A., *Lincoln's Last Hours*. (New York: Order of the Loyal Legion of the State of New York, 1909).

Lewis, Lloyd, *Myths After Lincoln*. (New York: Harcourt Brace, 1929).

Long, David, *The Jewel of Liberty*. (Gettysburg: Stackpole Books, 1994).

Mahoney, Ella, *Sketches of Tudor Hall and the Booth Family*. (Bel Air, MD: Franklin Printing, 1925).

May, John F., "The Mark of the Scalpel." *Records of the Columbia Historical Society* 13 (1910): 49–68.

McHale, John E. Jr., *Dr. Samuel A. Mudd and the Lincoln Assassination*. (Parsippany, NJ: Dillon Press, 1995).

Moore, Guy, *The Case of Mrs. Surratt, Her Controversial Trial and Execution for Conspiracy in the Lincoln Assassination*. (Norman: University of Oklahoma Press, 1954).

Mudd, Nettie, *The Life of Dr. Samuel A. Mudd*. (New York: Neale Publishing Company, 1906).

Neely, Mark E., Jr., "Was the Civil War Total War?", *Civil War History* 37 (1991): 5–28.

Oldroyd, Osborn H., *The Assassination of Abraham Lincoln*. (Washington: O. H. Oldroyd, 1901).

Peterson, Merrill D., *Lincoln in American Memory*. (New York: Oxford University Press, 1994).

Pitman, Benn, *The Assassination of President Lincoln and the Trial of the Conspirators*. (New York: Funk and Wagnalls, 1954).

Poore, Ben Perley, ed., *The Conspiracy Trial For the Murder of the President*. (Boston: J. E. Tilton, 1865.) Reprint. New York: Arno Press, 1972).

Reck, W. Emerson, *A. Lincoln: His Last Twenty-four Hours*. (Jefferson, NC: McFarland, 1987).

Rhodehamel, John and Taper, Louise, eds., *"Right or Wrong, God Judge Me:" The Writings of John Wilkes Booth*. (Urbana: University of Illinois Press, 1997).

Roscoe, Theodore, *The Web of Conspiracy: The Complete Story of the Men Who Murdered Lincoln*. (Englewood Cliffs, NJ: Prentice Hall, 1959).

Shelton, Vaughan, *Mask For Treason, The Lincoln Murder Trial*. (Harrisburg: Stackpole Books, 1965).

Smith, Gene, *American Gothic: The Story of America's Legendary Theatrical Family—Junius, Edwin, and John Wilkes Booth*. (New York: Simon and Schuster, 1992).

Starr, John, Jr., *Lincoln's Last Day*. (New York: Frederick A. Stoles, 1922).

Steers, Edward, Jr., *His Name is Still Mudd*. (Gettysburg: Thomas Publications, 1997).

——. *The Escape and Capture of John Wilkes Booth*. (Gettysburg: Thomas Publications, 1983).

Stern, Philip Van Doren, *The Man Who Killed Lincoln*. (New York: Literary Guild of America, 1939).

Taft, Charles Sabin, *Abraham Lincoln's Last Hours*. (Chicago: Blackcat Press, 1934).

Tidwell, William A. with Hall, James O. and Gaddy, David W., *Come Retribution: The Confederate Secret Service and the Assassination of Lincoln*. (Jackson: University of Mississippi Press, 1988).

Tidwell, William A., *April '65: Confederate Covert Action in the American Civil War*. (Kent, Ohio: Kent State University Press, 1995).

Trindal, Elizabeth S., *Mary Surratt: An American Tragedy*. (Gretna, LA: Pelican Publishers, 1996).

Turner, Thomas, *Beware the People Weeping*. (Baton Rouge: Louisiana State University Press, 1982).

U.S. Government, *Trial of John H. Surratt in the Criminal Court for the District of Columbia, Hon. George P. Fisher Presiding*. 2 vols. (Washington: Government Printing Office, 1867).

Weichmann, Louis, *A True History of the Assassination of Abraham Lincoln and of the Conspiracy of 1865*. (New York: Vintage Books, 1977).

Wilson, Francis, *John Wilkes Booth: Fact and Fiction of Lincoln's Assassination*. (Boston: Houghton Mifflin, 1929).

INDEX